The *Second* Greatest

Greatest

Disappointment

"Every American bride is taken there, and the sight of the stupendous waterfall must be one of the earliest, if not the keenest, disappointments in American married life."

– Oscar Wilde, after a visit to Niagara, 1882

The **Second**
Greatest

Karen Dubinsky

Disappointment

Honeymooning

and Tourism at

Niagara Falls

Between the Lines

First published in Canada 1999 by Between the Lines, Toronto, Ontario

First published in the United States 1999 by Rutgers University Press, New Brunswick, New Jersey

Between the Lines gratefully acknowledges financial assistance for our publishing activities from the Canada Council for the Arts, the Ontario Arts Council, and the Government of Canada through the Book Publishing Industry Development Program.

Every reasonable effort has been made to find copyright holders. The publisher would be pleased to have any errors or omissions brought to its attention.

Canadian Cataloguing in Publication Data

Dubinsky, Karen
    The second greatest disappointment : honeymooning and tourism at Niagara Falls

Includes bibliographical references and index.

ISBN 1-896357-23-7

1. Honeymoons – Niagara Falls (N.Y. and Ont.) – History – 20th century.
2. Tourist trade – Niagara Falls (N.Y. and Ont.) – History.
3. Niagara Falls (N.Y. and Ont. – Social life and customs.
4. Niagara Falls (N.Y. and Ont.) – Description and travel.   I. Title.

FC3095.N5D82 1999   971.3'39   C99-930376-7   F127.N8D83 1999

Editor: Robert Clarke
Design: Gordon Robertson
Cover collage: David Laurence

Front cover images:
Flags: A Picture History of Niagara Falls, 1953; native woman: Niagara Falls Ontario Public Library; film poster: "NIAGARA" © 1953 Twentieth Century Fox Film Corporation. All rights reserved; couple on bench: courtesy of Joanna Fitzgerald; bride and groom: The Procter and Gamble Company; Maid of the Mist boat and souvenir store: Niagara Parks Commission; all by permission.

Back cover image: Niagara Parks Commission, Niagara Falls, Ont.

Printed in Canada by Transcontinental Printing

1 2 3 4 5 6 7 8 9 10   TP   06 05 04 03 02 01 00 99

THE CANADA COUNCIL | LE CONSEIL DES ARTS
FOR THE ARTS | DU CANADA
SINCE 1957 | DEPUIS 1957

Canadä

Between the Lines, 720 Bathurst Street, #404, Toronto, Ontario, M5S 2R4, Canada
(416) 535-9914   btlbooks@web.net   www.btlbooks.com

For my parents

Contents

Acknowledgements   ix

ONE   Introduction: Practising Heterosexuality at Niagara Falls   1

TWO   "The Pleasure Is Exquisite but Violent":
The Imaginary Geography of the Nineteenth Century   19

THREE   Local Colour in the "Contact Zone": The Spectacle of Race   55

FOUR   The People's Niagara at the Turn of the Century   85

FIVE   Boom and Bust in the 1920s and 1930s   117

SIX   "A Laboratory for the Study of Young Love":
Honeymoons and Travel to World War II   153

SEVEN   Honky-Tonk City: Niagara and the Postwar Travel Boom   177

EIGHT   Heterosexuality Goes Public: The Postwar Honeymoon   213

NINE   Conclusion: The Sublime Becomes Ridiculous   239

Notes   247
Illustration Credits   285
Index   287

Acknowledgements

All books are collaborative efforts, and one of the best things about writing this one was that a lot of people had a lot to tell me. For many years friends, family, colleagues, and students—even students' parents—have clipped Niagara or honeymoon-related articles for me, lent me their photographs, told me their Niagara holiday stories, and bought me Niagara memorabilia. This has not only had a remarkable impact on my household and office decor, but also helped to create a substantial and extremely useful archive of "Niagarana," for which I am very grateful.

I am also grateful for the help I received from an able group of research assistants: Stephen Connacher, Elise Chenier, Mike Dawson, Jessica Hamilton, Janet Hueglin, and Rebekah Warner. I must also thank the funding agencies that allowed me to pay these people: the Social Sciences and Humanities Research Council and the Advisory Committee on Research at Queen's University. I especially want to thank my "native guide," Niagara Falls resident Janet Hueglin, for helping me line up interviews and reading the local paper until she was bleary-eyed, even after the grant ran out. Thanks also to my various hosts: Adam Givertz and Jennifer Steele, as well as Ted Ho, in Toronto, Cecilia Morgan and Paul Jenkins in Niagara-on-the-Lake, Kelly Dubinsky and David Lahey in Ottawa, and Marty Gross in New York, for making my research travels so comfortable.

At my workplace, the History Department at Queen's University, Sandra den Otter, Jane Errington, and Geoff Smith offered daily encouragement, on this book and much else. Their sunny dispositions always help to warm the climate; I am lucky to have such friends. I am also lucky to have a keen, smart group of students, who teach me much more than they realize. My friend and mentor Roberta Hamilton helped me in countless ways, especially, as always, by example. Her courage while negotiating the treacherous waters of university administration helps the rest of us feel, on good days, a little less like outsiders in the world of big books and big ideas. On good days and bad days alike I have enjoyed the support and irreverence of other colleagues at Queen's, especially Mary Louise Adams, Jackie Duffin, Margaret Little, and Eleanor MacDonald. And while our paths cross much less these days than they once did, I'm still thankful for my "virtual" community of feminist historians who, through the miracle of e-mail, keep me conversant with gossip, complaints, witticisms, and new books; especially Nancy Forestell, Annalee Golz, Deborah Gorham, Katherine Harvey, Franca Iacovetta, Kate MacPherson, Lynne Marks, Maureen McCarthy, Cecilia Morgan, Suzanne Morton, Tori Smith, Becki Ross, and Susan Whitney.

Many colleagues, students, and friends improved this book by reading parts of it and providing me with honest assessments and fresh insights: thanks to Mary Louise Adams, Antoinette Burton, Mike Dawson, Ena Dua, Ellen Furlough, Roberta Hamilton, Paul Jackson, Ruth Pierson, and Geoff Smith. I am especially grateful to those who made their way through the entire manuscript while it was in various stages of lucidity. Caroline Dawson took time to read the words of a total stranger and offered encouraging and insightful comments. My fellow traveller in tourism history, Cecilia Morgan, swapped Niagara-area lore with me and provided excellent commentary on the manuscript. My colleague Ian McKay possesses a great and formidable brain, which he generously lent to me not once but twice, reading two versions of the manuscript and offering me wise and thoughtful counsel. The anonymous reviews from publisher's readers were also most helpful.

I also want to thank Niagara Falls local historian Dwight Whalen for his generosity, which reminded me how absurd the petty rivalries of academic historians can be. Many other Niagara Falls residents, especially the people I interviewed, welcomed me into their community and, often, their homes. Coffee, tea, old photographs, and vivid memories were bestowed liberally, and this book is much richer because of these conversations.

Librarians at a number of institutions and archives have also been extremely helpful. Thanks especially for the knowledgeable assistance I received from Inge Saczkowski and Andrew Porteous at the Niagara Falls, Ontario, Public Library, Donald Loker at the Niagara Falls, New York, Public Library, and George Bailey at the Niagara Parks Commission. All publicly funded libraries and archives are suffering in these times, and all deserve more support. But this project has made me realize the tremendous importance of local history collections held at public libraries, and I wish that their significance was more strongly recognized, socially and financially. Thanks also to Greg Brown at the Ontario Archives, and librarians at Queen's University, the University of Toronto Archives and the Thomas Fisher Rare Book Room, the Toronto Metro Reference Library, the Royal Ontario Museum Library, the National Library, the New York Public Library, the Museum of Television and Radio, the New York Historical Society, the Buffalo and Erie County Historical Society, the Kinsey Institute Library and Archives, and the British Museum.

This book was midwifed initially by two men. Geoff Smith helped me to find a good home for my manuscript, and his enthusiasm for this book, as well as his kind spirit and remarkable generosity, will never be forgotten. At Between the Lines, Jamie Swift helped navigate the route to publication. I'm also grateful to Ruth Bradley-St-Cyr and Paul Eprile at Between the Lines, and Martha Heller and Leslie Mitchner at Rutgers University Press, for their encouragement and for coming up with a co-publication arrangement that made everybody happy. Thanks also to the talented Robert Clarke, for his sharp editorial eye.

In another era Susan Belyea might have been referred to as my "travelling companion," which is especially funny since she insists she hates to travel. Recently she has conceded that tourism with a historian makes vacations more interesting. I want to thank her for her presence on at least some of the many excursions necessary for the evolution of this book: from our first odd but enjoyable visit to Niagara Falls, which hatched this project, through several years of research and conference travels thereafter. Her intellectual presence has been as rewarding as her physical presence, and I thank her for her eagerness to engage with history and her constant assurances that it was not boring.

This book is dedicated to my parents, Wallace Dubinsky and Marguerite Dubinsky. Their life together did not work out as they had hoped during their honeymoon in 1955. But, with love and hard work, they managed to raise four children who have become, if I may say so, decent and compassionate adults. Something worked.

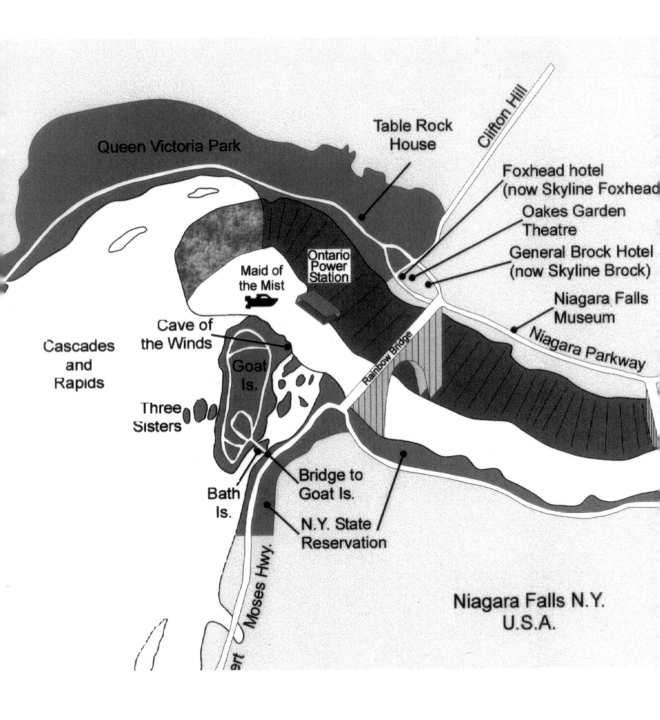

Queen Victoria Park

Table Rock House

Clifton Hill

Foxhead hotel (now Skyline Foxhead

Oakes Garden Theatre

General Brock Hotel (now Skyline Brock)

Niagara Falls Museum

Niagara Parkway

Ontario Power Station

Maid of the Mist

Cave of the Winds

Cascades and Rapids

Goat Is.

Three Sisters

Rainbow Bridge

Bath Is.

Bridge to Goat Is.

N.Y. State Reservation

Robert Moses Hwy.

Niagara Falls N.Y. U.S.A.

FRANK LESLIE'S
ILLUSTRATED
NEWSPAPER

No. 1,256—Vol. XLIX.]   NEW YORK, OCTOBER 25, 1879.   [Price 10 Cents.

Introduction:

Practising Heterosexuality at Niagara Falls

Dodge's Log Lodges. When I was growing up this phrase was a kind of magical incantation for my parents and us, their children. I can recall few moments of affection between my mother and father—their marriage ended in divorce when I was in my early teens—but I well remember those words. Dodge's Log Lodges was where they spent their wedding night, the first stop on their honeymoon trip to Fort William, Ontario, in 1955.

Because their final destination of Fort William was neither a romantic honeymoon resort nor an adventurous new discovery—the Northern Ontario industrial town was where my father grew up, and where he and his new bride were to spend the next thirty years of their lives—I imagine that Dodge's Log Lodges symbolized, for them, their brief visit to the world of romance and motor trips, the search for love, nature, and nation. The relationship between mass travel (represented in my parents' era by the neon-lit, phonetically innovative roadside cabin or motel), and the public declaration of heterosexual citizenship (the honeymoon) had taken about a century to create and celebrate, and by the time my parents rolled into Dodge's Log Lodges the ritual was at its height.

Honeymoons, travel, and heterosexual citizenship were everywhere, it seemed, in that era, but for my parents and for the many other 1950s newlyweds who went on to divorce each other, the relationships implied were not especially durable. I do not, of course, fully understand the meaning that Dodge's Log Lodges held for my parents. I remember it as a phrase reserved only for their usage, but as their eldest child I experienced a flood of relief whenever it was invoked. Whatever had happened in Dodge's Log Lodges that August night in 1955, its memory made my parents smile, even laugh sometimes, and laughter between my parents was special enough that the phrase stayed with me.

As a child I thought they laughed because the words sounded so funny, like a nursery rhyme or a Dr. Seuss story. Now I am more aware of the cultural codes represented by the "newlywed-couple-in-motel-on-honeymoon," and I have a wider range of possibilities to imagine. Maybe they were remembering their own nervousness, or maybe the place itself—like many enterprises catering to the postwar honeymoon trade—was excessively, humorously, romantic. Quite possibly Mr. and, very likely, Mrs. Dodge made a special fuss over these newlywed visitors who betrayed themselves with telltale new shoes, bits of confetti, or a rapidly wilting corsage. I cannot help but filter this picture through the lens of their subsequent marital unhappiness; maybe they were laughing ruefully, even bitterly, at their own willingness to create a fairy tale in a roadside cabin on the way to Northern Ontario.

This book is about the creation of millions of such fairy-tales—honeymoon vacations. It also explores the attractions Niagara has held for millions of other visitors: travelling families, couples celebrating anniversaries, people who turned up—and continue to visit—from virtually every corner of the globe to witness this remarkable place.

In many ways my inspiration is personal. My research was prompted and spurred along by my own adult curiosity about the culture in which my parents came of age, and into which I was born: the good life of plenty and optimism attained by a surprisingly large number of white North Americans after World War II. (That the culture had recently changed in distinct and unprecedented ways was evident, if only because the middle class now, amazingly, included people like my father, whose own Eastern European immigrant parents would not have been invited into the circle two or three short decades earlier.) As I dug deeper, my research triggered long-forgotten memories of familial happiness. While I now realize that the view from the back seat was different from that in the front, I remember our vacation trips by car through Ontario in the 1960s as a source of unimpeded joy, unfolding in the vast outdoor swimming pools of motor hotels, attractions such as "Santa's Village" or "Story Book Gardens" that dotted Ontario's highways, and endless campgrounds. That such adventures generally took place in locations like Wawa, Sudbury, or Owen Sound (on our way to our annual visit to my mother's family in Southern Ontario) did not diminish their exoticism one bit, at least for the children.

One year Niagara Falls was a stop at which we, like travellers since the late nineteenth century, disappointed the tourist industry by staying only a few hours. The best stop that year was Expo '67, the World's Fair in Montreal, an enormously successful event for the tourist industry, English/French relations in Canada, and my family. Sadly, such harmony, within the family and the nation, was short-lived, an oddly symmetrical coincidence that made 1967 a fitting date at which to end my research, and this book's history.

My other personal reason for writing this book comes from my adult life. I have not had a honeymoon, nor am I likely to. Yet I did, in spring 1991, take a short, utterly romantic motor trip around southwestern Ontario. Celebrating the beginning of a new relationship and, almost as happily, the end of many years of graduate student deprivations—years of isolation and poverty—my partner and I stopped in at Niagara Falls. The place beckoned, as it had to generations of tourists before us, because it was famous, nearby, and cheap. And for my girlfriend, raised on the east coast, it was new. We did not choose Niagara for our holiday for either its gay camp potential or a postmodern honeymoon parody. Yet the irony of our experience—it seemed as though we were the only non-heterosexual couple around for miles—was not lost on either of us. Heterosexuality elsewhere still does not tend to announce itself so openly as it has done, I have since learned, for two centuries at Niagara Falls. Having stumbled upon what appeared to be the greatest theme park of heterosexuality I had ever witnessed, I decided I must find out more.

These memories, observations, and impressions have helped to shape this book. So too have more general, less personal preoccupations—the sorts of questions other historians of sexuality, tourism, and popular culture have been grappling with. This book is a study of the history of tourism—especially but not only honeymoon tourism—at Niagara Falls in the nineteenth and twentieth centuries. In the following pages I survey the history of what British sociologist John Urry calls the "tourist gaze," by which he means the manner in which tourist attractions and experiences have been invented and organized.[1] Niagara has been a remarkably durable cultural icon in North America, and the tourist gaze has shifted dramatically through the years. Thus this book joins what is becoming a minor industry of "Niagarana": productions by writers who, like the nineteenth-century travellers before us, are intent on deciphering the cultural meaning of Niagara.

A recent and important contributor to this research, Canadian historian Patricia Jasen, locates Niagara at the centre of the search for "wild things" that captivated the pallid, urban middle class through the nineteenth century. Geographer Patrick McGreevy explores Niagara's long association with death, danger, and human mortality. U.S. historian William Irwin examines how electrical and industrial developments created Niagara as an emblem of North American ingenuity and technical progress. The pioneer of modern Niagarana, art historian Elizabeth McKinsey, examines changing artistic depictions of the waterfall to see how Niagara has represented "the sublime" for generations of Americans.[2]

Because I am curious about the long-time association of Niagara Falls with honeymooning, my contribution is to decode the waterfalls' gendered and sexual imagery, which I believe is central to the cultural meaning or "imaginary geography" of Niagara Falls.

Bricks, Mortar, and the Intangible Forces

I begin by following the trail of the nineteenth-century travellers and guide-book writers as they gaze upon, and play with, what many of them called the "Queen of the Cataracts." In the imaginary geography of Niagara—that is, in the way travellers speak about the waterfall as though it were female and invest it with dangerous, alluring, and quite sexual powers—are the origins of the Niagara/honeymoon association. Since the early nineteenth century, Niagara

Falls has been—implicitly and, later, explicitly—a place of forbidden pleasures, and a tourist industry emerged early on to facilitate this tendency. The culture of Niagara was linked to the history of the honeymoon in the nineteenth century. Sex and marriage manuals, literary sources, and honeymoon-themed pornography all reveal (or lampoon) the unfolding of proper honeymoons, and they show how the ritual varied with changes in gender roles and sexual politics.

Of all the ways to promote a waterfall, why honeymoons? The answer to this question is not, it turns out, a simple one. The Niagara Falls honeymoon was commodified, popularized, and advertised in the twentieth century, but it was not invented then. It was not conjured up by a clever tourist entrepreneur, for it has a much longer and more complicated history than a mere tourist-promotion gimmick. It has been shaped and reshaped by the prevailing climate of sexual politics, relations between the women and men, state of the tourist industry, and imaginary geography of the waterfall at any given moment.

Cultural critics such as Urry have argued convincingly that there is nothing natural about tourist attractions, even waterfalls. But why do tourists make the choices they do? After all, plenty of waterfalls, fishing villages, and shopping malls exist in the world. Why have some become famous and thus culturally desirable to "do" while others have avoided the tourist gaze entirely? To answer this question, we must place the symbolism or semiotics of tourism in the context of what I think of as the bricks and mortar: the network of hotel owners, hack drivers, guides, and other public- and private-sector entrepreneurs who created the modern tourist industry. The two-centuries-old history of Niagara's tourist industry reveals an extraordinarily complex relationship between sellers and buyers—in the tourist, as in other, marketplaces. Niagara Falls has been both a business *and* an image. Tourism-as-industry is connected with tourism-as-gaze.

Capitalism, as historian Victoria de Grazia notes, is a semiotic as well as an economic system. In writing the history of consumption, we face the challenge of relating metaphor or symbol to actual social life or, as de Grazia puts it, of linking "the imaginary world around consumption with the structural changes giving rise to modern consumer society."[3] The history of Niagara Falls tourism illustrates well not only how complicated—and profitable—it has been to turn such intangibles as love, nature, and nation into marketable commodities, but also, therefore, how necessary it is to understand the intersections of commerce and emotion.

For two centuries Niagara's tourist boosters have engaged in fierce and competitive struggles to attract and keep the right sort of tourist. They have debated which attractions and pastimes were appropriate to the proper appreciation of the waterfalls, and they have battled with each other, and with governments, about who has had the right to act as Niagara's "handler." Because the waterfalls were shared, often uncomfortably, between two countries, their handlers also encountered a tourist market with fluctuating ideas about national identity, patriotism, and whether crossing a border to holiday was or was not a good thing. Niagara's two-century-long status as a honeymoon resort also meant that tourist success was shaped by (and played a role in shaping) dramatic changes in relations between women and men and the meanings of marriage.

To take one example: by the 1940s the honeymoon trade at Niagara was experiencing one of its many boom periods, and publicity about the pleasures of a Niagara honeymoon was everywhere. But this carried a price, for after World War II intensive honeymoon promotion helped to reinvent Niagara as a sleazy, "honky-tonk" clip joint. As well, through all the periods of its history, Niagara Falls residents had to fend off criticism that making a living from promoting the waterfalls was an act of disrespect for nature's bounty. As a thoughtful (and, compared to nineteenth-century commentators, restrained) Canadian journalist wrote in 1954, residents of tourist towns had always evinced "a hint of corruptibility."[4] That those voicing these criticisms did so from the comfort of the hotel rooms, restaurants, and various other vantage points created and serviced by the tourist industry illustrates a central irony in the history of tourism: it is impossible to get off the beaten track.

While corruption and greed would never be foreign to Niagara's tourist industry, the moral politics of tourism make the study of the tourist industry complicated. Sellers of wheat, lumber, or automobiles have not, usually, faced such censure. Most importantly, perhaps, Niagara Falls is not just a metaphor or an icon but also a real place, in which real people have long lived and worked, people who themselves helped shape the cultural meaning of the waterfall.

When we examine the people who became the purveyors of Niagara, it becomes clear that many of the criticisms tossed their way arose because they challenged the Anglo gentlemen's club that had theretofore defined Canadian business. In the nineteenth century these people were Jewish museum owners, Native souvenir sellers, Irish hackmen, and black guides. In the twentieth century, until very recently, they were women tourist-home operators and Italian or Eastern European restaurateurs or motel owners. While plenty of Anglo gentlemen also made their living from Niagara (both in the tourist industry and in the massive hydroelectric projects of the early twentieth century), the most-noticed and complained-about people were the cast of "Others," those who lacked, as legal theorist Patricia Williams puts it in another context, "separate worth, distinct power, [and] sufficient rights to manipulate commerce."[5]

Visitors always tended to view Niagara's entrepreneurs and labour force as fascinating but problematic spectacles, and control of the tourist industry has always been hotly contested. By the end of the nineteenth century the issue had become a matter of public policy, including a little-known Royal Commission into abuses at Niagara Falls convened by the Ontario government in 1873 and the better-known campaign to nationalize the area around the waterfalls, which culminated in the creation of state-run parks on both sides. Legend has it that the Niagara parks were created by far-seeing governments in the United States and Canada to—as they put it—"free" Niagara of commercial hucksters. Less well-known are the racial dynamics of this story: for example, how the Royal Commission blamed the tourist industry's Jewish and black workers specifically for the problems at Niagara. Furthermore, the early operations of the Niagara Parks Commission (the government body charged with regulating the waterfall in Canada) included political corruption, nepotism, and commercial activities that were virtually identical to those carried out by private entrepreneurs. Niagara was never "freed." It was simply placed in different, more culturally acceptable hands. Then too, in the optimistic days of the early twentieth century, the townspeople of Niagara Falls created a vision of their future that combined tourism with industrial development, and they foresaw no contradiction between the two.

The early twentieth century, especially the 1920s, was a growth time for the tourist industry, particularly as vacations began to include the middle, and not solely the upper, classes. The advent of automobile tourism and the expansion of accommodation alternatives beyond stately hotels changed vacation patterns and the tourist industry itself. Niagara Falls was already experiencing deep divisions between public-sector and private-sector tourist entrepreneurs. In the 1920s intense rivalries also developed between (male) hotel and campground owners and (female) boarding house operators, tensions that deepened during the 1930s as more would-be businesspeople chased fewer and fewer tourists. Despite the setbacks of the Depression, tourism was to play an important and visible role in discussions and plans for the town's progress. "Tourist consciousness" was spreading, both locally and in emerging tourist bureaucracies within governments.

In the first few decades of the twentieth century the honeymoon was also changing. As travel possibilities expanded, so too did the honeymoon, which, for the middle class, was acquiring a new status as a culturally necessary prelude to married life. As the public culture of heterosexuality changed in the early decades of the twentieth century, more and more commentators—sex experts, doctors, filmmakers, and journalists—set themselves the task of representing the honeymoon and defining how and where it ought to unfold. These were the transition decades, between the "private" upper-class wedding tour of the nineteenth century and the considerably more public, populist honeymoon of the post-World War II era.

The tourist industry in Canada boomed in the 1940s and 1950s. In that era tourism—always defined narrowly as Americans visiting Canada—became understood as wholly and unquestionably a good thing. The tourist industry was able to generate enormous, nationwide enthusiasm for itself in large measure because of its ability to dress private enterprise in the garb of community spirit, civic pride, and patriotism. Niagara Falls had a special place in the postwar boom. As the history of the place makes clear, tourism was not a plot foisted upon a pliant or unwilling public. Indeed, it was the apparent democracy and openness of the tourist industry that gave it its appeal. Just about anybody could be a tourist, and almost anybody, it seemed, could become a tourist entrepreneur. Over one billion dollars were pumped into Niagara-area tourist development in the 1950s, and motels, restaurants, and tourist attractions seemed to spring up overnight. In the summer of 1953, the year the Marilyn Monroe film *Niagara* was released, thirteen million people visited the Falls.

Mass travel meant mass honeymoons, and after the war the honeymoon became, like the automobile or television set, a standard, affordable consumer good. But what was being purchased had changed considerably. Public discussions of the honeymoon had expanded enormously after the war, as did the promotion and advertising efforts of the tourist industry at Niagara Falls. Thus the honeymoon, and Niagara Falls as a honeymoon destination, acquired a much more overly sexual meaning in the popular imagination. When a sophisticated Cary Grant declared to a young and petulant Grace Kelly in the 1955 film *To Catch a Thief,* "What you need is ten minutes with a good man at Niagara Falls," everyone knew he was not referring to sightseeing or nature appreciation. In the history of heterosexuality, the 1950s hold a special place. In that era, the dominant culture demonized the pathological homosexual; a sexual cold war helped to reinforce gender and sex-role conformity. But the emergence of the happy heterosexual also forms a key part of this story, and nowhere was this more evident than at Niagara Falls. In the reinvented Niagara Falls honeymoon of the post-World War II era we can see how changes in leisure time, family life, and consumption resulted in an altered experience of heterosexual companionship.

Although the phenomenon of the modern honeymoon lingers on and, indeed, shows no sign of abating as we move into the next century—even though the sensibilities surrounding the institution have changed dramatically—Niagara has experienced a long, slow decline as a honeymoon destination. Today an underside of thinly disguised racial and class-based hostilities lurks beneath the surface of Niagara's place in contemporary culture. Niagara became passé to the European and North American upper class when the middle class began to arrive there at the turn of the century, and the working-class tourist boom of the 1940s and 1950s, as well as the later popularity of Niagara with Japanese tourists, had a similar, more widespread effect. People have long been amazed by the sheer magnitude, and the power, of the waterfalls themselves, but they have also long been laughing at the place as a whole, even as they visit it. And rarely do we consider the cultural and social anxieties represented by mass tourist destinations such as the Falls.

Niagara as Disappointment

Some might assume, from my title, that I am intending to join the chorus of commentators who, since at least the 1830s, were disappointed by their visits to Niagara. *The Second Greatest Disappointment* evokes Oscar Wilde's often-quoted remarks about Niagara, that it was "the second greatest disappointment of American married life."[6] Along with the obvious sexual allusions, Wilde was also, I suspect, having a bit of fun with Niagara's aesthetic reputation, for he was not the first or the last to evoke the theme of disappointment in describing the Falls.

Disappointment was a by-product of Niagara's fame, and, for many, image was far more impressive than reality. As early as 1838 the British writer Harriet Martineau was saying she "expected to be disappointed" at her first sight of the Falls.[7] She, happily, was not, but throughout the nineteenth century, as more and more people flocked to the Falls, disappointment became an almost mandatory response to Niagara. For upper-class visitors, disappointment helped to set one apart from the rabble. Almost all who wrote about their visits used disappointment as a yardstick or a measure of the experience. They expected disappointment and they got it, or, like Martineau, they expected it and were not. Some, such as Frances Monck, were disappointed but able to correct it, in her case by selecting a different vantage point from which to view the Falls.[8] Guidebooks also used the language of disappointment to sell themselves, promising that their pages would help readers avoid disappointment.

This chorus of complaints did not, at least in the nineteenth century, sound a death knell to Niagara's popularity, for as other historians of tourism have found, "People still flock to sights labelled disappointing by the guidebooks, if only to show that they are sophisticated enough to agree when they get there."9 At modern Niagara, disappointment still reigns, though it can often turn quickly into hip parody or, in Urry's words, "post-tourism," a kind of self-conscious mockery of tourist clichés. *Time* magazine was an early proponent of modern Niagara-as-camp, declaring in 1965 that "it's so out it's in," and almost every account of a visit to Niagara since the 1960s strikes a tone somewhere between the poles of sneering, patronizing, and bemused. A proposal floated by Canadian magician Doug Henning and the Maharishi Mahesh Yogi in 1991 to build a new age theme park at the Falls did little to encourage a more respectful attitude towards the place, nor did the opening of a gambling casino in 1996.

In the end, the irony of appropriating this early expression of gay camp sensibility for my own project—the nineteenth century's most famous homosexual making fun of the era's most famous heterosexual spectacle—proved impossible for me to resist. But in appropriating the language of disappointment for my title, I do not intend to strike the same haughty pose as the world-weary upperclass traveller, rolling his or her eyes at the working-class excursionists frolicking on Niagara's shores in the 1880s. Even the cynical Oscar Wilde saw something magical in the place. He declared Niagara "a melancholy place filled with melancholy people, who wandered about trying to get up that feeling of sublimity which the guide books assured them they could do without extra charge." But still he was enchanted with the waterfall. "I do not think," he said, "I ever realized so strongly the splendour and beauty of the mere physical forms of nature as I did when I stood by the Table Rock."10

I want to explore and explain these often contradictory feelings people have at Niagara Falls. Disappointment is part of the story, but so too is awe, wonder, and pleasure. Nor shall I portray the honeymoon in terms of a simple-minded outsider's critique of the rituals of heterosexuality; "stupid het tricks," if you like. The endurance of these institutions (Niagara Falls, heterosexuality, and the honeymoon) resists such an uncomplicated perspective. I do intend, however, to ask difficult and critical questions about heterosexuality and tourism.

Heterosexuality, Tourism, and Cultural Change

Someone remarked to me, as I was wondering aloud at the beginning of this project about how my long-standing interest in the history of sexuality fit with a book on the history of tourism, "Well, you don't go on vacation alone." Maybe so, but I don't think it is as simple as that. Sex and tourism are inexorably linked, overtly in the sex trade of countries such as Thailand and the Philippines and only slightly more subtly in the images of Caribbean, Hawaiian, and Mediterranean bodies that beckon winter-weary North Americans and Europeans from billboards and magazine ads.[11]

This sexualization of place through tourism is not new. The Caribbean Club Med, for example, flourished in the 1950s as an "isolated and recuperative Eden" that emphasized physical health, beautiful bodies, and an erotically charged climate, all located in an exotic, primitive setting: a "reconfigured colonialist adventure," as Ellen Furlough describes it, "that could be purchased." In the nineteenth and twentieth centuries, the Mediterranean became a homoeroticized space, thanks to a convergence of its image in history, poetry, and novels and its actual popularity with homosexual British travellers. Tiny bits of other countries have also been claimed as gay holiday spaces through the twentieth century, such as Fire Island's Cherry Grove in New York, and Brighton, England, which itself offers a most remarkable example of the reinvention and sexualization of space through tourism: from aristocratic haunt, to the heterosexual "dirty weekend" of the interwar years, to the gay mecca of the 1950s and 1960s.

Even such apparently not-sexual places as the Canadian Maritimes have acquired such a subtext, for, as Ian McKay argues, images of earthy, virile peasant sexuality were part of what constituted the exoticism of "the folk" so eagerly sought by visiting urban-dwelling Central Canadians and Americans.[12] Much of this is reprise, for, as we will see, the links between travel, sexuality, and the exoticized "Other"—the object of the gaze—were forged in countless travel books, scientific writings, and exploration stories of European conquerors as early as the sixteenth century.[13]

Places have a sexual, as well as political and economic, dimension. So when places become commodities and are bought and sold—which is, of course, what tourism is about—sexual images and meanings abound. What is unusual about Niagara Falls is that it has acquired a much more precise sexual meaning than the (apparently) hedonistic Caribbean or the (reputedly) wantonly sexual gay resorts. The honeymoon might be considered the original form of sex tourism, but it was always respectable. Even in the post-World War II era, when the honeymoon became a slightly risqué symbol of heterosexual passion, Niagara's sexual allure became consistently both highly regulated and permissible. Niagara Falls was where you went when you had your sexual "papers," a place that welcomed the only officially sanctioned form of sexual expression in Western culture—that which took place between two married heterosexuals. Armed with marriage licences and, for a time, even "official" honeymoon certificates, Niagara's newlywed visitors had the stamp of cultural approval. Because of this, Niagara Falls is an ideal place in which to observe the development of and changes in heterosexual identities. At Niagara Falls, the "Honeymoon Capital of the World," the hegemonic, taken-for-granted qualities of heterosexuality are rendered plainly, obviously, visible. You can't miss them, even if you wanted to.

Just as we are learning that men have a gender, and white people have a race, heterosexuals, odd as it sounds, have a sexual identity. Moreover, heterosexuality, like homosexuality, changes dramatically in different times and different places. The lens of the honeymoon reveals some of these changes. Understood, in different eras, as a retreat from home ground in order to accommodate the sexual innocence and embarrassment of the bride, the celebration of a return to normalcy in gender and family relations after periods of great social upheaval (the world wars), a companionate transition period for both husband and wife, a declaration of entry into the world of consumption, and, most recently, an orgy of sexual athleticism, the honeymoon, like heterosexuality, does not stand apart from its culture. In the outpourings of advice from sex experts about how one ought to behave on a honeymoon, in honeymoon-themed romance novels and films, including pornography (some of which parody honeymoon conventions quite revealingly), and in the particular flavour of Niagara honeymoon promotion through different eras, we can observe the changing rules of the game, as heterosexuals learned what was expected from them in entering public sexual culture. Changing honeymoon rituals—facilitated by changes in everything from the tourist industry to medical views of human sexuality to social class—have played an important role in shaping the contours of heterosexual identities.

A popular slogan, for instance, has adorned many a button and T-shirt in lesbian and gay circles. It goes "*heterosexuality isn't natural, it's just common.*" By investigating how heterosexual identities are acquired, rather than assuming that they are naturally, biologically fixed, historians of heterosexuality such as Mary Louise Adams and Jonathan Katz have also shown that the boundary separating "normal" from "abnormal" is not simple or easy to determine.[14] As teachers have learned, one of the most entertaining ways to introduce students to the notion of sexuality as a social and historical construction is to describe the moral panics of previous generations. As students convulse with laughter at the notion of the moral dangers of ice cream parlours and Chinese restaurants—both considered risqué in the late nineteenth century—they move, perhaps, into a better position to train a critical eye on our own culture's list of moral dangers: lesbians and gay men, the transgendered, and that timeless figure, the prostitute. The history of the honeymoon also makes complicated the notion of an enduring, unchanging norm—heterosexuality—set against a variety of other sinful practices.

Consider, for example, American novelist William Howells's fictional character Isabel March, an upper-class newlywed on her way to Niagara Falls with her husband in 1871. Her main concern about this excursion, voiced plaintively to her husband Basil, concerns privacy: "We will not strike the public as bridal, will we? My one horror in life is an evident bride."[15] This is about as far away from the culture of the 1950s bride, who was welcomed at Niagara with roses, complementary cocktails, and a stunning array of public promotional devices, as the Chinese-restaurant-as-moral-danger scenario is to students of today. Yet

Isabel March, the 1950s bride, and even the 1970s bride (who might have found herself in one of Niagara's playboyesque motel rooms, complete with red velvet curtains, hot tub, and circular bed), are all heterosexual, and all of them are observing the same ritual. For something that is allegedly natural, heterosexuality has changed dramatically over the years and requires enormous legal, social, and cultural support. The honeymoon was, officially at least, where it all began.

Tourism as History and Politics

Like Urry, I think travellers—honeymooners and other tourists—crave difference, and that the tourist gaze is formed "in relationship to its opposite, to non-tourist forms of social experience and consciousness."[16] But tourism raises many other political and philosophical questions, on which there is all manner of opinion. Some historians have argued that changes in tourism and leisure patterns over the last two centuries reflect the general democratization of North American culture. Mass tourism, from this perspective, signifies the vitality of North American capitalism, which has distributed social benefits such as leisure and travel much more widely than was the case a century ago, when only the very rich partook of the grand tour. Along the way, tourism has become, in historian John Sears's words, "nearly a universal cultural experience," and tourist attractions themselves offer "a common ground to all."[17]

Others are much more critical about the social benefits of tourism. Louis Turner and John Ash, for example, call tourism quite simply an opiate. Contemporary tourism, they argue, is simultaneously a safety-valve for First World nations (buying off working-class discontent with two-week holiday packages) and a conservative influence on Third World destinations (entrenching stereotypical and racist notions of how an "African" or "Jamaican" ought to look and behave, and forcing governments in tourist destinations towards status-quo policies to stabilize the country so as not to scare off visitors).[18] Others have detailed the devastating effects of mass tourism in places such as the Caribbean, mounting convincing evidence against the popular notion that tourism is a successful development strategy by showing the negligible economic benefits to host countries as the industry becomes increasingly centralized in First World hotel chains, airlines, and tour companies.[19] Since at least the sixteenth century, travellers have used their excursions to invent racial and cultural difference between Europe and everyone else. In the European imagination whole continents became, as South African novelist Christopher Hope has put it, adventures, rather than places, which travellers "made up as they went along."[20]

Rather than "broadening the mind," tourism does tend to reinforce social divisions, especially those of race and ethnicity. But the tourism-as-opiate theory, or the view of tourism only as voyeuristic, First World racism, has several problems. Such criticism, for example, tends usually to blame tourists themselves for this state of affairs. Turner and Ash, for example, writing in the 1970s, label tourists the "new Barbarians." Two decades earlier, U.S. scholar Daniel Boorstin argued that modern tourists had been hoodwinked by a series of what he called "pseudo-events." Tourist attractions, declared Boorstin, "offer an elaborately contrived indirect experience, an artificial product to be consumed in the very places where the real thing is free as the air. They are ways for the traveller to remain out of contact with foreign peoples in the very act of 'sightseeing' them."[21]

Boorstin blamed tourists for causing pseudo-events, rather than being targets of them. Thus he joins a long line of intellectuals who have dismissed tourists for getting it "wrong." But to blame tourists for tourism makes about as much sense to me as holding female readers responsible for badly written romance novels or blaming poor shoppers for junk-laden dollar stores. Tourists, like other consumers, are quite capable of ignoring the script, of wandering off stage and finding their own pleasures, imposing their own rhythms or subverting the official agenda.[22] The Niagara honeymoon has historically been reserved for those with stamped invitations—that is, married heterosexuals—which is why the place has long been irresistible to homosexual travellers, from Oscar Wilde to Walt Whitman to almost every gay person I know today.

Intellectual dismissals of mass tourism also overlook important dimensions of tourist history. Those who contrast the philistinism of the tourist with the high-minded, refined adventurousness of the traveller ignore the historical class relations of tourism. Mass tourism may hasten the ruin of a pristine waterfall, but elite travel was undemocratic and operated within a host/guest hierarchy in which the advantaged (European or white North American) guest was very well looked after by the host. Even the Lone Ranger, as Canadian historian Tina Loo remarks, was never "alone," and the notion that brave European souls in earlier centuries had more authentic or natural travel experiences is an illusion.[23]

Those who accurately identify the lopsided power relations of tourism tend to couch their analysis in the discourse of anti-pleasure moralism, a language all too common to the political left and feminists alike. There is nothing inherently *wrong* with vacations; nor is curiosity about other landscapes, other climates, or other people by definition an exercise in appropriation or exploitation. What is wrong is that, in the past as in the present, all people have not been allowed to give their curiosity free reign; some have been almost permanent guests, while others have remained hosts and walking tourist attractions.

What is wrong, also, is that too few tourists have recognized their privileged place in the host/guest hierarchy. Few have been as perceptive as Martin Amis, who wrote of his encounters with people in St. Lucia: "Although you wouldn't call them hostile, they are no more friendly than I would feel, if a stranger drove down my street in a car the size of my house."[24] Perhaps, as my sister commented to me as we watched our umpteenth sexual negotiation between a young local woman and an older European man (on the beach in liberated Cuba, of all places), if the world were such that North American or European men thought that Caribbean men might turn up in *their* towns, eating more than them and flashing great wads of cash in the faces of *their* children, they would stop acting like such jerks when they left home.

What follows is an idiosyncratic tour of heterosexuality, tourism, and honeymoon culture as they have played out at Niagara Falls. Although most readers have probably been to the Falls already, I hope that on this particular trip you just may see a few things you hadn't noticed before.

2

"The Pleasure is Exquisite but Violent": The Imaginary Geography of the Nineteenth Century

Like heterosexuality itself, the honeymoon is a commonplace, taken-for-granted aspect of our culture. The same goes for Niagara Falls. It is one of North America's oldest tourist destinations, and it is hard to imagine a time when people were not lined up alongside it, transfixed. But the honeymoon—as we understand it now—is a surprisingly recent invention, and Niagara Falls has been invented and reinvented with dizzying speed over the past couple of centuries. Originally, as we will see, this unusual combination—Niagara Falls and honeymoons—was not a tourist industry invention. Rather, the early association of Niagara with the honeymoon had something to do with the way in which countless people—visitors, local businesspeople, and writers and readers of travellers' tales—imagined the place.

The Origins of the Honeymoon: "My One Horror in Life Is an Evident Bride"

"The Cave of the Winds," wood engraving, from William Cullen Bryant, ed., *Picturesque America* (New York, 1873).

The modern honeymoon evolved from the nineteenth-century upper-class custom of the wedding tour (also known as the bridal tour), during which the bride and groom, often accompanied by relatives, visited other relatives who could not attend their wedding. The wedding tour, which had become a regular

The Wilcox and Mead Wedding Party at Niagara Falls, September 1867.

feature of middle-class weddings by the mid-nineteenth century, signified something quite different from today's honeymoon. Rather than a moment of romantic seclusion for two people, the wedding tour affirmed the bonds between the new couple and their family, community, and wider social network.[1]

The private honeymoon had appeared on the scene by the 1870s. But, while the Victorian honeymoon was an occasion for intimacy, sexual rituals did not figure prominently in its activities, and the popular culture of the day rarely discussed the event in sexual terms.[2] This had not always been the case. The wedding tour itself was an adaptation of the bridal night of sixteenth- and seventeenth-century England, a night that was an explicitly sexual milestone. As historian Lawrence Stone describes it, the couple were accompanied into the bedroom by relatives and friends, who provided plenty of horseplay and crude jokes, and were only left alone "once the curtains of the four-poster bed were closed." Such public sexual rituals ebbed at the end of the eighteenth century, when upper-class English couples began to shun practices such as the firing of guns at weddings, the display of the bride's garter, and even the parson's public kiss of the bride.[3] As part of the general attack on what has been called the "fundamental ritual order of Western culture"—the feasting, drinking, fairs, wakes, and other spectacles of the preindustrial era—the honeymoon was, by the nineteenth century, a much more modest and discreet affair.[4]

Some critics would have preferred to see the end of the ritual altogether. In 1886 Canada's Methodist newspaper, the *Christian Guardian*, called the wedding journey a "double evil" because it forced couples to "begin marriage in a state of lavish, artificial happiness" and "rendered them destitute" at the same time. B.G. Jefferis and J.L. Nichols, authors of a popular 1900 sex manual, *Searchlights on Health*, lamented that many newly married couples considered the ritual necessary for "connubial joy," since there was "nothing in the custom" to recommend its practice. "After the excitement and overwork before and accompanying the wedding," they continued, "the period immediately following should be one of rest." As late as 1923 a Quebec priest, Father Henri Martin, was charging that the honeymoon was a "deplorable custom which renders so many marriages sterile."[5]

Most people in the nineteenth century dealt with the growing gulf between the bridal night's overtly sexual history and public demands for sexual modesty by submerging the erotic features of the ritual. The Victorians simply unsexed the honeymoon. Sex experts Jefferis and Nichols, for example, recognizing that their main message, "don't," would go unheeded, instead joined other authorities in devising an intricate set of rules to be observed by newlyweds. Rule-making is inherent to the project of sex experts, and twentieth-century writers would also dispense volumes of professional, medical expertise; but later advice tended to be devoted to heightening the pleasures of marital sexuality, usually by coaxing recalcitrant brides and instructing bumbling grooms. Nineteenth-century experts focused their attention firmly on the dangers of sex.

Sex experts thought that wedding-night dangers arose from an unfortunate convergence of three problems: exhausted wives, oversexed husbands, and the rigours of travel. Wedding planning and organization fell squarely on the bride's shoulders, which could have disastrous consequences. "Who," asked Sylvanus Stall, author of the 1897 manual *What a Young Man Ought to Know*, "has not seen brides, with pallid cheeks and colorless lips, whom the white wreath and the long veil made appear more like the bride of death, than the woman who was about to assume the sacred duties of wife and mother?" Feminine frailty—for white, middle-class women—was a highly sought-after ideal at the time, but this frenzy of female activity was particularly unfortunate, for, as Stall continued, "If there is any time in the life of a young woman when she needs the largest store of physical endurance and glowing health," it was on her wedding night.[6]

The rigours of travel added considerably to the bride's burden. While rail and steamship companies, guidebook writers, and the nascent tourist industry were busily promoting the ease and benefits of tourism, all of the sex experts condemned long, arduous honeymoon journeys. Typical was physician George Napheys, who declared in 1880 that "to be hurried hither and thither, stowed in berths and sleeping-cars, bothered with baggage, and annoyed with the importunities of cabmen, waiters and hangers-on of every description, is enough . . . to test the temper of a saint."7 Some, like Napheys, were gender-neutral in their negative views of travel for newlyweds, while others were more faithful to their culture's view of vastly different male and female physicality. Jefferis and Nichols, for example, reminded a husband that "his bride cannot stand the same amount of tramping around and sight-seeing that he can. The female organs of generation are so easily affected by excessive exercise of the limbs which support them that at this critical period it would be a foolish and costly experience to drag a lady hurriedly around the country on an extensive and protracted round of sight-seeing."8

The alter ego of the timid, fragile Victorian woman was the sexually voracious Victorian male; and the newlywed husband described by sex experts could be a frightening creature. An early marriage manual, *The Physiogy of Marriage*, published in 1856, decried that a new husband tended to treat his wife as a "good and faithful beast of burden," and thus the first months of marriage were often "little better than a season of prostitution." The words "rape" or "legalized rape" were used by many commentators to describe the actions of brutish husbands upon their exhausted, innocent wives. Jefferis and Nichols, for example, argued that "many a young husband often lays the foundation of many diseases of the womb and of the nervous system in gratifying his unchecked passions," and they urged men to "prove your manhood, not by yielding to unbridled lust and cruelty, but by the exhibition of true power in self control and patience with the helpless being confided to your care!"9

It would be simplistic and wrong, though, to conclude, based on this evidence, that nineteenth-century honeymoons were passionless, unhappy endurance tests for both bride and groom. We cannot, unfortunately, contrast these public discussions of the ideal with the private realities of sexual practice, for the Victorians were notably reticent about setting pen to paper to record their innermost sexual feelings. While some of them did write about their honeymoon journeys, those accounts tend to read as standard nineteenth-century travelogues rather than sexual or romantic journeys. For example, in the memoir *My Honeymoon Trip*, published in 1897, the author Jean Brassey, a middle-class New Yorker, tells about taking his bride to Niagara Falls, stopping also at different points in New York state along the way. Like many of his contemporaries, Brassey submerges the erotic aspects of the ritual, but it is possible to read his account of the first evening with his bride as a story rich in sexual codes and metaphors. He is nervous, and like many honeymooners he displaces his anxieties into travel problems. He forgets to purchase his train tickets to Niagara until the last minute. He recounts his wedding night as a battle against nature: "It rained in torrents during the night and I had to get up and close the window, and to do so it was necessary to pull the awning down, which was too much of a struggle; but in a little while I succeeded in getting it down." By that time, he says, the lower part of his pyjamas (which he was not accustomed to wearing) "had fairly left my body."[10] Perhaps this passage stands as sexual metaphor or, to paraphrase Freud, perhaps sometimes a rainstorm is just a rainstorm. In any event Jean Brassey was one of the few of his generation who saw fit to record his honeymoon story.

Yet judging from another source of honeymoon wisdom, nineteenth-century pornography, Victorians were not completely successful in their attempts to put a new, sexually cleansed public face on the ritual. Pornography is always where the repressed and forbidden tend to lurk, and nineteenth-century pornographic writings subverted the dominant honeymoon script in fascinating ways. In titles such as *Honeymoon Confidences by the Bride Herself* (1909), *A Dialogue between a Married Lady and a Maid* (1900), and *Letters from Laura and Eveline* (1883), readers are treated to robust wedding-night tales, in which bride and groom alike display voracious sexual appetites.

Written, as their titles imply, as first-person communications between the bride and a female friend (though the sex of the author remains unknown), these stories often have a quasi-instructional tone. In *Mysteries of Venus* (1882), Sophia, who is about to be married, implores her friend and bridesmaid Cecilia to tell her about her own wedding night, for "I should like to know what I am to do and how to act." Similarly, Minnie frames her story, *First Three Nights of Married Life*, as a letter to her friend Nellie: "I am in the zenith of my happiness and . . . I will remember one girl friend and write her a letter that I hope will not only be interesting but instructive. I only hope that you for one will be blessed with the same concert of bliss that I now revel in." What Sophia, Nellie, and the other expectant brides in these stories learn is that sex—described in explicit detail, in infinite variations—is fun.

While the men in these stories are clearly the leaders and initiators (indeed, in these tales women are thankful for sexually experienced men, because they make better lovers), their wives prove willing and eager students and quickly declare their approval: "I tell you, Nellie, experiences were coming thick and fast. I did not think there could be such pleasure in the world." Minnie's only moment of unhappiness came when her husband, declaring he would not "act the brute" on his first wedding night, bid her goodnight the first evening without sex. "Imagine, now, my disappointment. Death at this moment would have been a welcome deliverance. . . . For the first time I was dying for a taste of that nectar ambrosia that gives the young their highest happiness."[11]

Pornography overturned almost every Victorian wedding-night convention. Honeymoons, in these stories, existed solely for the purposes of sexual initiation and pleasure, and brides as well as grooms were quickly aroused and sexually insatiable. Some stories also extended the sexual awakening beyond heterosexuality. Newly sexualized Minnie muses about her other friend, Kate, "the gayest and loveliest girl in the crowd," and declares: "How I would like to be the man who sleeps with her the first night of her wedded life. What bliss of heaven he would find in her arms and between her plump and tender thighs."

The most subversive of the genre, *Letters from Laura and Eveline*, is a remarkable story of the mock wedding of two pairs of homosexual men, complete with homoerotic decor ("splendid silver-gilt candlesticks, each one of which represented the emblem of our worship a huge priapus, set straight up as we like to see them in life, the bases being composed of finely moulded testicles"), two cross-dressing "brides" ("no one would have known us from lovely girls of seventeen or eighteen"), and a sexual initiation scene that brilliantly parodies

"THE PLEASURE
IS EXQUISITE
BUT VIOLENT":
THE IMAGINARY
GEOGRAPHY OF
THE NINETEENTH
CENTURY

24

heterosexuality: a tangle of the bride's "splendid clitoris," "arse cunt," and the groom's "foot long, muscular cock."[12] This is about as far away from the apparently chaste, modest ritual encouraged by marital experts as it is possible to get. Yet both are products of the same culture, and together they suggest that the nineteenth-century transition to the passionless private honeymoon was not simple or uncontested.

Advice manuals also offer clues as to why the public wedding tour was transformed into the private honeymoon. Since at least the 1880s, marital experts decried the "harassing" wedding tour, which was deemed both physically debilitating and immodest for the bride. Part of the problem with lavish travel, according to Sylvanus Stall, was that it exposed the couple to the "staring gaze" of crowds, and the bride, especially, was likely to suffer when made "the object of public attention and remark."[13] Newlyweds Gertrude Fleming and her husband Sandford Fleming learned this hours after their lavish society wedding in Ottawa, as they arrived in Montreal to embark on a European wedding journey in 1891. The couple was recognized when they walked into the dining room of Montreal's Windsor Hotel, and as Gertrude explained, "A guest dashed at us with loud congratulations." Gertrude Fleming—who grew up as a socially prominent daughter of the Ottawa elite, and whose wedding was front-page news—was rendered "miserable and self-conscious" by this attention and left hoping that "this newly-married feeling will soon wear off—I am ill at ease."[14]

Despite its problems, the private honeymoon had one important advantage over the more public wedding tour: it allowed the couple to escape the prying eyes of friends and relatives. It was horribly unpleasant for the bride to pass through "the ordeal of criticism and vulgar comments of acquaintances and friends" after the wedding. As one young woman complained to Mary Wood-Allen, author of *What a Young Woman Ought to Know*, she "did not want to be stared at or commented on by strangers" on her bridal tour. "Let us go to some quiet spot in the mountains or by the sea, and let us live with each other and with nature," she suggested as an alternative.[15]

Nature held out great promise as a honeymoon destination. Rigidly separated from "culture" in that era, "nature" was inherently private. That some humans lived there—Indians, for example—scarcely counted. Furthermore the country acted, in the nineteenth-century imagination, as the purifying and restorative tonic for many of the ills of the city. Just as nature might cure delinquent youth, wayward women, criminals, and sick people, so too might it work its magic on heterosexual romance. As one doctor put it, "Studying and admiring nature together . . . is the great cementer of hearts."[16]

American novelist William Howells's fictional characters, Basil and Isabel March, illustrate this attempt to combine public modesty with private romance. Howells's 1871 novel *Their Wedding Journey* follows Basil and Isabel on their tour from Boston through Niagara Falls and points east. The couple took their journey several weeks after their wedding ceremony, for which Isabel, especially, was extremely grateful. "How much better," she declared, "than to have started off upon a wretched wedding-breakfast, all tears and trousseau, and have people wanting to see you aboard the cars. Now there will not be a suspicion of honeymoonshine about us."[17]

Even during the Victorian period, everyone—as Isabel March feared—knew what a honeymooning couple stood for. In a culture that only considered sexual relations permissible within the institution of marriage, the wedding provided heterosexual couples with a social licence to become sexual beings. In earlier times, this was acknowledged and celebrated as part of the post-wedding ritual. For Victorian couples of the middle and upper classes, the private honeymoon was a way to reconcile the embarrassment of this passage into adult sexual citizenship with their culture's demands for public sexual modesty.

Even so, as Isabel March fretted about, and Gertrude Fleming experienced, newlyweds were marked and highly visible, and the private honeymoon was an illusion. When the first North American hotel to feature a honeymoon suite, New York's Irving Hotel, opened its new space to public viewing in 1847, the *New York Tribune* gushed at the elegance of what it called the "fairy boudoir," decorated with lace and white satin.[18] But the "privacy" of a honeymoon suite designated for the exclusive use of newlyweds was, like the honeymoon itself, a contradiction, as many honeymooners would have learned when they were spotted and mocked in hotel lobbies or on board trains headed to Niagara.

"How they gushed and spooned, and gazed idiotically," wrote a correspondent for *Frank Leslie's Illustrated Newspaper* of the honeymooners he travelled with to Niagara Falls from New York in 1879. As James Maloney, head porter at Niagara's Cataract House hotel in the 1880s, recalled, "A bride and groom didn't want anybody to suspect that they'd just been married. Seemed as if they'd almost rather be caught stealing!" While innuendo about honeymooners filled pages of Niagara journalism in the mid-twentieth century, even in the nineteenth century the newly married could be "distinguished by the practised eye of the hackman and the [hotel] clerks on sight, and the bridal chambers are seldom, if ever, assigned to the wrong couple."[19]

The lengths to which some honeymooners would go to avoid the public embarrassment bestowed by their new status are apparent in another honeymoon-themed novel of the early twentieth century, H. Perry Robinson's *Essence of Honeymoon*. Along the way, Robinson's book also reveals the precarious route taken by couples to acquire a comfortable, "natural," heterosexual identity. Euphemia and Jack decide that when they take their honeymoon trip in England they will pretend to be an old married couple. This is Euphemia's idea. She hates the notion of being an "evident bride" and, as an actress, thinks her new role as wife will be an easy one to pull off. She is dead wrong, and within the first five minutes of their journey they give themselves away. At the train station Jack purchases their tickets and returns to his wife:

> From a distance I could see Euphemia standing by the book stall where I had left her; and as I approached the perplexity assailed me. Ought I, or ought I not, to raise my hat? Did husbands take off their hats to their wives after leaving them for five minutes in a railway station? Yesterday I would have done it, but today? Why had I never noticed how married men behaved? Why was there no manual to tell one these things?

In the train, registering at the hotel, and especially at breakfast in the dining room the next morning, Jack and Euphemia learn that there is nothing natural about heterosexuality. Despite her acting skills, Euphemia cannot perform seasoned heterosexuality in a manner even remotely convincing, nor can Jack. At each turn their attempt at "passing" fails miserably, albeit humorously.

> Wherever I looked the guests peered at us, and were whispering confidentially to one another "Honeymoon! Honeymoon!" There was knowledge in the accusing eyes of every waiter. I believe Euphemia was no less comfortable than I. "If that old lady," she said at last, "doesn't stop staring at me, I know I shall have to throw my bread at her." "My bit is crustier," I said, as I passed it over to her. "It will hurt more."[20]

"THE PLEASURE
IS EXQUISITE
BUT VIOLENT":
THE IMAGINARY
GEOGRAPHY OF
THE NINETEENTH
CENTURY

28

The "Honeymoon Craze": Why Niagara?

French philosopher Michel Foucault describes the honeymoon as a "privileged or sacred or forbidden" place, set aside for those who are in a state of crisis. Like the menstruating woman, the pregnant woman, or the adolescent, the honeymooning couple exists nowhere, passing through this moment of crisis outside "conventional geographical markers."[21]

Nineteenth-century honeymooners had a peculiar relationship to their culture; they were, for a moment at least, decided oddities and outsiders. Social conservatives voiced their firm disapproval for the ritual, doctors and sex experts thought honeymooners should be given dire warnings and then, for a period, banished, and pornographic writers delighted in mocking social convention by exposing the main premise of the institution: entry into heterosexual culture. Yet honeymooning couples do not completely exist outside conventional geographic markers, for one such location, Niagara Falls, has been privileged as a honeymoon site par excellence for the past two centuries. Indeed, Niagara Falls was the first and, for a long time, the only honeymoon resort in the world.

The association of Niagara Falls with honeymoons is almost as old as tourism at the Falls itself, dating from the early nineteenth century. The legend, now a staple of Niagara Falls tourist promotion and local history, that the first honeymooners were the U.S. statesman Aaron Burr's daughter Theodosia and her husband, who visited in 1801, or Napoleon Bonaparte's brother Jerome and his wife, who came in 1803, has been challenged by historian Elizabeth McKinsey, who dates the origins of what she calls the "honeymoon craze" at Niagara to the late 1830s. Scattered references to honeymooners crop up in travellers' writings of the 1830s and 1840s. That era also saw perhaps the first Niagara honeymoon reference in popular culture, a celebrated 1841 ditty called, simply, "Niagara Falls." Its first verse goes:

Oh the lovers come a thousand miles,
They leave their home and mother
Yet when they reach Niagara Falls,
They only see each other.[22]

Visitors seemed to take honeymooners for granted as part of the Niagara landscape, but while newlyweds probably felt conspicuous, no one paid them much attention. During her stay in 1864, English visitor Frances Monck simply noted the presence of "several bridal couples" at her hotel. She also wrote approvingly that "they look very loving." Occasionally the presence of newlyweds provided another reference point for visiting Europeans to distinguish themselves—for good or ill—from North Americans. Captain William Butler, visiting from England in the 1870s, commented tersely that he saw several "newlywed couples conducting themselves in that demonstrative manner characteristic of such people in the New World."[23]

Niagara's fame as a honeymoon resort was, then, taken in stride by visitors through the nineteenth century, yet the first obvious hard sell of the region to honeymooners did not occur until almost one hundred years later. The honeymoon, like travel itself, was long a luxury, not an item of mass consumption, and so it was not really advertised or promoted in the nineteenth or early twentieth centuries. There were faint attempts at marketing the Niagara Falls honeymoon in the 1920s, such as specific references to honeymooners in general tourist promotion. These were piecemeal measures, hardly an ad campaign, particularly when contrasted with the real selling of Niagara as a honeymoon haven—including the creation of honeymoon certificates, honeymoon hotels, and other promotional devices—that would begin during World War II. Why, then, did huge numbers of honeymooning couples "vote with their feet" and visit the Falls in the nineteenth century, without being directly encouraged by anyone?

This raises the question of how certain sites become designated as popular places to visit, as well as of how particular places become invested with specific qualities. Consider, for example, the British seaside, a popular tourist destination for several centuries. Seaside resorts were popular because they were close to cities and towns and relatively easy to get to. But this was not the only reason that British holidaymakers flocked to seaside towns. They were also attracted to the sea because of its supposed health-giving properties. Later, in Britain as elsewhere, people began to think of the sun, not the sea, as healthy and rejuvenating, though in recent decades the depleting ozone layer has been changing this phenomenon as well.

In Canada nature tourism became popular in the nineteenth century and was, like trips to the British seaside, based on the notion that the woods provided a pure and nourishing environment. Throughout the early part of the twentieth century, the Ontario government, for example, sold the province, and especially the North, as a place of health, rest, and transformation. A "rest cure in a canoe," as *Rod and Gun in Canada* dubbed it in 1909, was just the thing to cure the ailments of white-collar urbanites.[24]

Places are more than simply locations; the spatial is also socially constructed, and places can mean different things at different times. Social divisions are often spoken of in spatial terms—the "wrong side of the tracks," for example. Like individuals, places can become labelled: Paris is romantic, New York is scary, Canada is boring (except for Montreal, which is sleazy). This combination of social divisions and spatial metaphors becomes incorporated into what geographer Rob Shields calls "imaginary geographies," so much so that certain sites become associated with "particular values, historical events and feelings."[25] Tourist promoters can take these associations of places with values,

"THE PLEASURE
IS EXQUISITE
BUT VIOLENT":
THE IMAGINARY
GEOGRAPHY OF
THE NINETEENTH
CENTURY

30

events, and feelings and create successful enterprises from them. But these efforts have their limits. As Michael Moore's documentary *Roger and Me* revealed, in the 1980s lots of money and grand planning could not turn the decaying industrial town of Flint, Michigan, into a tourist mecca, under any guise.

For Niagara Falls to become a popular honeymoon spot—especially in the absence of massive promotion—there must have been something there to begin with. The answer to this puzzle—honeymoon popularity a century or so before honeymoon promotion—lies in how romance, sex, and danger were incorporated in the imaginary geographies of nineteenth-century Niagara Falls visitors.

"First-Class" Tourists:
Niagara Falls as a Nineteenth-Century Resort

An English visitor, sketching the Falls, 1872. From *The American Tour of Messrs. Brown, Jones and Robinson: Being the History of What They Saw and Did in the United States, Canada and Cuba* (New York, 1872).

The tourist industry began in Niagara Falls immediately after the War of 1812. The first tourist entrepreneur was William Forsyth, an American from Buffalo, who in 1822 built the first hotel, the six-storey Pavilion, on the Canadian side. He promptly fenced in his property, so that only paying hotel guests could view the Falls from his vantage point. The first hotel on the U.S. side, Parkhurst Whitney's Eagle Hotel, also dates from this era. The opening of the Erie Canal in 1825 brought more visitors, as did the opening of the Welland Canal in 1832 followed by construction of railroads and bridges linking the two countries during the 1840s and 1850s.

While increased tourism was the result of easier access, the industrial possibilities of the waterfalls were the motivation for most of the investment in transportation. Backers of the Erie Canal saw visions of textile machinery and grist and saw mills fuelled by power generated from Niagara, and in due course manufacturing plants began to line both sides of the river. Niagara Falls, New York, was renamed, for a brief period, Manchester, a telling indicator of industrial optimism.

By the 1840s Thomas Cook was whisking hundreds of English tourists around on the world's first package tours. That decade too saw the launch of the first

The original Clifton House, the Ontario side's grand hotel. It stood at the base of what is now Clifton Hill from 1833 to 1898.

Atlantic steamship service, and Niagara Falls was hosting more than 40,000 visitors per year. Until the American Civil War, the Falls were especially popular for the Southern U.S. aristocracy, whose members wished to escape the summer heat on the plantation by attending the Niagara "Season." The grandest hotels in the area were built in the 1830s: Canada's Clifton House, "an abode of almost unparalleled gaiety," built by Monty Chrysler in 1833, and the U.S. Cataract House (also owned by Parkhurst Whitney). Each featured balconies and verandas with spectacular views, as well as gardens, billiard rooms, baths, and nightly balls and parties. The Clifton House even kept a pack of hounds should guests decide to venture out for an afternoon of sporting. In its fine dining room the hotel employed French and German waiters to act as interpreters for European guests. Many more fine hotels opened their doors in the 1850s and 1860s, most of them owned by the Falls Company, a consortium of seven men who took over much of the land adjacent to the waterfall.[26]

The second Clifton
House, 1906-32.

In this period everyone who could afford it went to Niagara, often as part of the Northern Tour, the American equivalent of the European Grand Tour. Other stops in North America included Boston and Quebec City. Visits to scenic attractions became important cultural currency for the U.S. upper classes. In the same way that an earlier generation regarded visits to the great cities of Europe as a central component of good breeding, early nineteenth-century Americans learned that the consumption of scenery closer to home demonstrated their gentility.[27] While the occasional early visitor claimed Niagara as "the great centre of attraction to all persons of every class," its upper-class aura held until at least the end of the American Civil War, which, according to a guidebook published towards the end of the century, cut off the summer pleasures of the Falls' "remunerative southern patronage."[28]

The waterfall was the main attraction, but always with plenty of sidelines. Two of the most popular attractions, both instituted in the 1830s, were (and

A drawing from *The American Tour of Messrs. Brown, Jones and Robinson* (1872), one of the only publications in the nineteenth century to suggest that some tourists lacked the masculine spirit of adventure.

remain) the U.S. side's Cave of the Winds and the Canadian side's Table Rock tours, in both of which people could walk through the Falls, buffeted by wind and water, and view them from "inside." Another popular attraction, the *Maid of the Mist* steamer (named after a fake "Indian legend" of virgin sacrifice), began its journeys to the base of the waterfall in 1840. Thomas Barnett's museum of "rare and exotic" curiosities (such as deformed animals and Indian and Chinese handicrafts), opened in 1827, and the villages on both sides of the Falls boasted bathing palaces, billiard rooms, bowling alleys, and public gardens. Entrepreneurs competed to claim the best viewing site. The Terrapin Tower (collapsed in 1873), built in 1833 on the U.S. side, on Goat Island, rivalled the Canadian Table Rock land formation (most of which collapsed in 1850). The view from various hotel balconies was also widely promoted. Battlefields were also an important part of the early tourist experience. Travellers would hire guides who claimed to have been survivors of the War of 1812 and be taken to Lundy's Lane, to the monument to English war hero General Isaac Brock (constructed in 1824), and to other famous war sites.

Entrepreneurs also found creative ways of embellishing the waterfall itself. The first major tourist gathering occurred in 1827, when hotel owner William Forsyth had a condemned schooner filled with live animals go over the Falls. Some fifteen thousand people (many of whom would have paid Forsyth and other landowners for the privilege of watching the event from their properties) gathered for the spectacle. Feats of human daring were also important (and massively advertised) audience builders. Daredevil Sam Patch jumped over the

The same Brown,
Jones, and Robinson
taking the view from the
American side, 1872.

Falls in 1829, and the most famous Niagara Falls stunt artist, the great "Blondin," performed his high-wire act over the Falls in 1859, repeating it the next year for another huge and appreciative audience, including the visiting Prince of Wales. Other tightrope walkers followed Blondin's lead, including an Italian woman, Maria Spelterini, who dazzled crowds in 1876 with her costume—a scarlet tunic, green bodice, and flesh-coloured tights—and her added twist: her feet were encased in peach baskets as she made her way across the wire.

High-wire acts were eclipsed by the "barrel craze," beginning in 1886 (by which time Niagara was already passé for the prestigious holiday-goer). The first person who successfully went over the Falls in a barrel was a woman, a widowed school teacher named Annie Taylor, who plunged over in 1901 (and has ever since been the subject of misogynist lampooning in Niagara Falls tourist history).[29]

Niagara Falls was also sold in the popular and high culture of the period. As McKinsey's book demonstrates beautifully, Niagara Falls was the most-often painted subject in early American art. The place became the first example of Canadian scenery depicted on a movie screen and was a hugely popular subject for filmmakers and photographers at the turn of the century.[30] It was also the

HARPER'S WEEKLY

JOURNAL OF CIVILIZATION

VOL. XXXV.—No. 1797.
Copyright, 1891, by Harper & Brothers.
All Rights Reserved.

NEW YORK, SATURDAY, MAY 30, 1891.

TEN CENTS A COPY.
INCLUDING SUPPLEMENT.

THROUGH THE CAVE OF THE WINDS, NIAGARA FALLS.—Drawn by W. T. Smedley.—[See Page 402.]

Sheer fascination: Messrs. Brown, Jones, and Robinson seek a better view, 1872.

subject of plays and novels as well as of some inventive visual spectacles, in the United States and abroad. In New York a popular play, *A Trip to Niagara, or Travellers in America*, took place in front of a moving panorama depicting the scenery between New York City and Niagara. In the 1840s two museums, one in London and P. T. Barnum's American Museum, exhibited scale models of the Falls. The most unusual spectacle toured the United States in the 1850s: a moving "panorama" featuring a thousand-foot-long canvas that took one and a half hours to unroll, with depictions based on two hundred paintings of the Falls.

Niagara Falls became a fashionable and desirable tourist resort in the early and mid-nineteenth century in part through mass spectacles and promotional gimmicks, but also because as a celebrity itself the Falls was visited by a veritable who's who of nineteenth-century luminaries.[31] In this first period of prestigious tourism, celebrity tourists helped make Niagara a cultural icon. Niagara became famous for being famous, and fame did not—as it would in the twentieth century—render the place boring or passé.

Not for the faint of heart: negotiating the Cave of the Winds wooden stairway, 1891.

Indeed, fame helped, so much so that visitors such as English author Isabella Bird were excited to visit because of the familiarity of the place: "From my

The visiting Englishmen atop Terrapin Tower (1872), not long before it collapsed.

earliest infancy I had been familiar with the name of Niagara and, from the numerous pictures I had seen of it, I could, I suppose, have sketched a very accurate likeness." Another visitor in the 1870s agreed: "Its fame has gone before it, so that no person approaches it without expecting more of it than probably any other show place or natural wonder in the world." Niagara was one of the "canonical sights" of the New World: "What the pyramids are to Egypt . . . so is Niagara to North America," exclaimed another visitor in the 1870s. Another said it "beats Michael Angelo" [sic] for artistry. A guidebook contended that Niagara was to waterfalls as Shakespeare was to poetry.[32]

Guidebooks like that one create the tourist gaze in multiple ways; once a location becomes entrenched in a guidebook, its fame is guaranteed. Niagara was blessed three times over: it was in all the guidebooks (according to estimates, over a thousand different gift books and guidebooks about Niagara were published in the nineteenth century); it was a celebrated and beloved icon in paintings and photography; and it was visited by the rich and the famous. It would also, of course, become the favourite destination of honeymooners.

The Imaginary Geography of Niagara Falls: The "Queen of Cataracts"

The main objective of visitors was quiet contemplation of the waterfalls. To really "do" Niagara, the visitor stayed for a long period of time and watched the Falls in awed silence, from different vantage points and in different lights. "Words are powerless, guides are useless," wrote *London Times* correspondent

Nicholas Woods in 1861. "He who wishes to see and feel Niagara must watch it for himself."[33]

We know a lot about what the nineteenth-century traveller felt and thought about Niagara, because a good many of them took the trouble to write down their impressions. In the nineteenth century, travel was a literary activity; the travelling class was also the reading class.[34] Literary celebrities published accounts of their visit to the Falls, as did a host of less famous travel writers, poets, and diarists. Guidebooks and gift books also contained pages and pages of descriptive writings. Charles Dickens is probably the most often cited writer of Niagarana; passages from his travel journal, published in 1842, were quickly repackaged in countless guidebooks, and he continues to be quoted by tourist industry promotional literature to this day.

But the imaginative outpourings of hundreds of other obscure or even anonymous writers also found their way into print. The desire to offer impressions of Niagara was institutionalized by the tourist industry; the proprietors of Table Rock House provided guest books in their sitting room, where people would write a few lines about their experiences after taking the Table Rock tour under the Falls. At least two anthologies from this album were published as souvenir books in the 1840s and 1850s.

Travellers were determined to "read" the waterfall, and a number of different meanings appear in the writings of nineteenth-century visitors. Travel writing provides a revealing commentary on the place of the narrator—the self—in relation to the surroundings. Many Americans, for example, imagined Niagara as a symbol of their nation. In paintings that depicted bald eagles, stars and stripes, and flag-draped young women standing before the waterfall, Americans—intent on national definition and celebration—appropriated the Falls for the spirit of their young country.[35] Because the Falls were shared by another nation, and the Canadian Horseshoe Falls was the larger and more compelling of the two, this claim was rather complicated to sustain.

The U.S. visitors who commented on the Canadian waterfall often did so jokingly, expressing remorse or envy. Novelist William Howells admitted that he watched the "mighty wall of waters" on the Canadian side "with a jealousy

almost as green as themselves," and an anonymous scribbler in the Table Rock album expressed the same sentiment in verse: "My pride was humbled and my boast was small, for England's King has got the fiercest Fall." U.S. President John Quincy Adams turned the history of Canada/U.S. border battles into an act of God. "It is as though," he mused, "Heaven had considered this vast natural phenomenon too great for one nation."[36] Canadian writer Agnes Machar's patriotic delight that "our Canadian falls are the grandest" was a theme taken up by surprisingly few Canadian visitors.[37]

The waterfall also acquired an important religious identity. For many tourists, Niagara had all the trappings of a sacred shrine, a view that achieved official recognition in 1861 when Pope Pius IX established a pilgrim shrine at Niagara Falls. Many referred to the place as a "cathedral," and others suggested it was "where God himself baptizes." "I feel as if I had entered a living temple of the Eternal," wrote one visitor, who invited others to "come and worship at the shrine of Niagara." Irish poet Thomas Moore probably spoke for many when he wrote in a letter to his mother in 1804: "Oh! Bring the atheist here, and he cannot return an atheist!"[38]

Religious sentiment about the Falls helped shape another type of meaning: the moral power of Niagara. Niagara was the setting of several didactic Christian children's books, and the Canadian social purity movement also found Niagara Falls a powerful visual metaphor to illustrate its agenda. The "Mighty Niagara of Souls" was an image used by the Canadian Salvation Army to arouse concern for the plight of countless lost souls—the drunkard, the gambler, the sensualist, the society lady and her "fallen" sister—who were "fast being hurried over the 'Niagara' of life into the whirlpool of eternity."[39]

Nineteenth-century moralists found Niagara Falls a powerful symbol of damnation and destruction because of another long-standing set of meanings evoked by the waterfall: its association with both pleasure and terror. From the first written description of the Falls in 1683 by Father Louis Hennepin, who called it "the most Beautiful, and at the same time most Frightful Cascade in the World," such ambivalence has characterized much writing about Niagara. "The pleasure is exquisite but violent," wrote one visitor in 1821. Yet the lure of Niagara was as potent as its danger. As another early nineteenth-century traveller commented, he could "hardly consent to leave this seemingly dangerous, and enchanting spot."[40]

Despite the voluminous accounts of visits to Niagara Falls, writers again and again expressed the difficulties of describing the experience. "There is no term of our language too high, or idea of our imagination adequately comprehensive, to describe this profound and impressive scene," wrote one anonymous guidebook author. Another Table Rock album contributor agreed:

I came to see;
I thought to write;
I am but—dumb.[41]

One device many writers used to describe the indescribable was to attribute human feelings and emotions to the rushing waters. Some simply compared the waters to humans. "When one has looked at the waters for a certain time one feels certain that the mass is alive," declared a typical visitor in 1873.[42] Isabella Bird described the U.S. rapids: "rolling and struggling down, chafing the sunny islets, as if jealous of their beauty," they then "flung [themselves] upwards, as if infuriated against the sky." She concluded, "There is something

HIS LATEST CRIME

Niagara Falls as woman. This cartoon, published in the *Niagara Falls Review* in 1926, refers to a dispute of the day between Canada and the United States over diverting water from the Niagara River. The strangler's sweater carries the words "Chicago Water Steal."

very exciting in this view, one cannot help investing Niagara with feelings of human agony and apprehension."[43]

Others were less self-conscious than Bird in their use of human imagery, but no less expansive. The rapids were seen as "a symbol of life and human passion. . . . The helplessness of its frenzied sweep saddens your heart." These characterizations, varying in mood and emotion, fill volumes of Niagara Falls prose. The rapids "gambol along in a sportive mood," then become "possessed by demons." The mist is like "children of the air," and the "greedy" waters evoke a "sullen majesty," a "haughty grandeur," or "dance and curl in rapture." Cliffs "frown," billows are "angry," shores too are "sullen." Novelist Henry James saw the Horseshoe Falls as an exhausted swimmer, "shrieking, sobbing, clasping hands, tossing hair."[44] Others saw the river "telling its tale—at first in broken syllables of foam and flurry, and then . . . in rushing, flashing sentences and passionate ejaculations." Niagara Falls, declared the Niagara Parks Commission, gave tourists the opportunity to see the "awe inspiring spectacle of nature in one of her turbulent moods."[45]

That last passage indicates another common descriptive device: the waters were not simply personified, they were given a gender, and most of the time this was the female gender. To almost all writers who used gender in their descriptions, Niagara was a woman: the "Queen of the Cataracts," the "Water Bride of Time," the "Daughter of History," and the "Mother of all Cascades."[46] Niagara Falls has always been an icon of femininity.

While incorporating female imagery into their descriptions of Niagara, many writers also projected suitably heterosexual responses, which sometimes took the form of simple flattery, particularly of the "costume" of the waterfall. Niagara "wears a garb that wins from man . . . wonder, awe and praise." At "her" base, she would "wrap herself saucily in the rainbow robe" of mist. During the reign of "King Winter," Niagara dons a "coat of crystal" and sparkles like "a gem in the diadem of nature." One particularly poetic writer saw, amidst Niagara's winter scene, trees "bowed down to the earth with their snowy vestments, like so many white nuns doing saintly homage to the genius of the place." Others saw Niagara's mist as a veil, sometimes bridal, at other times ghostlike. Writers also described the electrical illumination of the waterfalls using metaphors of fashion, though not always positively. Lady Mary McDowell Hardy was horrified to see Niagara "dressed up like a transformation scene in a pantomime. It was like putting a tinsel crown and tarlatan skirts on the Venus of Milo."[47]

To many observers Niagara was *like* a woman; others were more literal. British visitor William Russell claimed, "I never looked at it [the waterfall] without fancying I could trace in the outlines the indistinct shape of a woman, with flowing hair and drooping arms, veiled in drapery." The invented tale of the Indian "Maid of the Mist," who went over the waterfall, fuelled many such fantasies. Promoters of Canada Steamship Lines tours to the Falls in 1915 invited tourists to imagine that "instinctively we see the Indian maid in her flower-bedecked canoe approach the apex of the Falls, her body erect, her demeanour courageous." Images of naked "Indian maidens" going over the waterfall adorn postcards, souvenirs, and advertising, as well as "high art," to this day.[48]

The positioning of the waterfall as female and the viewer as male enhanced the pleasure of "doing" Niagara. Not surprisingly, then, sexual imagery abounds in descriptions of the Falls. The spray from the mist was often described as a "kiss." The sound of the water rushing was a "moan." Islands rest on the "bosom" of the waterfall, and the "soft shales" of the cliff "gradually yield before the attack" of the rushing water. The "clinging curves" of water "embrace" the islands, and water "writhes," "gyrates," and "caresses the shore." The whirlpool is "passionate." Some writers recoil from the "mad desire" of the waters. For others, "no where else is Nature more tender, constrained, and softly clad." Niagara— "nature unclothed"—was "seductively restless" and "tries to win your heart with her beauty."[49]

Niagara certainly won many hearts. "Like a beautiful and true, an excellent and admirable mistress," wrote George Holley in 1872, "the faithful lover may return to it with ever new delight, ever growing affection."[50] Poets spoke of the "smooth, lustrous, awful, lovely curve of peril . . . cruel as love, and wild as love's first kiss!" Another evoked the image of Sappho, "that immortal maid—

enchantress sweet." One poem published in a 1901 collection illustrates the "exquisite pleasures" of Niagara in no uncertain terms:

"THE PLEASURE

IS EXQUISITE

BUT VIOLENT":

THE IMAGINARY

GEOGRAPHY OF

THE NINETEENTH

CENTURY

44

> Nymph of Niagara! Sprite of the mist!
> With a wild magic my brow thou hast kissed;
> I am thy slave, and my mistress art thou,
> For thy wild kiss of magic is still on my brow
>
> I feel it as first when I knelt before thee
> With thy emerald robe flowing brightly and free
> Fringed with the spray-pearls and floating in mist
> That was my brow with wild magic you kissed

The author continues, describing how the waterfall has "bound" him.

> . . . thy chain but a foam-wreath, yet stronger by far
> Than the manacle, steel-wrought for captive of war
> . . . While the foam-wreath will bind me forever to thee,
> I love the enslavement and would not be free.
>
> Nymph of Niagara! play with the breeze
> Sport with the fawns 'mid the old forest trees
> . . . I'll not be jealous, for pure is thy sporting
> Heaven-born is all that around thee is courting
> Still will I love thee, sweet Sprite of the mist
> As first when my brow with wild magic you kissed! [51]

Fictional treatments of visits to Niagara also recounted the magnetic sexual lure of the waterfall. Agnes Machar depicts Niagara as the first stop in her story of a holiday journey of several young Canadians. The protagonist, May, is joined at Niagara by her cousin Kate and Kate's cousin Hugh, whom May had not previously met. Young May is initially shy around Hugh, but after their first look at the waterfall together (a "curving, quivering sheet of thundering surge . . . dazzlingly pure in its virgin beauty"), May looks at Hugh in a new light. She feels "much less shy" around him and notices him physically for the first time. She is mesmerized by his "heightened colour" and the "absorbed expression of dark blue eyes."

Hugh, it turns out, is also transformed by his view of the Falls. "I never felt," he tells May, "as if I had got so near the state of self-annihilation, the 'Nirvana' we read about." May had "much of the same feelings herself," though she was "too reserved to say it out." As the party continues its journey, going across Lake Ontario and down the St. Lawrence River, the romantic tension between May and Hugh heightens, and by the end of the trip Hugh proposes marriage, asking May to "travel down the river of life together."[52]

Isabel March, the reluctant honeymooner in William Howells's *Their Wedding Journey*, was similarly transformed by Niagara, though she was ambiguous about her feelings. Howells treats Isabel's determination not to reveal herself as an "evident bride" with gentle humour, particularly because she is one of countless "evident" newlyweds at Niagara Falls. This parody of Victorian manners comes to a crescendo when Isabel, positioning the waterfall as a sexual male, confesses that she cannot contain herself any longer: "I'm tossed upon rapids, and flung from cataract brinks, and dizzied in whirlpools; I'm no longer yours, Basil; I'm most unhappily married to Niagara. Fly with me, save me from my awful lord!"[53]

The waterfall could also—befitting a female of many moods—turn ugly, and many horrified but fascinated visitors commented on the fatal lure of its waters. "As you gaze upon the rush you feel a horrid yearning in your heart to plunge in and join the mad whirl and see the mystery out," declared one. Some suggested scientific explanations for this experience, positing that the sight of such a "frightful eminence" caused a rush of blood to the brain, which in turn produced a "partial derangement."[54] Yet most others relied less on science than common discourses of feminine sexuality, depicting the waterfall as an alluring and enchanting female, bewitching and sometimes entrapping legions of male suitors.

"With all this fear," wrote one promoter in 1856, "there is something so imposing in our situation as to render it pleasing. . . . We are in the presence of the enchanter." "The beautiful stream permits itself to be toyed with," wrote another visitor. "Its smiling accessibility is most alluring, but is most dangerous. Every rock and ledge has its story of the fatal attraction of the waters." Like a designing woman, Niagara Falls often uses wiles to trick the unsuspecting. "One of the chief charms of the Falls of Niagara is the familiarity with which they can be approached, but beware of their relentless power."[55]

The dangers were perhaps as widely promoted as the pleasures. Patrick McGreevy observes that metaphors of death abound in the human-made landscape around the waterfall. Wax museums depicting famous criminals and monsters, war monuments, and emergency hotline telephones positioned at prime viewing areas all testify to people's fascination with the waterfalls' deadly potential.[56] Vivid descriptions of accidents, suicides, and other deaths at the Falls have been a staple feature of Niagara tourist promotion for two centuries. Twentieth-century publicity focuses on the brave, heroic, and happy: the tightrope walker, barrel jumper, and, especially, the now legendary "miracle at Niagara," the story of a seven-year-old boy who went over the Falls in the summer of 1960 and lived. Nineteenth-century stories were decidedly more horrifying. Descriptions of the "hell of waters," their "angry fury," the "roar of ten thousand baffled demons," and the "hissing cauldron of spray" fill the accounts of the time. Niagara-area military history made these stories even more convincing. As one guidebook explained, "The lurid tales of conquest . . . have made the historical page of Niagara a record of blood."[57]

The fatal attraction of the waters was promoted and celebrated as an integral part of the Niagara experience. Stories of babies accidentally swept over the Falls as their mothers looked on helplessly, construction workers falling off bridges, "weak-minded" souls (usually female) who jumped from the cliffs, and intoxicated men (usually Native people) going over in canoes abound in guidebooks, and these tales obviously enhanced perceptions of the area's dangers. "You cannot tell," as one guidebook writer explained, "when or where the next tragic affair will happen. Perhaps, reader, the polite stranger who has

"THE PLEASURE
IS EXQUISITE
BUT VIOLENT":
THE IMAGINARY
GEOGRAPHY OF
THE NINETEENTH
CENTURY

46

The Ice Bridge at Niagara, as photographed for a postcard printed in Germany about 1900. Until the tragedy of 1912, strolling about and playing on the frozen falls were popular wintertime pastimes.

ridden with you . . . or chatted with you at the hotel table, or who even now, at your side, leans over the bridge, is on the point of—but we forbear; it is not well to regard those about you as suicidal suspects, unless their conduct is manifestly suspicious."[58]

The most popular accident story in the nineteenth century was the tale of Charles Addington and Antoinette DeForest. The two were picnicking with their families, who lived in Buffalo, on Luna Island in June 1849. Addington, aged twenty-two, playfully grabbed DeForest, aged eight, and pretended to throw her in the current. Antoinette fell in, and Charles jumped in after her. The two went over the falls and did not survive. This most "melancholy of all Niagara tragedies" was recounted in guidebooks and travel writing over the next fifty years, but how it was told varied markedly. Few guidebooks reported the ages of the two victims. Most told this as a story of two lovers who went over the falls "locked in each other's arms."[59]

The twentieth-century equivalent of the Addington/DeForest tale was the great Ice Bridge Tragedy of 1912. The Ice Bridge, a snowy hill that formed in winter at the base of the waterfall, was a popular attraction through the nineteenth and early twentieth centuries. Visitors could walk across the frozen river to the Ice Bridge and get much closer to the waterfall than they could in the summer. Children had fun sliding down the ice, and vendors set up booths nearby to sell hot drinks. But in February 1912 the ice cracked and broke apart, and three of the fifty or so people gathered on the Ice Bridge that day failed to make it to shore. Those three stood helplessly on an ice floe, unable to reach ropes that rescuers suspended from the bridge as they passed under it.

The dramatic story of these three—a young man from Ohio and a husband and wife from Toronto—would provide heart-wrenching copy for guidebooks and newspapers for some time to come. As one particularly vivid writer described the scene:

> Mr and Mrs Stanton went to their doom with a prayer on their lips. The man's courage was sublime. When he realized that all hope was gone he took off his coat, wrapped it about the woman, and together, they knelt on the ice in an attitude of prayer, the man with his arms about his wife. And thus when the first breaker of the rapids turned their frail ice craft over they plunged into the icy current. Many a prayer went up from the silent groups on the shore in unison with that uttered by the dying couple, and hundreds turned their faces away when the ice floe reached the breakers.[60]

Quite an account: yet later on the event would yield even better stories. The famous psychoanalyst Ernest Jones, who knew the Stantons through a mutual friend, and hence knew that they were childless after seven years of marriage, appropriated the story to illustrate his views about the sad effects of sterility for women. The very presence of Mr. and Mrs. Stanton in Niagara Falls that

"THE PLEASURE
IS EXQUISITE
BUT VIOLENT":
THE IMAGINARY
GEOGRAPHY OF
THE NINETEENTH
CENTURY

48

weekend, he suggested, revealed something of Mrs. Stanton's sadness about her childless state. As well as being known as a honeymoon resort, Niagara, Jones pointed out, was also well known as "the Baby City, from the high percentage of conceptions that date from a visit there." Thus he explained the "unconscious attraction" of the place to the childless Stantons; especially in winter, when "the idea of winter (death, cold, etc.) . . . was beginning to correspond with their attitude of hopelessness about ever getting a child." Mrs. Stanton's apparent passivity as she felt herself floating towards the icy whirlpool was, for Jones, not the result of panic but rather "a childbirth fantasy of a sterile woman, the floating on a block of ice in a dangerous current of water, in company with the lover, in sight of all the world and yet isolated from it."[61]

No less inventive were the stories, told repeatedly by enthusiastic writers and journalists working in the honeymoon-besotted post-World War II era, which portrayed the Stantons as a love-struck but doomed honeymoon couple. In the 1940s and thereafter, even one of the local Niagara Falls newspapers got into the act, commemorating the tragedy with tender stories of the "final embrace of the honeymooners."[62]

For my part, I am not arguing that guidebooks, tourist promoters, or travel writers should be reprimanded for sloppy research. Rather, I am suggesting that the relationship between self and other, which is fundamental to travel and to travel writing, is often more revealing about self. At Niagara, the gendered, sexualized descriptive imagery, fatal attraction of the waters, and tales of death and destruction, as well as invented stories of romance and tragedy, were all of a piece and helped create a romantic, sexual, and frightening image of Niagara Falls. Such imagery helped fix an image of the Falls as a place of forbidden pleasures: just the spot for a Victorian honeymoon.

And it wasn't just in their heads. Two of the most popular Niagara Falls excursions—the Table Rock and Cave of the Winds tours—*actually*, not just imaginatively, heightened these sensations of pleasure and danger.

Before the advent of the elevator, the tours behind the Falls through the Table Rock tunnels and inside the Cave of the Winds were quite elaborate undertakings. At the entrance to each tour, women and men entered separate change rooms and completely disrobed: "down to the skin," as one traveller marvelled, "with no thought of retaining even your underclothes."[63] The visitors donned a suit of flannel, covered by an oilskin coat, and then followed a guide through the maze of rock and thundering spray. At their final destination, travellers celebrated their accomplishment by frolicking in the waters. Upon their return they were awarded with certificates for successfully completing this most dangerous tour.

The costume itself was enough to startle many visitors. One called it "the scantiest set of garments in which I have ever appeared in public." Robert White, an English doctor visiting in 1872, was horrified by the outfit and relieved at the end of the tour to "resume the habiliments of civilization." Others tried to take the event in good humour; one commented that his party was "every way enlarged, with oiled cloth, india-rubber and tarpaulin," causing the women to look like "little, rosy Dutch butter women." Women and men wore the same outfit, which also caused some consternation to nineteenth-century visitors, so accustomed to rigidly gendered styles of clothing.[64]

Like many, Isabella Bird balked at the idea of disrobing completely, and when she emerged from the dressing room her "appearance was so comic as to excite the laughter of my grave friends." Perhaps in an effort to upstage Niagara, the actor Sarah Bernhardt—another popular female icon of the late nineteenth century—proudly transformed the costume with a silver belt and a corsage of roses.[65]

George Borrett, who visited in 1864, offers this vivid account of his tour to the Cave of the Winds:

> I cannot describe to you what a terrifying scene it was—how the waters roared around us, how the stifling spray beat upon our faces, so as to drive all the breath out of our bodies, how the wind, caused by the falling mass of water, blew about in a thousand blinding gusts . . . clashing the rain into our faces and chests, or driving it against our backs and legs. . . . I only know that I went down into this watery hell, and came up again uninjured, but very much out of breath and awfully frightened, half blinded, more than half deafened, and three-quarters drowned.[66]

The American Falls and the
Cave of the Winds stairway.

For some, the natural dangers were enhanced by human ones. Isabella Bird was one of many who expressed horror at finding a "negro guide of the most repulsive appearance" waiting to take her through the Table Rock tunnels. Others recoiled at the Irish and French-Canadians employed as guides. Even without ethnic markings, guides were objects of fear and fascination, "ghost-like figures," according to one visitor.[67]

"THE PLEASURE

IS EXQUISITE

BUT VIOLENT":

THE IMAGINARY

GEOGRAPHY OF

THE NINETEENTH

CENTURY

52

Yet after the sightseers had negotiated any number of possible demons, nat-ural and human, the experience of cavorting through torrents of gushing water, dressed in oilskin or rubber, was truly remarkable. One of the most blissful descriptions comes from U.S. visitor Frederic Almy, in 1896. He spoke of the water "foaming and rushing about your knees, and lugging at you with an invi-tation that is irresistible. I have seen grave men frolic in the water, their trousers and sleeves swelled almost to bursting with the imprisoned air. . . . To play so with Niagara brings an exhilaration that is indescribable."[68]

Others spoke of the "delightful, novel and strange sensation, of commin-gled terror and safety." Novelist Thomas Hughes, author of *Tom Brown's School-days*, was positively schoolboyish himself, exclaiming that the feeling of water "seizing and tearing" over his body was "marvellously delicious."[69] Even a most scholarly and upright Victorian gentleman, Professor John Tyndall, writing for a scientific journal in the 1870s, was enthusiastic about the "sanative effect" of the Cave of the Winds:

Quickened by the emotions there aroused, the blood sped healthily through the arteries, abolishing introspection, clearing the heart of all bit-terness, and enabling one to think with tolerance, if not with tenderness, of the most relentless and unreasonable foe. Apart from its scientific value, and purely as a moral agent, the play, I submit, is worth the candle.[70]

Most agreed that the experience was a "terrible ordeal, which no one should miss undergoing."[71]

Many people have speculated about why Niagara Falls became associated with the honeymoon, and the question has provoked an endless series of jokes, witticisms, and bon mots. One of my favourites is novelist H.G. Wells musing in 1905 that falling water was merely an alibi for honeymooners, a noisy "acces-sory to the artless love-making that fills the surrounding hotels." The answer does not lie in mimicry. Niagara could not have sustained its reputation as "Honeymoon Capital of the World" for two centuries because a handful of famous newlyweds turned up in the 1830s. Nor does another popular answer—

falling water creates negative ions, which cheer people up and make them think about sex—get us very far.[72]

Niagara Falls undoubtedly did make visitor after visitor think about sex, but the creation of the place as a honeymoon mecca was a complex process that brought together several strands: its reputation as an elite tourist resort; its proximity to a large, concentrated population; changing mores about the honeymoon itself in nineteenth-century social and family life; cultural depictions of Niagara as an icon of beauty, which were more likely than not expressed in terms of gender and heterosexual attraction; and the forbidden pleasures of sexuality, romance, and danger that countless travellers experienced while gazing at, or playing with, the waterfalls.

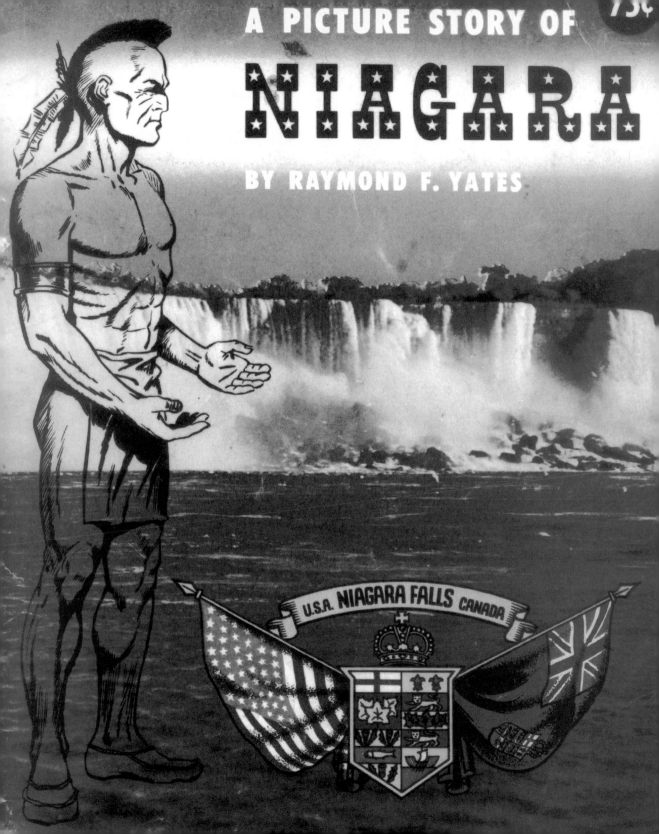

3

Local Colour in the "Contact Zone":
The Spectacle of Race

In the mid-1970s, U.S. sociologist Dean McCannell identified a new trend in tourist attractions. The distinction between what he called the "front regions"—what the tourists are supposed to see—and "back regions"—where the service personnel retire, relax, and prepare—was, he argued, becoming mixed up. Modern tourists, according to McCannell, had come to value the closer, more intimate relationships of the "back regions" more highly than the formality and distance of the "front." This explains why tourists had become increasingly interested in observing life behind the scenes, getting "in with the natives" (even though they are always ridiculed for failing to do this). But it also seemed that tourism was becoming a hodgepodge of front (Disneyworld) and back (tours of motion picture studios or grand, famous homes), which complicated an easy division between the two. It is always possible that what looks like a back region is really a front region, designed, with tourists in mind, to look natural or spontaneous. This sleight-of-hand has been termed "staged authenticity," making the whole world a kind of "living museum" in which tourists slip easily from front to back to front again.[1]

More recently, postmodern social commentators have argued that the categories of staged and real, or front and back, have completely collapsed. Today's tourists are enthralled by what anthropologists call "genuine fakes," attractions that everyone knows are inauthentic but have attained a certain quality of "realness" by virtue of their longevity or by how they are presented to visitors.[2] This also helps explain the popularity of literary landscapes—pilgrimages to

The cover of a tourist comic book published in Buffalo, N.Y., in 1953. For centuries now, Native men at Niagara have been offered up as being as thrilling and dangerous a spectacle as the waterfalls themselves.

Sherlock Holmes's apartment, or Dickens's London, for example—a popularity that upsets any easy division between fake and real. This collapse of modernist certainties has created a new kind of tourist, which John Urry dubs the "post-tourist." Post-tourists enjoy the staginess—even the campiness—of modern tourism. "They know," Urry says, "that there is no authentic tourist experience, that there are merely a series of games or texts that can be played."[3]

Plenty of famous North American tourist attractions are genuine fakes. One of the first times I discussed my Niagara Falls research with other historians was at a meeting of the Canadian Historical Association in Charlottetown, Prince Edward Island. I spent a few days at the Lake of Shining Waters Inn, a lovely old house that claimed to be the former residence of Rachel Lynde, well-known as the inquisitive neighbour of Lucy Maude Montgomery's fictional character Anne of Green Gables (whose own "home" was just down the road). If I had wanted, I could have dined at Matthew and Marilla's Pizza Parlour or shopped at Green Gables Groceries. The possibilities, in Cavendish, Prince Edward Island, are endless.[4]

Niagara Falls, though, is not fictitious. The authenticity of the waterfall is surely beyond question. What could be more real than a long, lingering gaze at nature? The more you look, the more the water keeps falling. But many different versions of Niagara beckoned the nineteenth-century tourist, and conflicts over these various versions of Niagara fuelled great changes in the 1880s, as governments on both sides of the river took over and created parkland.

Parks *look* natural, but they don't just happen. They are designed, and the parks on both sides of the Niagara River had a prestigious pedigree; they were created by the famous landscape architect Frederick Law Olmsted. Olmsted's work a decade earlier in creating New York's Central Park was deemed a smashing success, and this bestowed upon him tremendous cultural authority to define natural beauty.[5] Central Park was created as an urban safety valve, to bring the fractious and diverse multitudes of New York City together under the calming influence of nature. The movement to create public parkland around the Falls in the 1880s also had a social agenda. With the advent of one-day railroad trips from nearby industrial cities in the 1870s, "excursionists"—a code word for working-class and middle-class visitors, as opposed to upper-class "travellers"—were arriving by the trainload. The "wrong sort of visitor" was also having the wrong sort of experience. Rather than quiet contemplation of the waterfall, excursionists were treating it rather like a penny arcade or an amusement park; picnicking at its shore, watching it through camera obscuras, or having themselves photographed in front of it.

The activities of these excursionists point to a second, equally serious problem: the wrong sorts of entrepreneurs had established themselves on Niagara's banks. As one especially indignant visitor put it in the 1870s, "Vendors of Indian beadwork, itinerant philosophers, camera obscura men, imitation squaws, free and enlightened Negroes, guides to go under the Cataract—who should have been sent over it—spiritualists, phrenologists and nigger minstrels have made the place their own."[6] If the immediately apparent dangers of the Falls—not all of them real—had complemented nineteenth-century views of sexuality and made the place especially enticing for newlyweds, the imagined dangers of the Falls extended well past the waterfall itself, taking in many of the people who lived and worked there.

The back regions of nineteenth-century Niagara Falls are, surprisingly, a place few have ventured. While scholars have defined tourism as the interactions between "hosts and guests," most people who study tourism have done so from the perspective of the outside—the guests—rather than the inside—the hosts, especially the personnel of the tourist industry.[7] The many recent studies of Niagara Falls, for example, take the waterfall's fame as a tourist attraction for granted and tend to neglect the small army of hotel and museum owners, hack drivers, souvenir vendors, and guides who have collectively organized and managed the tourist experience. Tourism reflects the diminishing difference between staged and real, ordinary and different, but for millions of people it is also about day-to-day, immediate matters: it is their job. Niagara Falls was, since the early nineteenth century, a world-famous cultural icon, but it was also a town, a place people worked and lived. These people, in turn, helped to shape the image of the place in the larger culture.

Estimates of the number of people employed in the tourist industry around the world currently range from one in fifteen to one in nine. Researchers agree, however, that most tourist industry workers—the vast majority of them women and ethnic minorities—are clustered at the base of a "very steep pyramid" of low-paid, part-time, and seasonal workers. "In much of the world," writes Linda K. Richter, "tourism is something non-whites participate in only as employees, if at all."[8] Tourist brochures are one of the few places in modern advertising that feature black or brown faces, and this is true not just for Third World destinations. People of colour appear in a multitude of roles—mainly subservient—in tourist advertising around the world. They act as servants, entertainers, or vendors; and, as cultural markers, their "exotic" bodies and faces spice up the scenery for the guests, who are almost always depicted as white.[9]

This phenomenon is not new. The faces and bodies of non-European Others have constituted a central part of the tourist gaze for several centuries. Travel has long helped Europeans to define themselves as different from, and usually superior to, something they began to understand as "the rest of the world," as Mary Louise Pratt puts it in *Imperial Eyes*, her fine study of the history of travel writing.[10] Lopsided power relations are part and parcel of the tourist experience. What gets selected and promoted as a tourist destination, for example, often has less to do with the unique or desirable qualities of that place and more to do with its proximity to powerful, highly populated urban areas. Certainly, if it were not for its location Niagara Falls would never have become the place that it is; many other spectacular waterfalls in the world have not attained its iconic status. The host/guest relationship itself is a power relationship. As anthropologist Dennison Nash suggests, "If the tourist is to pursue peculiarly touristic goals, others must perform more utilitarian functions. . . . Others must serve while the tourist plays, rests, cures or mentally enriches himself."[11]

Let us not overlook, however, as many do, that these bodies at play and at work tend to have particular skin colours, facial characteristics, and cultural histories. Native North Americans, Africans, and Caribbeans are in and of themselves big tourist draws. A poster that appeared in Dominica in the early 1980s exhorted locals to "Smile. You are a walking tourist attraction." Viewed from the comfort of air-conditioned tour buses, black neighbourhoods from South Africa to Harlem have been transformed into harmless tourist spectacles.

The grand old days of colonialism are evoked—and purchased—in hotel bars in British Columbia and on the beach at Club Med. In most North American cities Chinatowns and gay ghettos alike have been refashioned from places of vice and crime into upscale shopping and dining areas. Whole land masses and economies in the Caribbean have been appropriated for European and North American tourism. Even in the poorer regions of North America—the Canadian Maritimes in particular—tourists are encouraged to search out and enjoy the "simple folk." In the face of all of this, the popular cliché that travel broadens the mind seems difficult to sustain.[12]

That North American Native peoples have long held a peculiar fascination for white visitors has been established. Less well-known is how the everyday experiences of travel released Europeans (and white North Americans) into the shadowy world of the non-Anglo service industry, which provided visitors with food, lodging, and enough local colour to fill volumes of guidebooks. At Niagara, travellers not only encountered a powerful natural spectacle but also found many new human curiosities. Non-whites constituted a good supply of the help, but they were also part of the show. Europeans described these encounters in a variety of ways—including fear, humour, and sometimes pity—and generally we have access to only one side of the conversation. Nobody published or preserved the opinions of the Indian souvenir seller or the Irish hack driver. Furthermore, lots of different kinds of people travelled in the nineteenth century and acquired sophisticated cross-cultural knowledge without producing travel writing. Some of Niagara's visitors would have brought along their own servants, for example, whose reactions to the waterfall, as much else, went unrecorded in travel narratives.[13]

These encounters, though, were a kind of conversation—even if one voice was louder—and not a monologue. The tourist experiences took place in what Pratt terms the "contact zone," the space in which people who have distinct social and historical experiences come into contact with each other. One side—the European travellers—had the upper hand, politically and economically. But in the context of unequal relations of power, the relationship between traveller and "travelee" (or colonizer and colonized) is not one of separateness and apartheid but rather of interaction.[14] This helps to explain the simultaneous fascination and repulsion with which travellers regarded the locals. Nineteenth-century imperialists claimed that colonialism was based on the "white man's burden" of helping the less fortunate. In our day, colonialism looks more like theft, pure and simple. But colonialism was about more than theft. It was also about imitation, fear, and fascination, the cultural relationships that formed to facilitate the processes of theft.

The spectacle of racial difference, then, proved to be immensely interesting to white Europeans and North Americans. Indeed, the world views of the colonizers contained an apparent paradox: they deplored the "savages" in their midst and at the same time made them central characters in their museums, exhibitions, circuses, fairs, and literature.[15] Mariana Torgovnick suggests that the Western fascination with things "primitive" is really about "imagining us," a revelation of the self that is inherent in the act of defining the Other.[16] In any case, nineteenth-century travel tales provide compelling evidence about the complicated and peculiar relationship between white people and "the rest of the world."

Many people have found travel writing a fascinating source of information about the clichés, conventions, and stereotypes that Europeans developed as they attempted to understand what appeared to them as the strange realities of the non-Western world.[17] The accounts of travellers to Niagara Falls show how Europeans helped to render the natural and human wilderness of the New World knowable and thus able to be claimed and owned. These acts of appropriation were produced through writing that created Niagara Falls as a highly sexualized icon of the savage and untamed. But this also happened economically, entrenching racial and ethnic hierarchies into the bricks and mortar of the tourist industry.

The Spectacle of Race: Native People as Tourist Attractions

One reason travellers came to Canada from abroad in the nineteenth century was to see "Indians." From travellers' descriptions of the sight of their "first Indian," to the variety of invented stories of Native tragedy and sacrifice associated with the legend of the Maid of the Mist, to the re-creation of an "authentic" Indian village in the 1950s, Native peoples have been woven into the natural history of Niagara Falls. Along with waterfalls and wax museums, Native people were established as tourist attractions, extensions of the natural landscape. The tourist gaze is created by symbols and signs, and thus one's journey consists of collecting—visually, through souvenirs or photographs—the appropriate symbols.[18] And nothing was a more important signifier of North America than the peoples of the First Nations.

Throughout the nineteenth century, Native people signified wilderness, the opposite of civilization. Like the explorers, traders, missionaries, and armies before them, European tourists carefully patrolled the civilization/wilderness border. They had a firm sense of the side they occupied, but they also evinced a strong curiosity about what, and who, lay on the opposite shore. The quest for "wild things" brought hundreds of thousands of tourists to Ontario in the nineteenth century, and Western Canada's tourist industry was also built by the tourist fascination with the original inhabitants of the land.[19] Niagara was no different than many other North American tourist destinations in this respect. It was tame enough to accommodate the standards of daily comfort demanded by the European upper class (after all, by the mid-nineteenth century at least six luxurious hotels stood on both sides of the river), yet wild enough to be interesting.

The Indians that Niagara's visitors strained to glimpse were probably from the Tuscarora nation. After decades of brutality at the hands of white settlers in the Carolinas, the Tuscarora had begun a forced march of migration to the Niagara region in the early eighteenth century. In the 1720s they joined the Iroquois Confederacy and were given land by the Seneca. In the first population estimate of the Carolina Tuscaroras, published in 1708, they had numbered 5,600 in fifteen communities, but their first community near Niagara Falls consisted of fewer than three hundred people, initially living on one square mile. By the time the tourists started arriving in the 1820s and 1830s, they had acquired more land, the village extended to ten square miles, and the population numbers remained about the same.[20]

This community, about ten miles from the Falls, near Lewiston, New York, became an important tourist destination, serving, as Patricia Jasen notes, as "a place where visitors could assess the residents' capacity for civilization while picking up souvenirs at the same time." As members of the Six Nations, the Tuscarora held perhaps an even more symbolic meaning for visitors. The former power and military prowess of the Iroquois Six Nations made them legendary, and Europeans most likely found tremendous excitement in viewing the "tamed" descendants of such famous warriors.[21]

The local Native peoples were absolutely "safe" and no longer restless, but they had not put too much distance between themselves and their exotic history. Furthermore, Niagara Falls was located sufficiently far away from the Tuscarora's compatriots in the western part of the continent, who, through the 1880s, stubbornly refused to be tamed. Yet the persistence of Native resistance elsewhere must have added to the allure. Wild-west adventure stories and especially the popular "captivity narrative"—stories of white people kidnapped by Indians—increased in both popularity and imagined viciousness as whites increased their physical control over Indian lands.[22]

This particular contact zone also gave European visitors a close look at one of the era's great divisions: the difference between "progress" and "degeneration." As Anne McClintock explains, degenerate types of people were necessary for the self-definition of the European middle class, for "the distance along the path of progress travelled by some portions of humanity could be measured only by the distance others lagged behind."[23] Measuring this distance was, for European travellers, a fascinating but clearly disconcerting pastime. As Lady Duffus Hardy remarked, observing her "first Indian" outside Montreal on her way to Niagara, "It is simply impossible to regard them as 'men and brothers.'. . . Looking on these people, with their low brows and the animal expression on their expressionless faces, we felt there might be some truth in Darwin's theory after all."[24]

Travel writers regularly noted the sight of their "first Indian" on the shores of the Niagara River, sometimes in a tone rivalling the excitement of seeing the waterfall. As soon as German composer Jacques Offenbach arrived at Niagara in the 1870s, his guide insisted, "You would like to see the Indians." British writer and illustrator George Sala "captured" his first Indian in his travel diary in much the same way he might have recorded sighting a bird: "He was the first North American Indian, in his own land, I had seen." William Russell declared, "Next to the purveyors of curiosities and hotel keepers, the Indians reap the largest profit from the crowds of visitors."[25]

Like most travellers, Offenbach, Sala, and Russell were disappointed with what they saw. Indeed, most accounts of first sightings of Native people provide a telling glimpse of "racial panic" as the travellers let loose a volley of invective at the spectacle of race before them.[26] Travellers' accounts of Niagara's Indians ran the full gamut of nineteenth-century stereotypes. The Indians were too ferocious or too tame, romantic figures or pathetic drunkards, uncivilized and unchristian, or boring (or ridiculous) in their attempts to mimic white lifestyles. Some writers felt cheated by their visits to the contact zone. As early as 1855 Ida Pfeiffer complained that the Tuscarora reserve was "now scarcely worth going to see, as the inhabitants, who have become Christians, go dressed like the whites, and build and cultivate their fields just like their neighbours."[27]

Contrary to Pfeiffer's account, and despite the efforts of Christian missionaries who arrived in their village in 1800, the Tuscarora did resist some European cultural impositions. The first Christian church was built in 1806, but by 1820 fewer than twenty Tuscarora had joined. By 1845 Europeans had constructed two schools, but most of the Indians spoke Tuscarora, not English. Still, the community had taken up farming, and reports of missionaries and other observers through the nineteenth century indicate that the Tuscarora were among the most self-sufficient of all the Six Nations. Pfeiffer's disappointment about Tuscarora apparel, however, was probably real enough. Tuscarora Chief Clinton Rickard, born on the reserve in 1882, recalled that in his youth it had not been the custom to dress "in Indian fashion," and when he began to reject European clothing in favour of traditional Indian dress, he was considered an oddity.[28]

The conflict between the assimilationist aims of government policy and the demands of tourism for difference and exoticism explains the introduction of stage-managed Indian events at Niagara Falls in the 1870s and 1880s. These included the "Indian burial ceremony" and "Great Buffalo Hunt," organized by Col. Sidney Barnett, who, with his father Thomas, owned the Niagara Falls Museum.[29] Barnett began these events in 1872, importing buffalo, steers, fifty Indians, and four Mexicans, as well as the famous Wild Bill Hickok, to perform an annual two-day "Wild West Show." While these pantomimes of colonial conquest were wildly popular throughout North America into the early twentieth century, Niagara's tourists seemed unimpressed. Only two thousand spectators showed up to see Wild Bill Hickok. Few travellers mentioned this attempt at staged authenticity in their reminiscences, and Barnett lost $20,000 on this event alone. The "Buffalo Hunt" received this stinging rebuke in an 1884 guidebook:

> The crowd assembles to witness a great treat of a most exciting kind, only to see a couple of old, decrepit buffalos from the Museum Gardens lazily feeding on the green pastures of the old Drummondville race course, and Buffalo Bill and his braves decked in gay trappings riding about the course. Several attempts are made to excite the buffalos into a run; but all the flogging, clubbing and prodding fail to develop a speed in the monarchs of the prairie above a trot. Finally, the "brave hunters" turn their attention to a few Texan steers, which had been secured from a passing train for the occasion, and after a great effort actually succeeded in getting them to run from their pursuers.[30]

Disappointment and cynicism about Indians at Niagara began to peak towards the end of the nineteenth century, which is not to say tourists were not still interested. Rather, the tone changed. Instead of expressing fear and disgust, travellers presented themselves as knowing, world-weary sophisticates by questioning the authenticity of the Indians they met. The "Oriental Dancing Girls" and "Indian Snake Charmers" at U.S. circuses in this era were often played by heavily made-up white people, and rumour had it that some of Niagara's Indians might also be theatrical inventions. Offenbach, in 1875, wrote that he "expected to find savages, but they showed me pedlars, men who produced articles de Paris. . . . Were they really Indian? I rather doubt it." Edward Roper, visiting Niagara for a second time in the 1890s, noted, "There are the same Indians about as of old; they say the squaws come generally from 'ould Oirland.'" Many visitors complained about "Irish Indians" or "Indian curiosities" made in New York (or England or France or later, of course, Japan), and by the 1890s one of the popular guidebook series edited by Karl Baedeker was warning readers that "the bazaar nuisance [at Niagara] continues in full force. . . . Those wishing Indian curiosities should buy from the Indians themselves."[31] From savage to boring to fake, Native people as tourist attractions generally disappointed, but they always drew.

The sight of Indians provoked more than the desire to gaze. While the European gaze itself, especially as expressed in scientific and travel writing, is proprietary (the "master-of-all-I-survey," as Pratt calls it), visitors claimed possession through a variety of other gestures. The Other was consumed imaginatively—when Europeans wrote their own scripts for fantasy conversations—and literally—when Europeans purchased Native-crafted souvenirs. Both of these encounters—imagining Native people, and buying from them—reveal the two-sided nature of relationships in the contact zone: exchange and appropriation.

Consider, for example, Sala's long discussion of sighting his "first Indian," an event that occurred, he says, as the two of them were gazing at the waterfall together. Sala begins with a familiar diatribe: the Indian is a "shiftless and degraded vagrant, who does not wash himself, who is not at all scrupulous about taking things that do not belong to him, who will get blind drunk on rum or whisky whenever he has a chance." Yet after this outpouring Sala returns to their mutual fascination with the waterfall, and the Indian changes from a human object of scorn to one of nature's victims. "I wonder what he's thinking, as we look at the Falls together; maybe he is thinking that all this used to be mine," Sala muses.

Sala narrates his Indian fantasy: "All this belonged to me, and now I am a vagrant and an outcast and the white man charges me for the birds I have slain." He ends his reflection with a return to the explicit imperial voice, but his tone changes from disgust to pity: "Poor copper hued child of the wilderness!"[32] This may be a matter of imperial guilt, genuine compassion, or the reinscription of racism, but it is certainly an exchange that can function only because of the imagined silence of one party.[33]

The passion for collecting Indian "curiosities" also signals something of the ambivalent relationship between whites and Native people in the contact zone. At Niagara Falls Indians had been granted permanent access to the tourist market by General Peter B. Porter, whose family owned much of the land immediately surrounding the waterfall on the U.S. side. As a reward to Indians for meritorious service during the War of 1812, Porter permitted members of the Tuscarora reserve to sell beadwork on his property, and this practice continued even after Porter's land was purchased to make up Prospect Park in the 1870s. Female beadwork vendors, such as the often-photographed sisters Delia and Rihsakwad Patterson, proved a great hit, for visitors seemed as interested in the merchants as the goods.[34] Yet most visitors complained about the "grotesque and gaudy" style of Indian handicrafts, "a miscellaneous stock of gewgaws," even as they purchased them. One visitor even claimed to have seen, on sale in an Indian bazaar, a "real scalp of an Indian, duly labelled and consisting of a triangular piece of skin," and speculated that the scalps of a group of Indian women sewing beadwork nearby might someday similarly become "a saleable ornament."[35]

By purchasing souvenirs travellers could prove that they had made the journey, and perhaps they could also pretend to attain a certain level of "Indianness." Some critics suggest that the European fondness for Native souvenirs reflects a European love/hate relationship with Native people, as though by collecting and consuming Indian artifacts white people might displace real live Aboriginals. The effect on Native people of this exchange is less clear. Women and children especially secured employment as makers and sellers of Indian crafts, and the participation of Native people in the tourist economy was, perhaps, one way for them to make the best of a bad situation. But the manufacture and sale of tourist commodities formed, at best, a rearguard, minimal defence.[36]

Part of what made the North American Indian such a spectacular attraction in the nineteenth century was, as Daniel Francis puts it, the widespread convic-

"The Indian Store," Niagara Falls, Ont., 1927.

tion that "they would not be around to see much of the twentieth."[37] When dire predictions that "progress" was bound to doom Indians to extinction failed to come true, twentieth-century tourists continued to see Native people as a colourful, timeless reminder of North America's tumultuous frontier. This accounts for the popularity of the model Indian villages established in Niagara Falls and elsewhere in North America in the mid-twentieth century. These representations of Indianness by non-Indians continued to reproduce the "imaginary Indian" of European fantasy.

The Maid of the Mist

The paradigmatic "first Indian" who provided a moment of panic and, sometimes, further reflection, was always male, which most likely indicates more

"Scene at Niagara Falls—Buying Mementos," a sketch from *Harper's Weekly*, June 9, 1877. Visitors complained about the "grotesque" Indian souvenirs—and the people who sold them—even as they freely purchased them.

about European notions of fitting representatives of culture than the sex of the Native person the travellers actually first saw. The visitors always spoke of Indian souvenir sellers as female—"an army of persistent saleswomen," as one guidebook put it—which indicates the distinct possibility that a "first Indian" might well have been a woman.[38]

Native women were by no means ignored by Europeans, as the centuries-old fascination with the Maid of the Mist legend indicates. This tale is the epitome of the genuine fake. Dating (possibly) from a story "commonly reported in the country" and circulated by a travelling fur trader in 1753, of an Iroquois man caught in a current above the Falls and swept over, the tale changed form through the nineteenth century to conform to European conventions of drama, romance, and sexuality.[39] Tales of sexual relations between whites and Native people were standard fare in nineteenth-century adventure fiction, and "Indian maids" were especially popular characters. But the white male who is charmed by the Native woman is doomed, and the only escape is the death of the Native woman, which allows the white man to concentrate on his real mission, which is to conquer or tame the land. These stories are merely the nine-teenth- and twentieth-century versions of a long-standing cliché of colonial

A sightseeing party, with guide, on Table Rock across from the American Falls, c.1860.

history. Africa, the Americas, and Asia were all eroticized by Europeans, and travellers' tales abounded with what McClintock calls "visions of the monstrous sexuality of far-off lands . . . a magic lantern of the mind onto which Europe projected its forbidden sexual desires and fears."[40]

In this case the Iroquois man became an "Indian maid" named Lelawala, who was forced by her unfeeling father, the chief, to descend the Falls in a canoe to appease angry gods. Sometimes the father, in a moment of remorse, joins her, while in other versions she is joined by her lover and rescued by him at the bottom of the Falls. Some stories have the two young Indians living there still, behind the waterfall, as man and wife.

Countless versions of this story have been told, in guidebooks, travellers' accounts, and tourist industry promotional literature, for two centuries. In 1910 the Pathé Cinematograph Company of France arrived at Niagara to film the story, setting a birchbark canoe, with a "dummy figure of an Indian maiden" inside,

adrift over the Falls. In 1928, several years after the Falls began to be lit by coloured lights in the evening, a "special illumination" had Queen Victoria Park "black with people" who crammed in to see the silhouette of the "Indian Maiden" pass over the Falls. In the 1940s the tale was retold as a honeymoon story; the "fairest maiden" was set adrift to become "the bride of Manitou." In the 1950s the crowning of "Miss Maid of the Mist" was a highlight of an annual Indian festival.[41]

Stories of exotic Indian maidens and savage customs such as human sacrifice certainly gave the New World a dash of romance and adventure. But these tales also fit well with white people's preconceived ideas about their own presence in the New World. Colonialism was presented as a good thing, because it reined in the barbarism and hypersexuality of the colonized. It was only in the summer of 1996 that the Maid of the Mist Steamboat Company finally listened to the protests of Native groups and ceased telling this tale as fact.

Unruly Locals—Problems at the Falls

Niagara was home to colourful characters and romantic stories, but its tourist industry, according to most visitors, left a lot to be desired. From almost the first time that Niagara was claimed for tourism, in the 1820s, travellers have expressed their disapproval with how the place was being run. By the 1830s visitors were sending out warnings. In 1831 Alexis de Tocqueville urged a friend to "hasten" to Niagara, because he didn't "give the Americans ten years to establish a saw or flour mill at the base of the cataract."[42]

Two long-standing complaints were that Niagara was being ruined and that a Niagara holiday was too expensive. Visiting in the 1850s, Isabella Bird resented the distractions of "parasitic guides, sandwich-eating visitors, vile museums, pagodas and tea-gardens," and William Ferguson agreed that Terrapin Tower, the staircases to the base of the Falls, and "some twopenny-halfpenny museums, which all cluster about the edge of the falls, spoil the effect sadly." In 1871 English visitor Henry Jones was astonished that the spectacle he had come so far to see was "choked in the horribly vulgar shops and booths and catchpenny artifices

A page from Raymond Yates's 1953 comic book "A Picture Story of Niagara" reinvents a long-standing genuine fake, the Maid of the Mist legend.

"A guide," most likely a Table Rock or Cave of the Winds employee, "in the prime of manhood, large and well built." From *The Village of Niagara Falls* (c.1880).

which have pushed and elbowed to within the very spray of the Falls, and ply their importunities in a shrill competition with its thunder." Another wrote, humorously, of the defilement by billboards:

As you stood on the Table Rock, the finest point from which to view the Falls, a huge board, which you could not possibly evade, informed you all the time that Jennings liver pills were sure, quiet but searching. The fine trees which frame every lovely picture on Goat Island had been let out to a wretch who had painted on every trunk the startling fact that "gargling oil was good for man and beast," and the lovely rocks on Luna Island resounded with the cry that Love's worm powder was never known to fail.[43]

Even worse, a sojourn at the place cost a lot. Amelia Murray, visiting from Britain in the 1850s, wrote sarcastically, "The English are accused of being a grasping nation in requiring fees for sights, but nothing I ever met with equals the charges for the contemplation of Nature here." Others noted the need for "well stuffed pockets" when visiting, and an anonymous reporter for the *Canadian Illustrated News*, visiting one afternoon in 1876, learned quickly that rather than "doing" Niagara, "Niagara was 'doing' me." He remarked, "The Falls were sublime, the cost of seeing them, ridiculous."[44]

Perhaps the most telling comment on the expense of Niagara is a handwritten message scribbled on the back page of the Toronto Metro Reference Library's copy of F. H. Johnson's 1865 *Guide to Niagara Falls and Its Scenery*. Someone, presumably the original owner of the guidebook, had totalled up the charges at

Joseph Lennox, an American guide, shows visitors the view in winter 1910.

the Falls, including the price of the book ($1.00) and fees for tolls, museums, carriages, and hotel. The cost came to $15.40. Beside that figure are three words written in ink: "Grandeur is Expensive."

The cause of both of these problems—expense and desecration—lay with one source: Niagara's tourist industry. Complaints about what one visitor to Niagara called the "disgustingly obtrusive civilization that crawls over its sides" were nearly universal. Tourists spoke bitterly of the "hateful race of guides . . . miserable little peepshows and photographers, bird stuffers, shell polishers, and collectors of crystals," who were everywhere. It seemed that "the very pick of the touts and rascals of the world had assembled here." One visitor, who counted fourteen different "hotel runners" at the train station, was constantly "dogged over every inch of ground" by "guides, photographers, shop-mongers and toll-gatherers." Occasionally a guidebook tried to mute such criticisms. One book advised tourists that they would be "using facilities and improvements which have cost large amounts of money" and that "are only remunerated for a few months."

Other guidebooks attempted to turn the frenzy of commerce into part of the allure: "Everywhere in the busy streets is heard the hum of merry voices and the tread of hurried footsteps. Glittering carriages, filled with entranced passengers, hastily diverge in every direction, to visit the various surrounding scenes of interest."[45] More often guidebooks turned the controversy to their advantage, claiming to be the only "original, correct and reliable" source of information or offering "special protection" for their readers. *The Humbugs of Niagara Falls Exposed*, published in 1884, was perhaps the world's first manual for the post-tourist. It filled more of its pages warning readers about the "fake" ("impositions") than the "real" (paid advertisements for "legitimate" photographers, hotels, and grocers).[46] By the 1880s Niagara was a "byword and reproach," calling up "visions of tawdry shows, extortionate hackmen and tradespeople, hideous factories, and the dishevelled outskirts of an ugly village." It was a place, according to a New York journalist, "no American can visit without feeling his face burn with shame."[47]

These are strong words, and especially so for the "age of industry," which makes the condemnation of commerce at Niagara Falls that much more paradoxical. The same newspaper that carried damning stories of the desecration of Niagara would also be singing the praises of industrialization in other towns, countries, and empires. The same travellers who were so put off by the sights and sounds of commercial activity at the Falls were men—and women—of commerce themselves, whose comfortable circumstances gave them the leisure time and income to travel great distances, away from office, factory, or workshop. Niagara Falls, from these descriptions, may well have been ugly and tawdry but so too, from all accounts, were the commercial and industrial centres of most of the nineteenth-century capitalist world. The ruin of Niagara at the hands of the rapacious free market, in particular, elicited widespread criticism and eventually led to (successful) calls for state control, and the criticism sprang from the elite, not wild-eyed radicals, trade unionists, or social reformers. Why wasn't similar criticism raised, for example, against the equally ruined condition of urban landscapes, or around the issues of health or housing?

British novelist David Lodge has commented on the cleverness of the English ruling class, who located their places of work—the industrial north—as far away as possible from their places of leisure—the seaside resorts of the south.[48] Perhaps this wry observation tells us a good deal about the situation at Niagara, which would long juggle, with varying degrees of success, its twin role as tourist and industrial centre. Yet it was not just the factories that marred the tourist gaze at Niagara. Nor were all visible signs of commercialism condemned with equal vigour. Visitors were well pleased, it seemed, with Niagara's hotels. While the food and service sometimes elicited negative comments, the hotels themselves were usually lovingly described, and the views, especially from the private verandas, were awe-inspiring. Even in the 1880s, as the "free Niagara" campaign moved into full gear, visitors remarked on the "world-wide reputation" of Niagara's hotels, in which the visitor "may agreeably extend his stay over several days."[49] Why, one might ask, did camera obscuras and Indian bazaars disfigure the place but hotels did not? How do some sites and practices of capitalist market relations become subject to vociferous, moralistic criticism, while others are either ignored or, under some political regimes, cheered on as the best, most natural form of social organization?[50]

The answer to this puzzle has something to do with the explosive mix of host and guest in the nineteenth century. When the guests were pampered members of the white upper class, and the hosts were—according to the guests—"saucy Negro" guides, "half tipsy" Irish hack drivers, and Jewish museum owners, tensions were bound to emerge.

Serving Colonialism: Drivers, Guides, and Waiters

The first suggestion of conflict between visitors and the tourist industry came as early as the 1840s. Two businessmen, Thomas Clark and Samuel Street, local merchants and mill owners, owned the ferry service, which took people back and forth across the river until the Upper Suspension Bridge was built in 1869. These businessmen managed to move in on a thriving Native-run ferry service, for Native men had taken passengers across the river in canoes since the 1820s.[51]

Clark and Street hired black and Irish men to make the trek across the river, and some travellers did not enjoy the ride. In 1842 a petition circulated complaining that the ferrymen were "addicted to habits of intemperance" and were thus "unaccommodating and uncivil to passengers." They were, it was charged, "also in the habit of extorting from persons larger sums" than their employers advertised. The ferry rides continued, as a novelty excursion, in the 1880s, although travellers still grumbled about the "surly Canadian Charon" who took them across.[52]

Niagara's hack drivers were, it was said, even worse. Some travellers considered these workers to be almost as famous—or infamous—as the Falls themselves. They were "harpies," "ruffians," "hideous," a "terror all over the civilized world." Well into the twentieth century, the "outlawry" of the hackmen would stand at the centre of the story of the "bad old days" as related by the apparently cleaner tourist promoters of the modern era.[53]

One of their major crimes, it seems, was persistence. In the last decades of the nineteenth century, an estimated 125 hacks serviced the train station on the Canadian side alone, following incoming tourists "like a hound at [their] heels." This was not an uncommon sight at train stations in tourist towns of this era, for hack drivers employed by the hotels at Banff, Alberta, also greeted incoming trains, "each shouting out the name and virtues of his particular establishment." At no other locale, however, did hack drivers generate the criticism they received at Niagara. The constant importuning caused one visitor to remark, "If they only worried their poor horses as they worried us, I can pity the poor horses from my heart."[54] Almost everyone found the solicitations annoying, but so too was the apparent arbitrariness of the rates. Many visitors reported a discrepancy between the estimated and actual price charged for a scenic tour, and some reported that the driver defended his price with his fists. An Indianapolis newspaper reporter tried to capture the essence of the Niagara hackman in verse:

He allus kept his eyes ahead
Whichever way he went.

He was up in his profession—he
Could buzz a passanger
Successful half a square, right through
The winder of a kyer,
And he knowed the human way so well,
He never missed a fit
When it came to making charges
And securin' his perkisit.[55]

Visitors believed that hack drivers were prone to harassment, cheating, and violence because of their race or ethnicity. A few hack drivers were black, but more were Irish, and the familiar stereotype of the pugnacious, alcoholic Irishman provided an easy answer to the problem. To many nineteenth-century visitors, the dishonest practices of Niagara's hackmen were of a piece with their appearance ("ragged," "demoralised") and their accent ("Begorra . . . the Falls are in illigant condition").[56] Niagara's hackmen, wrote Moses Jackson, visiting from England in 1886, "have the reputation of being the most extortionate of their race, and everywhere that race is noted for its propensity to cheat."[57] Whether Jackson was using the word "race" to identify Irishmen, or more generally using the term to embrace all hackmen, the meaning was similar: hackmen shared an identity—an unenviable one—that set them apart from the norm.

So, while nineteenth-century visitors "knew" their drivers would be problems from their first glance, what they likely did not know is that hack drivers were simply the front men for an elaborately organized tourist industry. As a labour newspaper pointed out, the hackmen, "poor fellows," were simply following "the example of their betters."[58] Several hotels, for example, had contracts with the proprietors of other points of interests at the Falls, agreeing to supply a certain number of guests for a flat fee. So the hack drivers employed by Niagara's hotels had little choice but to pick sights from a preselected list or to ignore visitors' requests to visit sights without such an arrangement. Similarly, independent hackmen operated on a sophisticated commission system with some of the larger tourist attractions. Table Rock House, the Cave of the Winds, one of the bridges, and one of the railway companies, for example, offered hack drivers a percentage of every admission ticket, souvenir, or photograph sold to tourists they brought in. This commission system remained substantially in place even after the state took over proprietorship of the attractions.[59]

Independent hackmen did, by some reports, devise their own methods of petty fraud, such as taking a disoriented passenger bound for the train station on needless and more expensive journeys across the river to more distant stations. No doubt many visitors were, indeed, cheated. But the constant complaints about Niagara's rapacious hackmen tended to overlook the relatively humble position of these workers in an expanding tourist industry, and thus displaced questions of commerce and business ethics onto the familiar territory of race.

Black service workers were another source of dismay to many travellers. Travellers would probably have encountered black workers on the train on the way to the Falls, because the position of railway porter represented a black male job ghetto through the nineteenth and most of the twentieth centuries. It was a job that held mixed blessings. Porters had relatively steady employment and, after a struggle, a trade union, the Brotherhood of Sleeping Car Porters. Stanley Grizzle, a veteran Canadian porter and union leader, recalls that in a world of rampant job discrimination, the job of porter was highly sought-after, and porters were well-respected in the black community. But porters also experienced the daily frustrations and humiliations endemic to the service industry, tensions heightened when the jobs were filled by people of colour. As Grizzle recalls, "This was a job where, every day, you were made to feel that you were beneath the passengers. You were a servant, the epitome of the white man's stereotype of the Black man."[60]

At the Falls itself blacks filled a number of different positions in the tourist industry. They were present from the earliest days of European settlement throughout the Niagara Peninsula, including a community called Drummondville, near Niagara Falls, which was organized in the early nineteenth century. By the 1830s black men were finding steady employment in Niagara's hotel industry, and beginning in the 1840s and 1850s black men were employed as ferrymen, guides, and hackmen.[61]

At least one black man, Robert T. Dett, was a hotel proprietor. Dett, remembered as a "picturesque figure among negro residents," was originally from Baltimore, Maryland. He had worked as a Pullman porter, a job that brought him regularly to Niagara Falls, where he met a local woman, Charlotte, who became his wife. The two settled in Niagara Falls, Ontario, where Dett ran a downtown hotel. Later the family moved across the river, where he operated the Keystone Hotel in Niagara Falls, New York. Dett's son, R. Nathaniel Dett, was a composer and professor of music in Virginia and the namesake of a British Methodist Episcopal Church still standing in Niagara Falls, Ontario.

Black women appear rarely in the memoirs of travellers. It is likely that Charlotte Dett, like other wives of hotel proprietors, assisted in the business, though she had the misfortune of being written out of her husband's will and did not inherit the Keystone Hotel after his death in 1921. Only one black woman, a "bright eyed mulatto girl" employed in the change rooms at the Cave of the Winds in the mid-nineteenth century, appears in the historical record of the tourist industry in this era.[62]

The presence of black guides at the Table Rock and Cave of the Winds excursions added to the sense of danger and the drama of those tours. Black guides at Niagara Falls had the same effect as Native steamship pilots and wilderness guides elsewhere in Ontario: the combination of human and natural dangers heightened the adventure. The rushing water or roaring rapids were almost indistinguishable from the ferocious men who navigated them.[63] Table Rock and Cave of the Winds guides of all nationalities—and there were some non-blacks employed there—were rugged, hyper-masculine creatures, "in the prime of manhood, large and well built" as one visitor wrote.[64]

When Isabella Bird's guide—a "black imp"—extended his hand to steady her during her expedition, she "shuddered even there as I took hold of it, not quite free from the juvenile idea that the black comes off." The "black" did, in a certain sense, indeed come off on Lady Bird, for when she was dressed in the costume required of those taking the tour behind the falls—a bulky oilskin rain-suit—she found herself crossing the line from civilization to something she could only recognize in racial terms: "I looked in the mirror, and beheld as complete a tatter-demallion as one could see begging upon an Irish highway."[65]

Other visitors voiced similar fears about their guides—"great ugly blacks," as Lord Acton remembered in the 1880s. "Strapping specimens of negro or mulatto, in thick solid ungainly boots," wrote another. Trying, perhaps, to repress such fears, other male visitors turned their guides into silly children. W.G. Marshall was annoyed that his guide, whom he constantly referred to as "my darkie," kept interrupting his own reverie about God and nature: "Look, colonel, look at it! Hain't it mighty, hain't it glorious?"[66]

Encounters with black waiters in the relative safety of hotel dining rooms could also be disturbing. Black waiters sometimes caused the same momentary racial panic as the sight of the "first Indian." European hotel guests remarked that they "could not get used to the negroes' attendance, I am always afraid lest they soil all they touch." Others found them objects of novelty: "pleasant, funny creatures" or "good, grinning curly pated Sambos," particularly when dressed in white servants' jackets. Some (especially the English) inverted prevailing racial hierarchies to contrast blacks favourably to the Irish: "awkward, stupid, noisy and slow, I confess they [blacks] are more bearable and amenable to counsel than their fair skinned brothers. . . . Irish waiters abound, and their character is by no means improved by being 'citizens of a free country.'"[67]

Travellers no doubt swapped these stories of importuning hackmen, exotic Indians, and fearsome guides over dinners in their dining rooms or while enjoying the summer air in hotel gardens and on hotel verandas. In this era the local press commonly referred to the regular influx of people at Niagara Falls not as travellers, tourists, or even visitors but as "strangers." This appellation is an accurate reflection of relations between visitor and resident. Segregated from locals spatially by class, race, and ethnicity, and by their more privileged place in the host/guest divide, a community of strangers formed, dispersed, and formed again.

Most travellers recounted stories of meeting fellow visitors along their path. A few were disturbed that other travellers—sometimes dismissively referred to as "pleasure parties"—seemed to spend their time gossiping about goings-on in the hotel, paying all their attention to each other, as John Sinclair complained, "as if Niagara had not been there."[68] Yet most travellers seemed happy to join the community of strangers, meeting each other over meals and spending the day exploring the Falls together. Even honeymooning couples, who by the late nineteenth century were supposed to be resolutely anti-social, might meet and mingle with others. Jean Brassey and his wife met an "amusing" Englishman their first morning at the Prospect House, and they happily spent the rest of the day and evening with him.[69]

While travellers formed a exclusive club, they did not have the place entirely to themselves, and they knew it and felt uneasy about it. Nor could they be completely sure that everyone was whom they appeared to be. There were indeed scam artists—"confidence men"—who made travellers their special prey. But as Canadian historian Keith Walden explains in his study of the Toronto Industrial Exhibition—another popular tourist destination of the time—travellers' anxieties were based not solely on fears of crime but rather on "the difficulties of identifying the real, the genuine, the trustworthy, the substantial, the reliable in an anonymous, mobile society."[70] That they were "strangers," far from home and familiar routines, was at once what travellers sought but also what made them nervous.

A story published in an 1871 magazine captures some of this anxiety. The author recounts a visit to Niagara before "the season," when the place was relatively quiet. Four gentlemen, unknown to each other, find themselves in the dining room of the Cataract House, and after supper they begin chatting. They decide to go for a walk together to observe Niagara in the moonlight, each of them happy not to have to venture out alone. A heavy mist hangs in the air as they make their way over bridges and through parks in the dark, each of them growing quiet and increasingly nervous. The narrator becomes convinced he has been set up by con-men who plan to rob him and throw him over the waterfall. "The dark wood was to see my fate decided." But, feeling helpless, he cannot leave the company of the others.

Suddenly the man he had "settled upon" as the "villain of the party" bursts out laughing, and he is quickly joined by the three others, including the narrator. "The tension to which my nerves had been subjected for so long made me an easy prey, and I roared with laughter till the tears rolled down my cheeks, and sheer exhaustion alone put an end to the extraordinary quartet." They had all, it turned out, been frightened of each other, each imagining the murderous intentions of the next. Their "mutual fear and suspicion" over, they become fast friends and spend the rest of their holiday together.[71]

This is a revealing story, for it suggests that a certain level of anxiety lay close to the façade of the "pleasure party." Even vacationing middle-class or upper-class gentlemen, quite accustomed to taking public space for granted, could become unsettled by unfamiliar surroundings.

That Niagara's visiting strangers were forced to rely on the services of an array of unfamiliar, and generally unliked, hosts made the surroundings not just unfamiliar but frightening. Soon stories of Niagara's "disgustingly obtrusive civilization" circulated beyond travellers' private conversations and writings and reached the ears of state authorities. A little bit of danger—sexual, racial, or "natural"—made a place interesting and exotic, but at the Falls too many rules were being broken, too many boundaries crossed, and it would soon be necessary for governments to regulate unruly hosts *and* guests.

Most nineteenth-century travellers were no more inclined to recognize the irony of their position—that their comfortable existence at Niagara was facilitated by the very presence of the waiters, guides, souvenir-sellers, and drivers they despised—than were middle-class and upper-class Europeans who encountered the Other in their households, their workplaces, their Empires. Yet in their travels in this contact zone, nineteenth-century visitors left a revealing commentary on racial and ethnic encounters, which in turn illuminates the subsequent history of the frantic scramble for control of the Falls.

Given that these excursions to the contact zone were narrated by travellers or visitors, we know very little about what the inhabitants of Niagara's back region thought about the encounters (or anything else). This apparent silence should not, though, be taken for simplicity or submission. For instance, one of the many black porters on the U.S. railway system in the 1940s was none other than Malcolm Little, known later as Malcolm X. That Malcolm X earned his living, in historian Robin Kelley's vivid words, "squeezing money from white men who longed for a mythic plantation past where darkeys liked to serve" should make us wary of easy stereotypes of servility.[72]

One surviving story from Niagara's back region illustrates how "walking tourist attractions" could occasionally take matters into their own hands. In the 1920s the U.S. government passed a law reversing a centuries-old Indian treaty right to cross the U.S.-Canada border without impediment. The young Tuscarora leader Clinton Rickard became heavily involved in a campaign against this discriminatory law. He found to his surprise that the mythical tourist-Indian could serve as an effective political weapon in the battle. Rickard spent a summer donning traditional dress and visiting tourist camps at Niagara Falls. While posing in headdress and buckskin for photographs, he also lobbied tourists about the unjust law and persuaded many of them to write to authorities in protest. The law was eventually repealed.[73]

4

The People's Niagara
at the Turn of the Century

In June 1873 Ontario Premier Oliver Mowat appointed former Member of Parliament Edmund Burke Wood to head a one-man "Royal Commission to Enquire into Alleged Abuses Occurring in the Vicinity of Niagara Falls." The authorities were finally moved to act on long-standing tourist complaints, for two reasons.

Firstly, through the 1860s U.S. visitors to the Canadian side had taken their stories of importuning hackmen and guides to Martin Jones, the U.S. consul stationed at Niagara Falls, Ontario. Jones, who seems to have been a particularly activist consul, collected twelve written depositions from unhappy visitors and claimed to have many more unrecorded stories. He regularly made these complaints known to Canadian authorities.

Secondly, Jones's campaign was inadvertently aided by the man deemed by most to be the chief villain of the piece: Saul Davis, owner of Table Rock House and the "Jewish museum owner," a man disparaged by many visitors. In 1868 the *Hamilton Times* published a series of stories about what it called "the cave of forty thieves at Niagara, otherwise known by a sign as the Table Rock House . . . a dangerous locality for strangers." Of all the unfavourable stories written about him, this one seemed to irk Davis the most. Perhaps it was because it was published close to home. More likely it was because the *Times* outed him as a convicted criminal—he had been found guilty of receiving goods under false pretences in Buffalo in 1847 and served three months in prison. Davis decided to fight back. He sued for libel, and lost.

Strolling through Canada's
Queen Victoria Park, 1920.

Commissioner Wood went immediately to work and delivered his final report in November 1873. After hearing testimony from several travellers and U.S. Consul Jones, as well as examining the documents in the Davis libel case, Wood had his story ready. Davis, he said, was the chief problem. Davis had been "concerned more or less in many of the outrages" investigated. Thomas Barnett, owner of the nearby Niagara Falls Museum and Davis's chief rival, was deemed "the unwilling instrument in a most vicious system rather than the abettor or promoter of it." Davis's "organized system of extortion and imposition," declared Wood, was a "scandal and a disgrace to Canada."[1]

Wood's choice of Davis as villain was not surprising. While the many attractions of Table Rock House—which featured a small hotel, fancy goods store, photographer's booth, restaurant, and the tours behind the Falls—were extremely popular, Davis himself was an object of considerable hostility. He was, in another thinly veiled anti-Semitic reference, the "miserable Fagan" who, along with his wife, "hissed on" a den of "saucy Negroes" to harass passing tourists.[2]

The feud between Davis and Barnett had gone on for years, beginning in 1860 when they gained a joint lease to share access to the waterfall for their respective establishments. Theirs was not a neighbourly alliance, and acts of sabotage between the two quickly developed. One burned down his rival's staircase and then passed out leaflets to tourists warning them that the descent to the Falls was not safe. The other erected a building to impede the flow of tourist traffic to his neighbour. In 1870 one of Davis's sons, Edward, was attacked by a gang of Barnett's men and ended up shooting one of them, William Price, a black guide. Edward Davis argued that he shot Price in self-defence, and he was acquitted of murder. During the trial the judge reprimanded Barnett for instigating the harassment.[3]

Yet despite what seems a mutual, bitterly contested competition between two equally zealous businessmen, people always seemed quicker to condemn Davis. Barnett certainly had better press. Two years after the judicial reprimand in the Davis case he was the subject of a flattering profile in the *Canadian Illustrated News*, which congratulated him for contributing to the "progress of knowledge" by opening his museum free to schoolchildren. "His public spirit and enterprise," the item declared, "have added important features to the attractions of that beautiful place, Niagara Falls."[4]

Davis was Jewish, and he employed a number of blacks in his establishment.[5] These facts were not unimportant in the Davis/Barnett rivalry. Witness after witness, at both the *Hamilton Times* trial and the Royal Commission hearings, told stories of their frightening experiences at the hands of Davis's "coloured men," who were known to demand large sums of money from tourists trying to leave the establishment. One told of being detained by "five or six negroes" who "shook their fists in our faces and spoke very excitedly." Another was reminded by one of Davis's men that "this—placing his fist in my face—is my authority." When another irate tourist told Albert Thomas, one of Davis's black porters, that he would tell the U.S. Consul about his threatening behaviour, Thomas allegedly replied, "Damn the U.S. Government."[6]

Davis was the ultimate victor in the rivalry. Barnett went broke in 1877, by some accounts because his own attempts to cash in on spectacles such as the Wild West Shows and Buffalo Hunts flopped. Davis purchased the Barnett museum, operating it for another ten years in Canada before moving it to the U.S. side. Barnett left the country for South America, but his son Sidney returned to the area in 1919.[7]

Other historians have told the story of the Barnett-Davis rivalry as a straightforward tale of "organized crime" at the Falls, accepting Wood's findings that Davis and his staff were thugs; and maybe they were. But Wood's investigation took place in a context of overt racial and ethnic animosities, and his report placed disproportionate blame for abuses on those who, like the Davises and their black and Jewish employees, were at the bottom of Ontario's nineteenth-century cultural hierarchy. Still, ironically enough, the episode did little harm to the Davis family enterprise, nor did it irrevocably harm Davis's reputation. In 1877 local newspapers published a retraction from the *Guelph Herald*, apologizing to Saul Davis for calling him "a veteran swindler."[8]

Some of Wood's other findings had a significant impact. He suggested that the civic officials, "elected, more or less, under the influence of those by whose vote they occupy their position," were "inefficient officers in the administration of justice," which stung the community of Niagara Falls, Ontario. The town council quickly passed a bylaw imposing a new set of regulations on hackmen, but the Commission's criticisms in general initiated a conflict between local authorities and provincial "reformers" that continued well into the twentieth century.[9] Wood's major recommendation was that the provincial government should assume control of the descent to the foot of the waterfall, currently shared by Barnett and Davis. The proposal unleashed a veritable genie of public debate, which could not be rebottled.

The Parks Campaign

Over two decades ago Canadian historian Gerald Killan called for a dramatic revision of the story of how the Niagara Parks system came to be. Generally, the tale has followed a familiar line: Canada's Governor General Lord Dufferin gave a speech to the Ontario Society of Artists in Toronto in September 1878, deploring the commercial and industrial ruin of Niagara and calling on governments on both sides of the border to establish an international park, restoring the area to nature. Dufferin's speech caught the attention of a group of public-spirited New Yorkers, including landscape architect Frederick Olmsted, painter Frederick Church, and journalist Jonathan Harrison. These men shared Dufferin's concerns, about Niagara and elsewhere; some of them had been involved in the campaign to create the United States' first national park, Yosemite, in 1864. An intense lobbying campaign began. This time, when "the people" came up against "the interests," the good guys won. As Thomas Welch, the first park superintendent on the U.S. side, liked to say, "Niagara was made free." On July 15, 1885, the New York State Reservation at Niagara Falls opened Prospect Park, and on May 24, 1888, the Niagara Parks Commission opened Queen Victoria Park in Ontario.

Killan has astutely pointed out several of the flaws in this story. For one thing, business interests—at least those on the Canadian side of the river—

were not, on the whole, opposed to this conservation movement. Indeed, the smarter ones got in front of it and made a place for themselves in the revitalized tourist industry that accompanied the new parks. The notion that farsighted intellectuals acted to rescue the area from industrial and commercial interests obscures the role of business people, during and after the campaign. The story should more properly be seen as one—familiar in Canada's national past—of resilient businessmen negotiating with government to forge a consensus about the "public interest," leaving untouched the basic structures of private capital.

Missing from both versions of this history is the extent to which the campaign to preserve Niagara mobilized both racial and class fears. Certainly, the working-class and middle-class day excursionists who arrived in large numbers in the 1870s were not having a fundamentally different experience at Niagara than their upper-class predecessors several decades earlier, for, as we've seen, there have always been diversions from nature at the Falls. But many *thought* they were. Frederick Olmsted, for example, concluded that tourists in the 1870s "had poor taste, were in a hurry, and were easily led by the arrangements made for them." As he wrote in a Special Report of the New York State Reservation in 1879: "The idea that Niagara is a spectacular and sensational exhibition, of which rope-walking, diving, brass bands, fireworks and various 'side shows' are appropriate accompaniments, is so presented to the visitor that he is forced to yield to it, and see and feel little else than that prescribed to him."[10]

Others were more haughty in their criticisms of excursionists, "second-class tourists . . . who are brought by the car-load," who "fetch their own tea and coffee and provisions" and enjoy "a rollicking dance in the Pavilion."[11] When these concerns about Niagara's visitors were combined with the perennial complaints about how the tourist industry was ruining the place, the result was a powerful movement for government intervention. It seemed to many that both hosts and guests alike were misbehaving themselves; perhaps governments could do a better job of controlling the place.

One of the most vocal propagandists for the public park was U.S. journalist Jonathan Baxter Harrison. A newspaper man originally from Indiana, Harrison had risen to national prominence in 1880 with the publication of *Certain*

Dangerous Tendencies in American Life. The book expressed his concerns about the threats to American democracy posed by an overworked, uncultured working class, and the growing cultural and political gap between workers and what he called "cultivated people."[12] This philosophy paralleled that of Frederick Olmsted, and the two became friends. Olmsted proved an important ally, for his power was mightier than the pen. He had established his reputation for using nature—properly designed—to solve social problems twenty years earlier in New York City.[13] In summer 1882 Olmsted and Harvard professor Charles Eliot Norton bankrolled Harrison for a month-long stay at Niagara. While there, Harrison filed a series of newspaper reports for several prominent U.S. publications, and he later went on to write a book, *The Condition of Niagara Falls and the Measures Needed to Improve Them* (1882), in which he laid out the concerns and philosophy of the Niagara preservation campaign.

No one had lost faith in the waterfall itself, a scene, according to Harrison, of "absolutely exhaustless vitality." The problem was people. Visitors had lost sight of the real reason for visiting the waterfall. "They come hither because it is the fashion . . . they sit in carriages at the top of the stairway . . . look at the Great Fall for a minute and a half and usually remark, as they pass onward, that it is a less curious and interesting spectacle than they had expected to see." This mindless and casual approach to nature exasperated Harrison and his colleagues. "Of course it disappoints, and must forever disappoint, all who look at it in this foolish, hurried way." This place, he said, "in its sovereign dignity and perfection . . . is to be seen, felt, not talked about."

Harrison made some enormously high-minded claims for the waterfall:

It offers to those who are weary from toil of any kind, of hand or brain, or from the wearing, exhausting quality which is so marked in modern life,— it offers to all such a vital change, the relief and benefit of new scenes and new mental activities and experiences consequent upon observing them. . . . There is a quickening and uplifting of the higher powers of the mind, and awakening of the imagination; the soul expands and aspires . . . self-respect becomes more vital.[14]

Despite this apparently classless rhetoric, Harrison was much more concerned about the poor missing out on Niagara's great opportunities than he was the rich. "The rich," he declared, "are better able to take care of themselves, here as everywhere." Much of Harrison's book, therefore, reads like a detailed instruction manual for those of "modest means" on the right and wrong way to "do" Niagara. The Cave of the Winds, Indian stores, curiosity shops, and illuminated waterfall were wrong, "debasing, vulgarizing and horrible in the extreme." The islands, "primeval" forests, and rapids were right, indeed, "indispensable."

Yet even with Harrison's precise tutelage, the tourist—rich and poor—was still likely to be "swindled." The problem, as Harrison saw it, ran deeper than the individual dishonest hackman or souvenir vendor. The towns of Niagara Falls were simply not suitable custodians. They had insufficient "intelligence, organizing powers, pecuniary resources and efficient public spirit, as is required for the direction of the affairs and enterprises of the local community in its relation to Niagara Falls." The second problem was related to the first: "the gradual, ever-advancing, total ruin of Niagara is inevitable, if the private, personal ownership of the lands under consideration is to continue."

Lest anyone be alarmed by the radical-sounding nature of this diagnosis, Harrison quickly explained himself: "There is really no such antagonism between practical business interests and those which are ideal and spiritual." As he saw it, "The mass of men must always toil," but let them toil somewhere else. "If the State should purchase these lands . . . the water-power could be utilized just as fully, and the mills and shops would be quite as valuable, a little farther away from the Falls."[15]

Harrison's arguments eventually won the day. While the preservation campaign ran into stiffer opposition on the U.S. side than it did in Canada—including a seemingly intransigent New York Governor Alonzo Cornell, who declared the Falls a "luxury," for which, like all such indulgences, people should pay—eventually governments on both sides of the river passed legislation to expropriate local property owners.[16] It had become a matter of national, even racial, duty. As *Outing and the Wheelman*, one of the United States' first sporting and nature magazines and a staunch supporter of the parks campaign, noted in 1885, "The two great branches of the English-speaking people—the British and the Americans—share in the control of Niagara; the Canadian province of Ontario and the American State of New York are simply their trustees."[17]

It certainly helped that the preservationists were able to mobilize the support of a long list of luminaries, including the U.S. vice-president and chief justice, members of the Canadian courts and parliament, and international literary figures such as Thomas Carlyle, John Ruskin, Ralph Waldo Emerson, Henry Wadsworth Longfellow, Francis Parkman, Oliver Wendell Holmes, and W. D. Howells. In all, seven hundred people, "leading men of literature and science," signed a petition, initiated by Olmsted and his colleagues, which deplored the commercial diversions around the waterfalls and argued that the Falls should not be "regulated solely by the pecuniary interest of individual land owners."[18]

But what also helped is that those local forces that might have voiced opposition to nationalization had, by the 1880s, been almost thoroughly discredited. The communities on both sides of the river had, it seemed, squandered the enormous gift they had been granted. Local authorities were, according to the Ontario government, "inefficient," perhaps even corrupt or, according to the U.S. preservation campaign, too backward and parochial to appreciate their responsibilities. The most visible of Niagara's residents, the people who worked in the tourist industry, had, after decades of outraged tourist complaints, almost no legitimacy whatsoever.

Yet the transparency of the high-minded claims made by the governments on both sides of the border when they stepped in to "free Niagara" is patently clear in the early operations of state-driven tourism. Niagara was not "freed." It was simply placed in different, more culturally acceptable hands. Conflicts over who had the moral authority to commodify and sell natural spectacles, and how those spectacles ought to be purveyed, continue to this day.

Marketing a "Free Niagara"

The opening of Ontario's Queen Victoria Park was greeted enthusiastically by the Toronto press, which had been especially invited to a "sneak preview" in

May 1888, a few days before the official opening. The Toronto *Globe*, describing the area as a "land of enchantment," noted approvingly (and erroneously) that mills, hotels, and the ubiquitous hackmen were "vanishing." The *Empire* called Niagara Falls a "lovely summer resort" and commended the Niagara Parks Commission for its "radical clearing out of annoyances."

Curiously, one of Canada's leading news and literary magazines, *Toronto Saturday Night*, remained unimpressed. While acknowledging that the sight-seeing public was, on the whole, better off under the hands of the Niagara Parks Commission than it had been previously, a magazine editorial commented, "It has to be admitted that matters are not yet by any means too satisfactory." What remained irksome was that, while the entire U.S. park had free entry, the Canadian park had a small charge for visiting its islands—ten cents for pedestrians. Although the main park, which encompassed the most spectacular, and previously private, views, was free, the matter of the islands was bothersome; so much so that the magazine declared, "We must confess that we fail to see much difference between its [the Parks Commission's] doings and those of the individual owners of the islands under the old system."[19]

Saturday Night was, at that moment, alone in this criticism. For several decades after the establishment of the park system, visitors and guidebooks alike paid tribute to the newly "freed" Niagara. Writing in *The Canadian Magazine*, E.A. Meredith enthused that visitors had been rescued "from the attacks of the crowds of sharks, hucksters and pedlars, who used to infest the place, taxing so heavily their purse and temper. All these pests are now banished as effectually as the vermin were banished from Ireland by its patron Saint, and the lover of nature is now allowed to enjoy in peace and quiet the beauty of the glorious scene before him."[20] This sentiment was to be extremely popular well into the twentieth century, but it was also absolutely wrong.

Historian John Sears suggests that the preservationists secured only a partial victory in their campaign. The "sensational version" of the Falls continued to operate on the periphery of the parks, and thus "two versions of the Falls settled down side by side to vie for the attention of visitors."[21] Indeed, visitors today continue to be jarred (and fascinated) by the quick transition from the bright lights and carnival-like Clifton Hill, the main tourist strip in Niagara Falls, Ontario, to the manicured, landscaped Queen Victoria Park. But in the early days there was no easy and obvious line between the private, hucksterish old Niagara and the public, free, people's Niagara. The Niagara Parks Commission began its tenure in 1885 with a commitment to "preserving as far as possible, what still remains of the natural and original" around the Falls.[22] Within a decade the NPC was selling snacks and souvenirs and leasing out both water power and tourist attractions. Travellers still complained of harassment, and local business men and women began asking why it was alright for the state to profit from tourism but morally repugnant for them to do so. As the *Saturday Night* correspondent asked, what really was the difference?

That the state might not do things so differently from the private sector was evident from the very beginning. The first superintendent of Queen Victoria Park, James Wilson, freely blurred the boundaries between public and private industry: while he ran the park, he was also a shareholder in two prominent private-sector tourist attractions. Before long, signs of nepotism and patronage appeared in almost every aspect of the NPC's operations. Ontario's Liberal Premier Oliver Mowat sent Wilson and Casimir Gzowski, the Commission's first chair, a list of approved applicants for staff positions; most were Liberals, some were relatives of commissioners. Prominent Liberals were also among those awarded contracts to supply the park with uniforms and construction materials.[23]

These practices seem to have led to little public outcry, perhaps because the Commission became adept at patronage, identifying and placating important local business interests to ensure the economic and political survival of the park.[24] The truce did not last forever. In 1905 the Conservative association of nearby Welland, Ontario, as well as local Conservatives, protested what they termed the "most bitter partisan principle," which had, they argued, governed the park from its inception. Provincial Liberal governments since the 1880s had run the park as their fiefdom, and partisanship, in "expropriating property, granting privileges and employing men and managers," was the order of the day. The result was "the poorest kept park that possibly can be found in North

America," full of "useless officials," an overpaid superintendent, and an "army" of unnecessary staff.[25]

Another citizen chimed in with his own story. R. M. Gonder said that when he applied to work for the Commission he was told that he would get steady work if he signed papers "binding" himself to vote for the Liberal government. He said, "There are about twice as many police in the Park as are needed and a lazier lot of time killers working in the park you never saw, and they are all Grits, too."[26]

Before long these complaints began to surface in other, more public quarters. In 1909 the *Canadian Horticulturalist* editorialized that Queen Victoria Park "has none of the finished appearance which such an old park should have." The reason for this was clear: the park was "periodically overturned by changing superintendents as if their views of what such a park would be were coloured by their political faith."[27] The muckraking newspaper *Jack Canuck* took up the same theme in 1915, publishing an anonymous letter headlined "Poor Man Gets It in the Neck," complaining about the salaries of NPC administrators. NPC officials struggled to address these skirmishes, saying, for example, in 1912, "We want to disabuse the minds of the public that the Park belongs to the Commission."[28] That was, however, exactly what many felt.

What had been relatively minor incidents of bad press erupted into something major in 1921, creating the first of many political scandals to rock the NPC. A number of Niagara residents forwarded a petition to Ontario Premier Ernest Charles Drury expressing their dissatisfaction with the reigning chairman, Philip Ellis, as well as his superintendent, John H. Jackson. The allegations were many and serious. Ellis was entertaining "a great many who may add to his influence, particularly from the city of Toronto, at the expense of the Commission." He was appointing people to park positions "without giving properly qualified local men or women fair or any consideration." He was selling supplies to the park from his own firm, as well as influencing park leaseholders into buying supplies from his company. The allegations against Jackson were more personal. Besides being unqualified for the position, he was said to be "narrow, biased and insulting."[29]

96

The ladies' waiting room in the Refectory, operated by the Niagara Parks Commission at Queen Victoria Park, 1927.

Ellis's response to these charges spoke volumes about the relations between the public and private tourist industries. In an interview with the *Niagara Falls Review*, Ellis denied that he had sold supplies or coerced concessions to buy from him and said it was government policy to entertain guests at Niagara Falls, which was certainly true.[30] The NPC's correspondence files—before and after this controversy—bulge with letters from provincial politicians seeking accommodation for themselves and, usually, family or friends, at the Refectory, the grand building that housed the NPC headquarters, a restaurant, and private sleeping quarters. Along with the nine bedrooms reserved for commissioners, the building contained forty other bedrooms.

In private, in a letter to Premier Drury, Ellis went further than merely

The Niagara Parks
Commission Refectory,
1927. Photo by E. Hodge.

defending himself. He also tried to locate the complaints in Niagara's fractious tourist history: "It is a notorious fact that for many years, until the Commissioners took the work in hand, the Niagara Falls district was a happy hunting ground for extortioners of various kinds. This has all been done away with. . . . It is not to be expected that such drastic reforms could be brought about without exciting local antagonisms."[31]

Jackson was also convinced that the affair was rooted in the lingering residue of the "bad old days." As he wrote in a memo to Ellis, "From the commencement of the park, an antipathy was started which has hardly yet died out in the minds of the generation of that day, and ever since I have been a resident of Niagara, for some twenty years, sparks of the old fire have readily come to light." Hackmen, in particular, were "always resentful" of the new regime, and citizens of Niagara in general had always been angered that the Parks Commission had "filled some offices with persons not resident of the district."[32]

This is more or less the version of the story believed by outsiders, including, apparently, Premier Drury, who did not act on the petition or reprimand Ellis or Jackson in any way. *Saturday Night* magazine was incensed by the charges made in the petition, calling it "contemptible piffle." It too located the real source of the story in the public/private feud: "The efforts of the Park Commissioners to prevent visitors from being robbed by unfair exactions is not calculated to promote its popularity with some of those who got up the petition." Using the same rhetoric that marked both the 1873 Royal Commission and the parks campaign, the magazine slighted Niagara's citizens for their small-mindedness:

> There are certain residents of Niagara who are sordidly opposed to the whole idea of preserving the beauties of the frontier. . . . The dirt and ugliness of certain parts of the American shore . . . fills them with envy. They would like to have the whole Canadian shore turned over to industries. . . . What they want is not a tourist's playground but factories, smoke and a real estate boom.[33]

Controversies of this sort emerged almost every decade through the twentieth century, usually during a provincial election campaign or when the government changed hands. A few years after this scandal, during the election campaign of 1926, local Conservatives enjoying a rally and picnic at Queen Victoria Park were told by the president of the local Conservative Association that all those wearing Conservative badges could make purchases from the government-run concessions in the park for half price. (Ellis later told the press that he was "incredulous" about this magnanimous offer and had not authorized it.)[34] A decade later the Liberals got their revenge. In July 1934, newly elected Liberal Premier Mitchell Hepburn appointed a Special Committee to probe the activities of the NPC.

Queen Victoria Park, c.1900, with a wall of factories in the background.

Prompted, said Hepburn, by complaints from residents about the lavish entertainment of government officials, as well as heavy financial losses, the probe also revealed that the system of financial kickbacks so despised in the nineteenth century was essentially still in place. A stream of taxi drivers told the investigators that they received a percentage of every sale made to tourists they took to NPC-run souvenir shops, as well as a portion of every ticket to Table Rock House, now under the management of the NPC. Irate transportation company officials also testified that the NPC made an exclusive agreement with one bus company that was allowed to take tours through the Park, while other companies were forbidden entry.[35]

These revelations, though raising questions about the extent to which Niagara had been "freed," were not the stories that received the most attention. The populist Hepburn was more concerned about the evidence of what the local press called "absolute extravagance," as uncovered by the probe. One widely circulated story was that of the staff chauffeur, whose sole responsibility was to travel to Toronto, in a newly purchased blue Packard automobile, to pick up the

469 government officials and their friends entertained—free of charge—at the park during the previous three years. The Special Committee concluded that the entertainment facilities of the Parks Commission were indeed used by "friends of the Government," and not on Commission business.

During the Depression of the 1930s these tales of taxpayer-financed opulence created a much greater stir than the stories of the inner workings of the tourist industry. Hepburn acted more decisively than previous premiers faced with NPC-related scandals: he fired all the sitting commissioners, the chairman, and the superintendent. While Niagara residents were hopeful that this new broom might sweep away partisanship and leave the ground free for local control of the park, in this they were to be disappointed. Hepburn's new appointments were Liberals, and only one was from Niagara.[36]

In some respects, state-driven tourism simply replaced one form of conflict—rival businessmen feuding over territory, spurred on by ethnic and racial differences—with another—the "who's in and who's out" system of patronage familiar to students of political history. But the "bad old days" narrative of Niagara's unregulated outlaw history gave park and government officials a ready answer for their critics: they were jealous; they were still opposed to nationalization; they were, in short, the small-minded tourist-gougers who proved the necessity for a government-run tourist industry.

So, while the administration of the people's Niagara did not match the claims made for state intervention by those who supported the parks campaign, did the scenery, at least, benefit? Was the waterfall itself "freed"? The NPC presented itself as being drastically different from what had come before. Some of the original buildings surrounding the waterfall (most of them, according to the NPC, "of inferior character and small value") were torn down. There were no plans to replace them, for the commissioners were of the opinion that "no hotels, refreshment rooms or booths for the sale of refreshments or other articles" would be allowed within the limits of the park. Within two years the commissioners changed their minds. Convinced, they said, by the length of the park (two and one-half miles), in 1887 they decided that "places for rest and for refreshment" were a necessity.[37] Over the following decades the com-

"Yesterday's Indian," the Maid of the Mist, canoes over the Falls—as usual, wearing no clothes. Detail from a 1915 Canada Steamship Lines brochure.

mission made many such compromises, and soon the promise of pristine nature was replaced by a series of souvenir booths and private franchisers, who held the rights to a railway and the Table Rock House (soon to be replaced by the Refectory restaurant), as well as by the continuing diversion of water power to electrical companies.

Each decision to diversify and commodify the people's Niagara was accompanied by a defensive reminder from the commissioners of how bad things had been before they'd been appointed. But this argument didn't always work. Some decisions, such as selling off water power, were extremely controversial. To be fair, this was not a new issue, and the NPC inherited a long-standing political conflict between those who favoured harnessing Niagara for electrical development and those who worried that diversion of water to power stations would ruin the grandeur of the waterfall. The hydro-promoters would win the day.

The task of winning popular opinion towards industrial Niagara was made easier by the common association of Niagara with femininity. When the "Queen of Beauty" met the "King of Power," the winner was, in this discourse of masculine conquest, foreordained. Canadian historian H.V. Nelles was struck by how hydro promoters used military metaphors to describe their attempts to "conquer" Niagara, turning the story of industrial development into a heroic and mystical "epic" of man against nature.[38] But, like all epics, this one was profoundly gendered. After the construction of massive hydroelectrical plants, travel writers enthused, "Man has accomplished here, with Nature as his handmaiden, some of the greatest achievements of any age." Some accounts combined this conquest of feminized nature with the element of racial domination. A Canada Steamship Lines brochure in 1915, for example, evoked the spirit of "yesterday's" Indian, the Maid of the Mist: "The hunting grounds of her fathers are peopled by a new race of strong, virile men. To them, the earth is their destiny, the things of the earth their heritage; this wonderful natural phenomenon but a potent natural force to be brought under human control."[39]

By proclaiming electrical development as the manifest destiny of white men, parks commissioners could also sidestep any conflicts between scenic preservation and industrialization. Stung by growing criticism from journalists, environmentalists, and recreation associations about the selling off of water power, the commissioners defended themselves. "The great works of the Creator were primarily and chiefly intended for the service of man," they said, "and that each succeeding generation witnesses some new achievement in the scientific adaptation of nature's forces, which is everywhere eagerly seized upon and utilized for the convenience, comfort and advancement of the race."[40]

When South African scientist Leo Weinthal visited Niagara in 1920 and declared, in a speech to the Empire Club in Toronto, that "Niagara is a lesson in harnessed power" and "so far as Victoria Falls and the Zambesi Falls are concerned, we have to go a long way yet," the commissioners' words seemed fulfilled: "harnessing" Niagara was masculine, Anglo-Saxon providence.[41] In the struggle between man and nature, the times clearly favoured man. Modern man had become busy, farseeing, and technologically sophisticated. How could nature compete? As the *Toronto Star* editorialized, "Scenery is a fine thing, but undeniably it is idle. It does not do anything. If left to itself it will merely persist."[42]

Yet even in this undeniably mechanical era, man and nature collided regularly at Niagara, and these conflicts were not always easily resolved. On several occasions in the early twentieth century the NPC hired Frederick Olmsted's firm, Olmsted Brothers, to report on the general condition of the parks and to make recommendations on renovations. In his 1914 report Olmsted was scathing. He was horrified by the souvenir booths and refreshment stands operated by the government. The Parks Commission, he declared, was "more keen to get the public's money by any device than to assist the public." The proposal to lease out the land downstream at the Whirlpool rapids to the Spanish Aerocar Company to erect a cable ride over the river "would be a very conspicuous human construct, constantly challenging attention in every view of the whirlpool as an evidence of man's domination over nature and flatly contradicting the impression which I believe ought here to be guarded." The photo stand at Brock's monument at nearby Queenston Heights was a "vulgarizing catch-penny device."[43]

It would no doubt have been difficult to mount a defence against these charges, coming from one of the most famous landscape architects of the continent and, indeed, a man who figured prominently in the campaign that created the NPC in the first place. The solution to the dilemma was simple: Superintendent Jackson simply suppressed the offending sections of Olmsted's report before it was presented to the commissioners. The next time Olmsted Brothers was hired by the NPC, in 1916, Olmsted's son wrote the report, and he struck a more diplomatic tone. While still objecting to the Aerocar at the Whirlpool— the idea was "unfortunate in its conception and executed with deplorable lack of intelligent regard for scenery"—he was strategically ambivalent in his discussion of the overall vision of the park: "To what extent it is properly a duty of your board to provide space for games and amusements of a sort which can be carried on as well in any other locality as they can along the margins of the great cataract, is difficult to determine."[44]

The NPC determined that amusements were not incompatible with the vision of a "free Niagara" as championed by Olmsted and other parks promoters in the late nineteenth century. By the 1920s Queen Victoria Park and the parks territory at Queenston Heights offered an array of services and amusements: pavilions that provided shelter for almost two thousand visitors, gardens, picnic tables and benches, regular band concerts, ice cream and soft drink stands, as well as the long-standing attractions, a railway tour, Table Rock House (newly decorated with Indians hired by the Commission for the summer), and Brock's

The Queenston Heights
Park Nursery, a crèche for
the use of visitors, 1927.

monument. Groups of day excursionists could rent plates and cups and purchase hot water for tea, and the Commission received hundreds of such groups
yearly: churches, employee organizations, unions, and service clubs. In 1921 the
park opened a crèche described as a "tribute to the work of women during the
war." The nursery allowed "tired mothers" to deposit young children in the care
of trained nurses, so the mothers could enjoy an afternoon relaxing in the park.
To encourage women to use the service, the NPC invited the Local Council of
Women to inspect the crèche, and the group members gave the new facility
their enthusiastic approval. The NPC also embarked on a publicity campaign in
the 1920s, not only hiring a public relations firm to give it advice on how and
where to advertise but also publishing a series of promotional guidebooks.

The claim made by an early NPC guidebook that Niagara was "a veritable
Eden in its natural state" was exaggerated.[45] But NPC officials did take to heart
the message stated repeatedly during the parks campaign that visitors had to be
taught how to enjoy nature properly. Responding, perhaps, to the presence of a

"rough element," allegedly from Niagara Falls, New York, who monopolized the swimming pond at Dufferin Islands through the summer of 1913, bylaws governing the "deportment of visitors" were quickly established. The rules prohibited indecent language, card playing or games of chance, fortune-telling, and intoxicating liquors. Parades, flag waving, and even the playing of musical instruments required the written permission of the superintendent.[46] The rules were enforced immediately and enthusiastically. Park officials considered banning the Socialist Party, which intended to have a rally in the park in 1914, but after some deliberation instead simply warned party leader James Simpson that the members of his group must "conduct themselves in an orderly manner." Perhaps park officials remembered the outcry that had occurred a few years earlier, when they attempted to ban the Salvation Army from meeting in the park on the grounds that its members would be "soliciting alms." After a flurry of negative press reports in Niagara Falls and Toronto, they had backed down.[47]

Park authorities also regulated personal behaviour and morality. An irate citizen from Niagara Falls, New York, was ejected from the swimming pond in 1914, apparently because his bathing costume failed to measure up to standards. Park officials defending this action declared, "It is our aim to have all persons using this swimming pond appear in modest and becoming costumes."[48] NPC police also kept a vigilant eye out for "curb cruisers" (men harassing women), vagrants, prostitutes, white slavers and runaways, "flim flam men" (con men who preyed on unsuspecting tourists), flashers, and people sleeping in their cars overnight.

NPC officials themselves were not immune from moral problems. They were occasionally caught drinking on the job, soliciting for private tourist homes, and acting as unauthorized paid tour guides—spinning stories for credulous tourists, for example, of Indians who, they claimed, still lived in Niagara's caves. Once an official was even suspected of raping a runaway girl. Yet their uniformed presence added to the air of order and dignity that park administrators were striving to establish. The uniform alone worked wonders. When Commission chairman Philip Ellis noticed that tourists taking the railroad tour through the park were paying very little attention to the commentary provided by the guide, he decreed that, like the police, the guides should be fitted with uniforms, which would "create a better impression on the public."[49]

Still, despite the authority bestowed by both culture and law, the "freed" people's Niagara did not meet the demands or expectations of many of its proponents. Blame for this failure might be placed on a combination of factors: the necessity of operating the park on a shoestring budget, the taken-for-granted system of partisanship and patronage that characterized much of political life in the era, and the racially loaded story of the "bad old days," which was a handy yardstick by which the government of the day—Liberal or Conservative—could measure, and defend, its own practices. With every criticism or scandal, the Parks Commission had a ready response: things were worse before.

To Frederick Olmsted a souvenir store on Niagara's banks was a desecration, pure and simple. To the Ontario government, a state-run souvenir store was a vast improvement over one run by a Jewish businessman and staffed by unruly blacks. Rather than pronouncing one vision of Niagara correct, we might more usefully reconsider the slippery and, in the end, futile distinctions between nature and culture revealed by these debates. In a highly technological culture, nature was understood as the Other to urban industrialism.[50] Given this distinction, the winner in conflicts over the proper appreciation of nature has more to do with prevailing power relations than with any "true," more authentic vision of the natural. A visit to Niagara, whether in the bad old days or in the early years of the people's park, was a *social* act, embedded in human relationships.

What the arrival of the Niagara Parks Commission did accomplish was the establishment of a permanent, and in many ways external, rival to local business interests. The result was the beginning of a curious and intriguing relationship between public-sector and private-sector tourism, which would continue through the subsequent history of the Falls. Sometimes the two tourisms ran on a collision course with each other; at other times mutually beneficial alliances were struck. The state was more than willing to regulate leisure, to ensure that appropriate social and moral benefits were achieved. In this respect the Niagara Parks Commission acted no differently than was customary for other state institutions in this era in domains such as dance halls, amusement parks, and other forms of recreation.[51] But it was rare for the state to engage in tourist entrepreneurship side by side with the private sector and thus to shape, modify, and sometimes prohibit local business initiatives. Even though, by some standards, the NPC's early vision of pure nature tourism failed, its existence imparted an odd moral imperative to the Niagara tourist industry. The "bad old days" narrative cast a long shadow over Niagara's tourist history, and throughout the twentieth century it stood as a powerful warning.

"In It, but Not of It": Tourism and Industrial Development

When *Saturday Night* castigated the residents of Niagara who began publicly criticizing the Niagara Parks Commission in 1921 for indulging in "contemptible piffle," one resident responded by writing a letter to the local newspaper. Angered by *Saturday Night*'s claim that Niagara's residents didn't care about tourism and preferred the get-rich-quick route of economic development through industrialization, the anonymous reader remarked: "One cannot help wondering whether it is really an ignoble ambition to desire a few factories at Niagara Falls, or whether we should be content to be a 'tourist playground' leaving the 'dirt and smoke' and incidentally, the greater part of our electric powers to benefit Toronto and its society editors."[52]

The letter nicely captures the local sentiment in the early decades of the twentieth century. Until the late 1920s, many Niagara residents had expressed a certain ambivalence about tourism. While local people were proud to live at "the world's most famous address," as local historians would put it later in the century, they were not committed to or dependent on tourism alone for their livelihoods. Indeed, it was not until the late 1920s that residents began to speak of the "tourist trade" or "tourist industry" as something vital to the town's progress. In the early years of the century Niagara Falls, like many other small towns across North America, had other things on its mind: attracting industry to provide jobs, building houses for its residents, improving the roads and sewage systems, coping with the mounting casualty lists of World War I, and in general fostering a community spirit. Niagara's citizens of British descent—the majority of the population—fretted about the increasing presence of foreigners, especially Italians, and wondered how they might maintain their cultural, as well as numerical, domination. All of these were familiar goals, constituting what urban historians have termed a kind of "boosterism" as communities wrestled with the promises and shortcomings of "modern" life.

Novelist Jane Urquhart has imagined ironically that Niagara residents in the late nineteenth century didn't understand what the fuss was about. As she writes in her novel *The Whirlpool*, set in Niagara Falls in 1889:

> Main Street was situated far enough up the hill from the river to be spared any of the garish tourist attractions that dominated the lower town and so, in appearance, it resembled the principal thoroughfare of any other Southern Ontario settlement of a similar size. Its inhabitants, therefore, were able to ignore the presence of the giant waterfall in a way the rest of the world seemed unable to.[53]

As the *Niagara Falls Evening Review* declared in 1925, "Living too close to a great natural phenomenon, one is apt to become too used to it."[54] Yet not only boredom was the issue. As Urquhart suggests, most of the residential, commercial, and leisure activities of the town took place just up the hill or down the river, away from the waterfall and the hotels and parks lining its banks. The distance in perception and culture was even greater than geography, for, as the 1921 letter writer observed, to be a "tourist playground" in this era meant catering to "Toronto society," that is, the metropolitan upper class.

The high-living elegance of the many guests of the Niagara Parks Commission would have added to this perception, as would the steady parade of famous visitors, whose tours (usually escorted by NPC and civic officials) around the Falls always made the front pages of the local papers. On any given day in the early twentieth century, Queen Victoria Park might just as easily have been filled with people most Niagara residents would feel quite comfortable sharing a picnic with, such as the members of the Danforth Avenue Methodist Sunday School or the

International Brotherhood of Blacksmiths Helpers, rather than luminaries such as the Prince of Wales, Lloyd George, or Prince and Princess Takamatsu of Japan.

Though, as we will see, the boundaries of class and race separating host and guest at Niagara in the early twentieth century were not as impenetrable as they had been a few decades earlier, other barriers, more difficult to ascend, remained. So when a group of citizens lobbied in 1918 for a plebiscite to authorize the purchase of a downtown lot to serve as a city park and playground, their efforts (ultimately unsuccessful) were lauded by the press on the grounds that "Queen Victoria Park is *in* Niagara Falls, sure enough, but it is not *of* it."[55] Many citizens, though this time not the voting majority, would have preferred to pay a bit extra for their own park: smaller, with a far less spectacular view, but closer to home and filled with neighbours and friends rather than visitors or "strangers." Living in a bustling tourist town provided benefits but had drawbacks as well, and both sides of the issue received public airing.

The Town of Niagara Falls, Ontario, was incorporated in 1881, encompassing the former villages of Clifton and Elgin. That town co-existed, for a time, alongside the Village of Niagara Falls (formerly Drummondville), until January 1, 1904, when the town and village of the same name were incorporated as the City of Niagara Falls. Across the river the U.S. villages of Niagara Falls and Suspension Bridge had amalgamated in 1892, and hydro and other industrial development acted to quickly double the population there from 9,000 in 1890 to nearly 20,000 in 1900. Hydroelectric development provided the impetus for amalgamation, and a "city" possessed greater powers of taxation and other rights than a series of villages and towns. From 1901 to 1905 the area was a hive of activity as the huge hydro plants were under construction and the area's industrial base exploded. The Niagara Falls, Ontario, Chamber of Commerce, formed in 1889, initiated a great industrial promotion campaign in 1905, which, on the whole, worked. Both communities, U.S. and Canadian, had geography and political economy on their side: they were accessible to labouring, consuming, and vacationing populations, and they were connected to markets by a good network of railroad operations. By 1916 Niagara Falls, Ontario, boasted fifty factories and a continuing expansion of hydro facilities. Silverware, chemicals, women's corsets, paper boxes, and the area's most famous consumer good, Shredded Wheat, were manufactured at the Falls.[56]

Civic officials were proud of Niagara's "moderate, sane and substantial" growth, but they were also concerned that the growth be balanced among different sectors of the economy. Too much tourism was, in those years, considered a problem, not a blessing, for the communities on both sides of the river. By 1912 local pundits were declaring that the community had "long since passed the stage of a mere summer resort."[57] That the majority of citizens should "turn their activities in other directions, to industrial and commercial pursuits," was of twofold importance. It was a way of establishing distance from the bad old days of tourist gouging (which still stung), and it also signalled the arrival of the community in the "modern" era of industrial progress. The Chamber of Commerce encouraged local manufacturers to display the words "made in Niagara Falls Canada" prominently on their products (as Shredded Wheat did) because, as one resident worried in 1919, "people outside of our own vicinity think that Niagara Falls Canada consists of a few hotels grouped around a railroad station near the cataract." That only 3 per cent of the population of Niagara Falls, Ontario, "pay any attention to whether tourists come or do not come" was, to the town's industrial promoters, a source of strength and progress. As anticipated by Scottish physicist Lord Kelvin, christened the "father of the harnessing of Niagara," it was a "happy thought" that "the poor people of the country will be industrious artisans, rather than mere guides and assistants to tourists."[58]

It was not that tourism was overlooked or unimportant. It was, rather, that the arrival of visitors or "strangers" had acquired a different meaning. Despite the almost hundred-year history of tourism, Niagara's residents in the boom days of the early twentieth century believed that there was something much better than a "visitor." Visitors might be convinced to become residents or, better still, factory owners or businessmen. "The stranger of today," declared the *Review*, "may be the citizen of tomorrow, if he is favourably impressed."[59] So when the Ontario government raised the cost of the bond required of those bringing a car across the U.S. border in 1915, from $4 to $20, the community circulated outraged petitions. Their concern was not solely that the new rates would keep tourists away. Rather, they feared that instead of being "visited and inspected" by wealthy Americans, such people might not bother to come, and thus "we on the other side of the river may miss scores of opportunities of being discovered as a possible home for industries by wealthy manufacturers who will be content to terminate their tours on the US bank of the river."[60]

This integrated vision fused tourism with industrial growth and civic pride. When the towns on both sides of the border co-operated, in 1910, to hold their first "International Carnival," boosters spoke of the event in this mixed language of industry, tourism, and civic-mindedness. "By dint of hustling principles and through the efforts of the wide-awake offspring of these two municipalities we have attained a comet pace in industrial and commercial growth," they declared. "Hence Niagara's International Carnival, which is our debut in affairs of its nature, and we bid outsiders welcome to see what we can do and to test our ability as entertainers."

Although entertaining "outsiders," then, was part of the vision, Niagara's citizens welcomed visitors mainly as an audience to appreciate the local accomplishments. Furthermore, Carnival planners reminded Niagara residents that, since the event was to last only one day, "the duties of hospitality could in no way become onerous."[61] Tourism was just one feature of civic pride; tourists were welcomed, but on the town's terms.

This unified vision of tourism and industrial and civic growth was also evident in debates about the future of the community. For example, in 1918, when the *Niagara Falls Review* asked its readers, "What does Niagara Falls need?" many responded practically, complaining about water quality, bad streets, and unsuitable houses. Others suggested that Niagara was lacking in less tangible items such as community spirit, a sense of patriotism, or the willingness to improve and beautify yards and neighbourhoods. No one answered the question by saying they wanted "more tourists." Rather, people framed their responses, especially those concerning the physical appearance of the town, around their embarrassment that the town was not as beautiful as the waterfall. As one editorial writer put it, "Niagara is every day being judged . . . by the strangers who visit our city."[62]

This debate continued in the town for a number of years, and one result was an annual campaign, initiated by the Chamber of Commerce in 1920, to "clean up" Niagara every spring. Here too, Niagara's tourist industry formed a backdrop for discussions of civic pride, but the campaign was not merely a tourist promotion gimmick. An enthusiastic supporter of "clean up week" put it in the hyperbolic language of boosterism: "We are visited by people from every part of the known world. . . . We thus have every opportunity of advertisement and our city should grow to the greatest, not only in the province of Ontario, but in the whole dominion."[63]

This fusion of industrial expansion and tourism was, in many ways, a product of the age. Travellers in the nineteenth century could express shock, dismay, and anger at the industrial desecration of Niagara with some reasonable expectation that *they might be listened to*, as indeed they were, after a fashion, by the parks campaign. By the twentieth century, however, what U.S. historian William Irwin calls the "happy synthesis" of nature and technology was in full flight.[64] To equate industry with desecration in the early twentieth century was to huff and puff on an extremely solid, well-built structure.

A few onlookers did complain. The Olmsted family continued to shake their heads at what governments on both sides of the border had done to their vision of a free Niagara. Not only was the continued presence of commercial amusements a problem, but also, as Frederick Olmsted Jr. wrote in a 1908 report commissioned by U.S. President Theodore Roosevelt, the manufacturing enterprises "form a skyline of colossal ugliness, insulting . . . the majestic beauty of the cataract."[65] Occasionally journalists joined this lament, and a flurry of concern appeared in publications ranging from *Scientific American* to the *Ladies Home Journal* about how hydroelectric development had "doomed" Niagara to early extinction.[66]

Local and provincial authorities were not unaware of, or unmoved by, the tensions between industry and nature at the Falls. In 1917, for example, an Ontario government official reported to the NPC that he had heard several stories of "injury being done to vegetation and foliage in the Niagara district, by certain plants operating in this locality," and asked him to look into it. Park superintendent Jackson agreed that the destruction of trees was obvious in the "vicinities of all of the manufacturing plants which emit poisonous gasses." He named one plant, the American Cyanamid Company, as a prime offender. After expressing these concerns to the company he received a terse reply: "We are not prepared to admit that the damage of which you speak is caused by gases from this plant." Jackson communicated his concerns to the provincial Board of Health in Toronto, but it is unclear what, if anything, came of the matter.[67] Most likely nothing did; a few years later, in 1922, a tourist visiting Niagara after a thirty-five-year absence complained publicly that hundreds of trees along the river were dying, and blamed gases from the Cyanamid Company.[68]

That an infrequent visitor touring the area for a short time could readily identify the source of the pollution suggests that people in the community were probably also aware of the problem. Many would have also been acutely aware of working conditions in the area's chemical companies, which were described by no less an authority than the Hooker Electrochemical Company's own historian as "unbelievable" and "appalling."[69] While an anonymous irritated resident might complain, as one did during "clean up week" in 1921, that "we should be telling the manufacturers to 'clean up' the grounds surrounding their plant," and while city council heard from the occasional delegation of residents requesting relief from the noise or odour of nearby factories, the downside of industrialization received little public airing in these years, from insiders or outsiders.[70]

Indeed, it remained far more common to champion the accomplishments of "man the conqueror," as commentators began to speak disparagingly of the "wasted energy" of preindustrialized Niagara. The area, declared Niagara Falls, New York, town historian E. T. Williams in 1916, was where "beauty and utility clasp hands." Industrialized Niagara was a tribute to all that was modern. A guidebook from the same era, citing the many electrical conveniences facilitated by Niagara power, declared that anyone even hinting at these inventions in "what we are pleased to call the 'good old days,' would have been . . . [burned] at the stake for witchcraft." Hydroelectric development simply became another object for the tourist gaze. In 1901, for example, visitors to Buffalo's Pan-American Exposition, in which the glories of electricity featured as a

The Spirella Corset Company, Niagara Falls, Ont., 1930. The building now houses the Niagara Falls Museum.

main theme, were treated to a detailed scale model of the power station at Niagara. Above it loomed a huge electrical sign spelling out "NIAGARA," with lightning shooting out from each letter, accompanied by the sound of thunder.

At Niagara Falls itself, virtually every aspect of hydroelectric development appeared on the tourist itinerary, from the construction of the massive tunnels to the majestic design of the buildings and, later, tours of the plants themselves. The vision, expressed by hydro promoters and industrialists, was of a seamless, uninterrupted transition between "nature" (the waterfall) and "culture" (industrial development). Some visitors declared themselves in favour of the latter. H.G. Wells commented, "The dynamos and galleries of the Niagara Falls Power Company . . . impressed me far more profoundly than the Cave of the Winds."[71]

Electric power was a key feature of what historian David Nye calls the "industrial sublime" at the turn of the century, and electricity-driven factories were the literal and cultural beneficiaries of this power. Like the production of electricity itself, the production of goods by electric power was an innovation that acquired great cultural significance, and across North America factories began to invent themselves as tourist attractions.[72] In the early twentieth century, several of Niagara's factories mounted extremely successful campaigns to combine manufacturing with tourism. These efforts could be quite magnificent. In one stroke companies such as Shredded Wheat, the Niagara Chocolate Company, and the Spirella Corset Company managed to make their products, silence critics of industrial desecration and pollution, and advertise their wares.

The Shredded Wheat company declared itself "another wonder of Niagara" and opened its doors to the public in 1901, timed to coincide with the Pan-American Exposition in Buffalo. In 1906 the plant erected the largest electrical sign in the United States to "welcome visitors." Soon one hundred thousand people a year were trooping through this model factory to observe the production of what founder Harry Perky called "nature's perfect food." The company positioned itself as a parallel icon to the waterfall—as one of its brochures proclaimed, "One might as well see Rome without seeing St. Peter's as to see Niagara Falls without visiting the Home of Shredded Wheat." The factory was located on lush, landscaped grounds and featured an observatory, tours of the cooking rooms, and examples of the many features of "social betterment" provided to employees, such as a cafeteria, library, auditorium, shower rooms, and hospital facilities.[73] "Tourists" and "customers" became one and the same, as visitors were invited to take home illustrated recipe books instructing them on a variety of ways to serve Shredded Wheat biscuits and crackers.

In the early twentieth century the Shredded Wheat plant was exactly the kind of place Niagara Falls was trying to become. It was both modern and beautiful, and it brooked no contradiction between industrial and scenic success. The relationship between tourism and industrial development was mutually beneficial. Industry, with a little effort and imagination, could double as a tourist attraction, and, as English visitor Yvonne Fitzroy noted perceptively of the waterfall, "If it hadn't of itself and unaided proved so remarkable a commercial success, they would have harnessed every drop of that plunging water, and the households of Canada and the States would have lit and warmed themselves with its lost majesty." Happily, she added, there was "enough left over for our awe and our delight."[74]

5

Boom and Bust
in the 1920s and 1930s

The ability of the tourist industry to diversify—and especially to rewrite the script to include industrial development alongside scenic splendour—was not the only challenge facing tourist entrepreneurs in the early twentieth century. They also had to adapt to the changing circumstances of visitors. Looking back on recent history in 1896, the *Niagara Falls Gazette* (N.Y.) noted the "pronounced and radical" changes the area had experienced and tried to come to grips with a paradox puzzling many in the tourist industry. Each season saw a steadily rising number of tourists, yet better profits were not accompanying the increased traffic. The culprit, it seemed, was the free public park. According to the press, the park opened the door to "the masses of people who could not afford extravagant prices for seeing Niagara Falls."[1]

Although the class base of tourists was indeed changing in that era, the local newspaper was dramatically overstating the case. The story works only if "the masses" refers to the numerically small middle class. Certainly commercial venues had become available to more and more people by the late nineteenth century. Ice cream parlours, roller rinks, and oyster bars beckoned working-class women and men in small towns and large cities across North America, tripping social alarm bells about the promiscuous mingling of the sexes, a worry that would sustain reform movements for decades to come. Yet working-class people in the nineteenth and early twentieth centuries still spent most of their time *working*. The amusements of most people in small-town Ontario were expanding, but they were still profoundly local. Most people had neither

Four-legged race, Queen
Victoria Park, 1927.
Photo by E. Hodge.

the time nor the money to venture much further than the Sunday picnic or the Saturday evening social or, if they were near a city or county town, the annual fall exhibition. A trip to Niagara was only likely to be undertaken as a special day excursion: perhaps a Victoria Day holiday outing to attend a church event or a union picnic, or to cheer on a sports team.[2]

By the early twentieth century, vacations with pay had been extended to middle-class professionals throughout North America and were a symbol of white-collar status. By the 1920s most white-collar civil servants in Canada and the United States were entitled to one or two weeks' paid leave annually, as were employees in about two hundred private companies with vacation plans. Among industrial workers, the battle to shorten the working day was a more pressing priority—by 1918 the goal of the eight-hour day had been attained by fewer than 50 per cent of U.S. workers. Industrial relations experts were beginning to popularize the notion that vacations improved the health, and thus the productivity, of *all* workers, but very few unionized industrial workers in North America were making headway in negotiating paid leave into collective agreements. Vacations with pay were not regulated by government statute, and thus available to all workers, until the 1940s.[3] Even if industrial workers had the time, they did not have the money, despite the free entry to the park. Toronto's *Star Weekly* lamented in 1921 that the cost of the steamship day-trip excursion from Toronto to Niagara Falls was well out of reach of most working people of that city.[4]

A wandering Jack London discovered that Niagara Falls was no place for "the masses" when he arrived there penniless in 1894. "Somehow," he later wrote, "I had a 'hunch' that Niagara Falls was a 'bad' town for hoboes." After spending the night "sleeping like a babe" in a farmer's field, he was quickly spotted by a local policeman. When he couldn't come up with a proper answer to the officer's question, "What hotel are you staying at?" he was hustled off to jail.[5]

More typical, and more welcome, tourists were William and Effie Baker, of Norwood, Ohio. The Bakers visited the Falls for three summers in a row, beginning in 1906. Each year they took the train from their town to Cleveland and then a steamship to Buffalo. They were exactly the sort of middle-class tourist the industry had to learn how to handle. Baker, the Norwood postmaster, looked forward to spending his one-week vacation with his wife and planned his trip to the Falls carefully. His vacation diary bulges with brochures and advertisements from various Niagara-area attractions. The Bakers were wealthy enough to travel and to hire a housekeeper to look after their three young children while they were gone. They took in all of the attractions at the Falls, visiting the Incline Railway, the Cave of the Winds, the Shredded Wheat factory, and the power plant. They took a ride on the *Maid of the Mist*.

But unlike the upper-class travellers of a few decades earlier, travel for the Bakers was not an act of unrestrained, showy consumption. The couple did not stay in one of the area's grand hotels but chose instead a private tourist home run by a Mrs. Ida Burdick in Niagara Falls, New York. They were interested in Niagara's attractions, but often Effie went off the see the sights alone. William was content to stretch out in Queen Victoria Park, napping, or to occupy himself by meeting other travellers. While Effie enjoyed a side trip to Buffalo or Toronto, William popped into the local post office to make new friends and compare their operations to his own back home. The most that they purchased on any of their visits was the occasional meal in a restaurant, a few post cards, and, on one trip, a lace collar for Effie (which she thought was a "great bargain").[6]

Even the frugal Bakers were bigger spenders than many of their contemporaries. The travellers of the late nineteenth and early twentieth centuries were not only cost-conscious, but also time-conscious. The Bakers spent most of their one-week vacation at the Falls, but others were not nearly so faithful to the place. Gone were the days when "strangers" put up at Niagara for the "season." By the 1890s the local newspaper was reporting, "Trolley lines carry strangers in and out of the city every few moments, attractions are provided to draw these people elsewhere, and their visit here is curtailed to the briefest possible period."[7] Despite the increased number of visitors, the local tourist industry had begun its long lament that "there is not as much money in catering to the tourist trade now as there was ten or twenty years ago."[8] Thus began a twofold campaign: to encourage a longer stay at Niagara; and to adapt to the new middle-class traveller by diversifying, and shortening, the experience of "doing" Niagara.

Guidebooks of the 1890s began to scold and shame travellers for attempting to rush the Niagara experience. If tourists found themselves disappointed with the spectacle, according to *Tugby's Illustrated Guide* of 1899, it was probably their own fault, for "the longer the visitor tarries, the more he enjoys and appreciates." "Niagara," declared one visitor, "cannot be done in a hurry. The person who tries to insults himself and insults the scenery." Another recommended the same advice that Oliver Wendell Holmes allegedly gave for seeing the British Museum: "Take lodgings next door to it, and pass all your days at the Museum during the whole period of your natural life."[9]

Recognizing, perhaps, that even the harshest rebuke would not bring back the days of lengthy, expensive sojourns at the Falls, the tourist industry concentrated its resources on providing plenty of paid alternatives to lounging on the banks of the river, and on advertising Niagara to the widest possible audience. "One who simply sees the Falls," declared promoters of the steamboat tours from Toronto in 1903, "sees only a part of the wonders and beauties of Niagara."[10] As well as the old standbys—Table Rock House, the Museum, and the Cave of the Winds—visitors could add to their itinerary factory tours, two railroad tours,

River Road, a busy tourist thoroughfare on the Canadian side, 1927.

the Aerocar ride over the Whirlpool, and, by 1921, airplane rides over the water-falls. Shorter amounts of time to play with the waterfalls became part of the strategy. The *Maid of the Mist* boat ride, for example, which took one hour in the 1890s, was forty-five minutes long in the 1920s. (By the 1970s it would last a mere fifteen minutes.)[11] In 1928 the region's first bowling alley opened, and shortly after there was enthusiastic talk of a new golf course. In summer 1925 Niagara Falls entered the Jazz Age with the opening of the Prince of Wales Club, located next to the Clifton Hotel on the Ontario side. The club's "danc-ing pavilion" boasted twelve thousand square feet of marble dance floors and billed itself as equivalent to New York's Arcadia Club and Toronto's Palais Royale. While the proprietor, Andy Melbourne, went out of his way to attempt to appease the sensibilities of small-town Ontario, allowing only British sub-jects and U.S. citizens into his club and banning "vulgar dances and improper dress," the place was soon the centre of heated controversies over Sunday danc-ing, loud music, and what some felt was its general inappropriateness next door to the waterfall.[12] A disgusted *New York Herald Tribune* writer echoed the fer-vour of an earlier generation of preservationists when he described the scene

Sightseeing surreys outside the General Brock Hotel, c.1940.

near the waterfall in 1926: "A huge wooden dance-hall, named the Prince of Wales—how flattered he would be if he knew about that!—blares jazz, a little flat in the high notes, into the crowded street. Peanuts and popcorn and fried potatoes are peddled lustily and every other building displays tauntingly a sight which announces in varying language that beer may be purchased within."[13]

Industrial Niagara, quickly absorbed into the general air of spectacle, provided a fitting tribute to the majesty of science and capitalism. But again Walden's observations about the Toronto Industrial Exhibition hold equally well for Niagara. "However impressive the business community's demonstration of hegemonic influence," he writes, "its attractions were matched by the transgressive pull of freaks, frauds and floozies."[14]

Ironically enough, the First World War also helped Niagara's tourist industry adjust to a changing tourist economy. The war interrupted the vacation plans of wealthy North Americans, the playgrounds of Europe having been made rather inaccessible to them. Canadians hoped that formerly "over-the-ocean" U.S. tourists might be persuaded to become "over-the-border" visitors. Niagara residents worked hard to counteract rumours circulating in the United

States that visitors to Canada would be instantly conscripted into the armed forces, or that passports and elaborate registration were now required.[15]

Rather than discouraging tourism, World War I actually did the reverse. The Canada Steamship Lines tried to use wartime patriotism to its advantage, inviting Americans to "come visit your Northern ally." During the war the steamship excursions from Niagara Falls to Toronto were completely repackaged. The advertisements had previously stressed glamour and luxury, but now the company conceded patriotically that "extravagant pleasures are not to be encouraged." Americans were reminded, however, that "water trips" promoted health and refreshed the mind, just the thing for the citizen who needed to "keep one's efficiency above par."[16]

The tourist promotion did not assume centre or sole stage in Niagara's sense of itself or its economic future. Yet tourist consciousness did grow, as different segments of the community began to co-operate to raise the region's profile. Hotel owners on both sides of the border organized themselves into an international association and took up the task of establishing welcome signs outside both towns. The Chamber of Commerce, still mainly concerned with industrial expansion, took tentative steps in the direction of tourist promotion. The Canadian side's Chamber, for example, distributed posters to local businesses, reminding U.S. tourists how much they could purchase duty-free in Canada. Across the river, two young American women, dubbed "Niagara's favorite daughters," were launched on a promotional tour of the United States in 1925, "telling of the beauties and advantages of the power city" and distributing promotional material. This venture led to an even more inventive scheme in 1928, when the chambers of commerce on both sides sponsored a joint publicity tour. A pair of Chamber representatives boarded a plane, christened (what else?) "Miss Niagara," and visited fourteen U.S. cities, where they gave radio broadcasts, illustrated lectures, and distributed publicity.[17]

By far the most ambitious project was the illumination of the Falls with coloured lights. This plan, concocted in summer 1924, was financially supported by both city councils, chambers of commerce, and the Niagara Parks Commission. The illumination of Niagara represents another version of the technical sublime, and the merger of electric and natural spectacles intensified the power of both.[18] A multicoloured waterfall did nature one better, showing off the miracles of technology with the flick of a switch. As the *Niagara Falls Review* enthused, "The marvel of the whole thing is that Niagara generates the power which shows herself off to such advantage. It is as if one held up a mirror to nature and saw her two-fold."[19] But it was no secret that the demands of the tourist industry also shaped this project. As Charles Newman, mayor of Niagara Falls, Ontario (and, not co-incidentally, proprietor of the Trennick Hotel), explained, "There are vacant rooms throughout the city [and] they would be filled if the Falls were illuminated because tourists who now only pass through the city would stop over to see the illumination."[20]

The reviews from out of town were mixed. The *Manchester Guardian* protested that "man has done so much to Niagara that I did not wish to see his handiwork at night as well as by day," and the *New York Herald* wondered sarcastically if an "orange-colored Sphinx" was next. But the strategy of lengthening people's stay at Niagara through the creation of an evening spectacle had the desired effect. By the mid-1920s the place was again packed with visitors.[21] It also did not hurt that a year after the initiation of the illumination project, prohibition was lifted in Canada but not in the United States. The result for the Canadian side was pandemonium, and in these times of abundance familiar questions resurfaced. What sort of tourists did Niagara Falls want? Who had the moral authority to benefit from tourist spending?

Modernization and Rivalries in the 1920s

The tourist industry happily expanded to meet new demands. Even though as late as 1922 only three of the area's hotels remained open through the winter months, between 1923 and 1929 eight hotels either opened or were renovated and expanded in Niagara Falls, Ontario, alone, bringing the total number of hotels to nineteen in 1930. The number of restaurants on the Canadian side increased from eight in 1920 to forty in 1930, and by 1930 there were eighteen

An array of tourist services at McGibbon's Inn, Niagara Falls, Ont., c.1920s.

purveyors of souvenirs.[22] The town got a glimmer of the stark trade-offs that would characterize its future in 1926, when two local businessmen who had remodelled an abandoned hat factory into an "inviting" King Edward Hotel were congratulated for "getting rid of an old eyesore."[23]

The tourist business continued to be a multi-ethnic industry. A correspondent with the *Belfast Evening Telegram*, visiting in 1912, noted approvingly that he was able to stay in an Irish-owned hotel and that "Niagara Falls City swarms with Irishmen, usually the sons of emigrants of a generation ago, who are now the leading businessmen in the places where their fathers settled." By the 1920s

The orchestra at the
Clifton Hotel, 1923.

Chinese, Syrian, and Jewish families operated many of the restaurants and some small hotels. Italians did not enter the tourist industry until later, in the 1930s and 1940s; for a long time all that was available to Italians was menial work in the larger hotels.[24]

The major players, however, were neither local nor "ethnic." When the grand Clifton reopened its doors in 1919, having been closed for a few years during World War I, it did so under the management of the United Hotels Company, a conglomerate that owned several major hotels in the United States and Canada. A more promising local venture was the General Brock Hotel, which still stands.

This project, organized or, as it was put at the time, "fathered" by a consortium in 1927, generated tremendous excitement. The community followed the construction carefully over the next two years, and at the opening ceremonies in June 1929 the *Niagara Falls Review* declared the building "one of the finest on the continent." The *Canadian Hotel Review* agreed that the hotel was a "triumph," particularly its 247 "colourful and inviting" guest rooms. The General Brock featured four private dining rooms, a ballroom, a roof garden with a fountain and a spectacular view of the falls, and a lobby furnished in antique Italian style.[25]

No one quibbled at the notion that this project should have been a local undertaking, even though only two of the eight members of the consortium were Niagara Falls men (the rest were businessmen from Hamilton and Toronto), the construction was done by a Hamilton firm, and almost all of the skilled staff positions went to people imported from the U.S. hotel industry. No matter: at the head of the board of directors was John Robinson, owner of a local automobile firm, who proudly told the community that only $5,000 of the money raised for the venture was American. The rest was raised locally and elsewhere in Ontario.

The General Brock possessed everything except timing. Within a year John Robinson was in court, defending himself on charges of defrauding the creditors of his automobile firm, and the manager of the General Brock was asking city council for a reduction in taxes, claiming a vacancy rate in its first year of operations of 40 per cent. By 1932 the hotel was in the hands of a conglomerate, the Association of Canadian Hotels.[26]

In this round of tourist industry expansion, hotels were no longer the only game in town. The automobile brought a tremendous change to the pattern of North American tourism, and especially in unlocking the monopoly of the hotel industry on accommodation. The number of automobiles registered in the 1920s soared. In the United States automobile registration rose from eight million in 1920 to twenty-three million in 1930. The comparable Canadian figures are two hundred and fifty thousand, rising to one million in 1930, but in Niagara the Canadian numbers scarcely mattered, for attracting U.S. tourists was virtually the sole preoccupation.[27] Niagara was not alone among Canadian tourist centres in this obsession. Indeed, it is sobering (especially for Canadians) to learn that when highway building began in earnest in Canada after World War I, most provincial governments, their eyes on the tourist trade, set as their priority the creation of links between Canadian and U.S. cities. Until 1946 it was not possible to drive across Canada without either detouring through the United States or driving on railroad tracks, and the country did not possess a high-standard national road system until the completion of the Trans-Canada Highway in 1970.[28]

With the coming of the automobile, tourists no longer had to stay in centrally located, downtown hotels. In the early 1920s, autocamping or "gypsying" became an increasingly popular alternative to railway travel. Autocamping initially appealed to the antimodernist impulses of the urban middle class, because automobile touring gave travellers in search of pastoral, rural simplicity the opportunity to venture off the beaten track. Usually they camped beside the road or in farmers' fields. Farmers did not particularly appreciate the company, and businessmen in nearby towns watched regretfully as self-sufficient autocampers sped past their shops and restaurants. By the mid-1920s civic authorities in many towns across North America were offering municipally run, free accommodation in autocamps. If travellers were lured into towns, the thinking went, they would be more likely to spend money on goods, services, and even tourist attractions.

By the end of the 1920s the line between the temporary middle-class "gypsy," the working-class family looking for a cheap vacation, and, worse still, the authentically poor seasonal labourer had begun to blur. As a *New York Times* travel writer sniffed in 1930, "The very fact that all the mechanics, the clerks and their wives and sweethearts were driving through the Wisconsin lake country, camping at Niagara, scattering tin cans and soda pop bottles over the Rockies, made those places taboo for bankers and chairmen of the board." In an attempt to separate the paying wheat from the sponging chaff, by the end of the 1920s the free camps had become subject to registration, regulation, and, eventually, privatization.[29]

The municipal autocamp at Niagara Falls, New York, seemed a smashingly successful example of this kind of accommodation. Opened in 1925, the camp kept up to 150 carloads of visitors a day entertained with moving pictures, mili-

Clifton Tourists Camp, Niagara Falls, Ont., 1927. The camp was opened by Earl McIntosh in 1926 on the south side of Clifton Hill. The tenting area is in the background, a communal kitchen on the right.

tary shows, and concerts by the Shredded Wheat Orchestra. Niagara Falls residents kept **abreast** of news of the camp through the publication of visitors lists in the local newspapers and marvelled that people from as far away as Florida, Mexico, and Cuba were stopping over. Locals were regularly invited to mix with tourists at free corn roasts and fish fries.[30]

Across the river the story took a decidedly different turn. As early as 1922 the *Niagara Falls Review* noted the huge numbers of automobile tourists leaving Canada to stay across the river, and the paper called for the establishment of an autocamp to encourage them to stay overnight. By 1924 four privately owned autocamps had been set up in town. The area's hotel owners, however, were not so welcoming. Niagara's hotels had long enjoyed a favoured place in their community. After all, in the nineteenth century hotel owners had escaped the many criticisms heaped by travellers on others in the tourist industry, and in twentieth-century Niagara their openings, renovations, and personnel changes had been the subject of sustained and generally enthusiastic press commentary. Hoteliers tended to present themselves to the public as a kind of hybrid of businessman and public servant. Citing their many free services (such as washroom facilities and information distribution), Niagara's hotelmen compared their businesses to schools, because "hotels were rendering just as necessary and valuable public service" as the school system.[31]

Niagara's hotel owners were not unique, for they were part of a national campaign through the 1920s and 1930s to defend hotel territory from the encroachments of others. Presenting hotels as quasi-public institutions was central to this defence. Nationally, the trade journal of the hotel industry, the *Canadian Hotel Review*, considered hotels "the social centre" or the "hub" of their communities, and in 1936 Canadian hotel magnate Vernon G. Cardy (owner of several major hotels in Quebec and Ontario) told delegates to the convention of the Canadian Association of Tourist and Publicity Bureaus that hotels formed "an integral part of the social and business interests of every citizen."[32]

This self-conception on the part of hotel owners perhaps explains the tenor of their campaign against autocamps. Hotelmen did not present themselves as businessmen facing unwanted competition by another group of businessmen—autocamp owners—purveying a cheaper product, which, of course, they were. Instead, they combined their traditional public-spirited discourse with the widespread cultural stereotype that autocamps attracted an undesirable combination of middle-class and poor people. The American Hotel Association distributed reports suggesting that "grave conditions of immorality" existed in fully 75 per cent of the nation's autocamps.[33]

Locally, class and race prejudices were similarly inflamed. Niagara's hotel owners petitioned the city council to ban autocamps from the vicinity, arguing that the camps were attracting "strangers from all parts of the country." By that time a "tourist" was a welcome, paying guest; but a "stranger" had become something quite different. As Howard Fox, owner of the newly renovated Foxhead Inn elaborated, autocamps were filled with the "wrong" people: "Women went around [with their] hair hanging and in bathrobes, and the men in suspenders." A local alderman declared that the camps resembled "wash day on some streets in Buffalo," suggesting a working-class, immigrant image that had no place in a tourist resort. Even the once enthusiastic *Review* backed down from its original support for autocamps, arguing that "very little money" was being spent by campers and that beauty spots such as Niagara Falls should not be "covered by the dirty washing of tramp motorists."[34]

Some aldermen directly addressed the unspoken agenda of the hotelmen, referring to the issue as one of "businessmen against businessmen" in which the council should not get involved. Others argued, to no avail, that a municipal camp would be able to regulate some of the alleged problems of the camps. The Niagara Parks Commission stepped into the controversy by announcing its plans to build an autocamp, complete with a dining room and stores, on its property at the Niagara Glen, a few miles out of town. But this plan seems to have come to naught.[35] Some local businessmen were strong supporters of the camps, reminding the council that they had just used taxpayers' money on the illumination scheme to encourage more people to stay in the area overnight. Local shopkeepers addressed the council on the economic benefits of the camps and defended the campers. "All people," declared one shopkeeper, "can't all stay in high class hotels." He added that it was "by no means the riff raff that assembles in the camps."[36] In the end the hotel owners won the day. The council acted to banish autocamps to the outskirts of town and prosecuted camp owners who disobeyed the law.

Emboldened by their success in banishing autocamps, hotel owners next took aim at another rival, tourist-home operators. Tourist homes, or boarding houses, had existed at Niagara since at least the 1890s. A "tourist home" was simply a private house that took in tourists—an early version of the modern bed and breakfast establishment and a place that provided cheaper accommodation than a hotel. Throughout the 1920s newspapers regularly reported that, during busy weekends, "hundreds" of private homes were thrown open to tourists, especially when hotels were booked. The first local publication to advertise tourist homes, the *Niagara Falls Illuminator*, published in 1926, listed fifty-seven establishments, most of them run by women.[37]

That same summer local hotel owners began complaining to city council about what they called "indiscriminate soliciting" by tourist-home operators. Within a couple of years, they were joined by the Chamber of Commerce, which voiced concern that soliciting was "causing considerable complaint" and called for a system of licensing and regulation of tourist homes.[38] Thus began a series of mass meetings, petitions, and council debates in which the major players—tourist-home operators, hotel owners, and city councillors—hurled all manner of accusations against each other. Hotel owners charged tourist-home owners with telling lies about hotel rates and paying no taxes. Solicitors, they claimed, were either professionals, hired by tourist-home operators, or children sent out to drum up business for their parents. Either way, they were causing havoc by chasing after tourists as they crossed the bridges, or sometimes even intercepting potential customers on their way into hotel lobbies.

Tourist-home operators, for their part, depicted themselves as struggling small businesspeople being crushed by more powerful adversaries. Although most of the tourist-home spokespersons were men, they often evoked femininity to buttress their position, repeatedly circulating the tale of the widow with several children who took in tourists to make ends meet. Yet, when necessary, they also used the resources of masculinity, rejecting, for example, municipal regulation and licensing on the grounds that city council "had no jurisdiction over a man's home." Those on the side of the tourist homes also tried to harness Niagara's tourist history to their advantage, arguing that "twenty years ago Niagara Falls was known as a place to get out of as quickly as possible because everything in the way of accommodation for tourists was so high."[39] Each side—pro- and anti-soliciting—claimed to have the interests of tourists in mind, and each claimed the support of tourists themselves. Occasionally tourists sent angry letters to the newspaper or civic authorities complaining, as one woman did in 1928, that soliciting was "disgusting, unsafe and everybody does it"—including, she reported, local police and even customs officials.[40] Still, when William and Effie Baker of Ohio were approached by a young child soliciting tourists for his mother's tourist home, they were happy for the help in locating accommodation.

The hotels fight back: hotel industry advertising, 1936 and 1939. The top ad suggests that hotels have been unfairly burdened by regulation, while the unencumbered tourist homes zoom ahead. The bottom ad was designed for billboards that would be placed "at strategic points throughout the province" during the month of August. According to the Hotel Association of Ontario, "The advantage of stopping at a recognized hotel, where true hospitality is available, is emphasized on this colorful sign."

This dispute was, in some respects, a matter of big against small, but it also had elements of male against female. Historian John Jackle has called city hotels "male habitats," established by and for an exclusively male clientele. Hotel services, such as barber shops, bars, and meeting rooms, were built solely with male customers in mind, and hotel dining rooms catered to the masculine palate: plenty of red meat, starch, and (when possible) liquor. Guest registers told the same story. The Statler Hotel chain, for example, estimated that four-fifths of its guests were men until the Second World War.[41] The Palmolive soap company tried to capitalize on the alienation of women from hotels in a series of advertisements published in the hotel trade press in 1930. Headlined, "One Reason Why Women Criticize Hotels," the ads declared, "There is a general feeling among women that a hotel is primarily a place for men," but the use of "little feminine things" such as Palmolive soap might attract and please female guests.[42]

Female travellers did not yet form a distinct market segment, but they also did not stand out quite so starkly as they had in earlier eras. Nineteenth-century travel magazines, for example, assumed a male readership and tended only to feature stories of women when they did something unusual. *Outing*, for example, seemed particularly fond of the "woman-on-camping-trip" story. The magazine ran four such tales in the 1890s alone. By the 1920s and 1930s women's magazines were attempting to convince their readers that "travelling has become such a simple matter that no woman need have the least hesitation about embarking alone on a trip." They offered helpful advice on packing, customs rules, and travel etiquette.[43]

This breezy, carefree tone most likely overstated the case, and certainly at Niagara the tourist industry was concerned that women alone could face particular difficulties. The Niagara Parks Commission, for example, warned its staff in 1920 that women who missed the transportation connections out of the city would find the local YWCA a "safe" place for them to stay overnight. A few years later the Travellers Aid Committee of the local Y stationed someone permanently at the train station for the summer to give advice and help to women travellers.[44]

In this climate of real and imagined dangers for women travellers, women may well have been drawn to the less expensive—as well as homier and more private—surroundings of the tourist home. Dorthea Miller of New Jersey certainly was. The tourist home, she declared after her visit to the Falls in 1929, was "so much nicer than a hotel when two ladies travel together."[45] In some respects, then, the hotel/tourist-home conflict was a rivalry between male space and female space. The hotel owners thought so. They ranted regularly against the "housewives, working for pin money," who, they imagined, ran substandard tourist homes and contributed nothing towards economic development in their communities.[46]

By the end of the 1920s the basic framework of the modern tourist industry had taken shape at the Falls. The Niagara Parks Commission was firmly in control of a large chunk of the physical and financial territory. While the NPC and the private sector enjoyed moments of mutual co-operation—the illumination project, for example—the two would also often eye each other warily, as mistrustful competitors. To the locals, the NPC never did completely shed its image as outside interloper, with access to the vast resources of a provincial budget that it spent lavishly and lopsidedly. For its part, the NPC was never quite satisfied that tourist entrepreneurs in "modern" Niagara were any less conniving than their predecessors had been several decades earlier. Within the private sector, international hotel corporations were beginning to show their dominance, but there was still room for local businessmen like Howard Fox, a hometown boy who began his hotel career at the tender age of fourteen as a bellhop and who, a couple decades later, had acquired sufficient connections and capital to build a small hotel. Further down the economic hierarchy, plenty of Syrian or Chinese families were willing to work long hours at restaurants. The "housewives" who rented rooms to passing tourists were less welcome in this marketplace, but they were indeed present. Each constituency served a fairly homogeneous tourist population—the middle class—which, by nineteenth-century standards, was lamentably poorer and more diverse but hardly the mass-consumption market that would explode on the scene after World War II.

But even though the 1920s crowd was but a prelude to the hordes of the 1950s, the tourist traffic had its downside. Just as some recoiled in horror at the sight of the coloured waterfall illumination, many also regretted the consequences of tourist popularity. Travel writers certainly did. Writing for the staid *Canadian Geographical Journal* in 1934, Frank Yeigh was one of the first journalists to highlight Niagara's historical attractions, such as Brock's monument and Laura Secord's house, and completely ignore the growing number of commercial amusements in the region. Reminding his readers that "the Niagara frontier is full of appeal to the intelligent traveller" was, perhaps, a not-too-subtle attempt to win the Falls back from the less sophisticated "tourists." A British journalist visiting Niagara in 1925 was more blunt: "The native tourist in his or her appropriate costume . . . meets the eye in swarms. The salient features of the ladies are rouge, chewing-gum and knickerbockers; of the men, shirts, chewing-gum and Palm Beach trousers."[47]

A sitting room in the Foxhead Inn, owned by local businessman Howard Fox, Niagara Falls, Ont., 1923.

But the behaviour—not just the appearance—of tourists also generated criticism. Through the 1920s occasional stories cropped up about "unwelcomed guests" in the region: tourists who set out their picnic baskets on farmers' fields or who stole fruit, tore down fences and barns for firewood, or left their rubbish behind for locals to clear away. Indeed, farmers, increasingly annoyed by the invasion of their territory by streams of urban "scoundrels" and "nabobs," acted individually and collectively to try to stop them. Farmers' associations and rural politicians lobbied against highway expansion in the 1920s, and individual farmers also turned to sabotage, scattering tacks or deliberately watering dirt roads and then charging extortionate sums to pull stranded cars out of the mud.[48] Other annoyances also received an airing. People complained, for example, about the arrogance of tourists in broken-down cars on the highways who expected to be pushed to their next destination by locals who happened to be passing by.

Many of these visitors were from another country, and because all tourist promotion schemes of this era at Niagara were directed towards the United States, the cultural stereotype of "American tourist" began to take on the negative connotations it would hold for decades after. "All of us are familiar with the blatant American tourist," sighed the *Niagara Falls Review* in 1929, reporting

Foxhead Inn, located at the foot of Clifton Hill, c.1940.

on a controversy brewing locally as residents began to object to the number of U.S. automobiles they saw displaying the Stars and Stripes. The flag issue threatened to become a major controversy, particularly when the Canadian Legion's provincial convention voted to make it compulsory that U.S. cars displaying the U.S. flag in Canada also display Canada's Union Jack. At Niagara the press counselled restraint, reminding readers that "the practice is due to ignorance." Many would no doubt have agreed with local hospital administrators, frustrated in their attempts to collect unpaid bills from U.S. tourists, that the tourist industry was "not an unmixed blessing" for the community.[49]

Despite these annoyances, the tourist boom of the 1920s began to change the town's sense of itself. By the end of the decade the geographical and cultural barriers separating visitor from local were not nearly as pronounced. Townspeople could not ignore the influx of visitors. No longer were tourists confined to the train station, stately hotels, and parks immediately around the waterfall. Tourists now drove their cars down the main streets, shopped for bargains in local stores, and clogged the bridges and highways in and out of the city. Visitors and residents would have increasingly shared the same commercial amusements, dancing at the Prince of Wales Club or dining at the same restaurants. As accommodation alternatives expanded to include autocamps and tourist homes, the tourists and residents might also, for a time, share neighbourhoods.

Tourism began to play an increasingly important and visible role in discussions and plans for the towns' progress. In spring 1928, for example, the Canadian side's Niagara residents were as always exhorted to participate in "clean up week," but for the first time the campaign was pitched directly as a relationship between tidy front yards and increased tourist spending. "First impressions are often lasting and have much to do with the success of the tourist business," editorialized the *Review*. "A clean and trim city is a standing invitation to visitors to remain and spend their money there."[50]

The transformation of tourism's place in the civic culture of the town would come to fruition in the 1940s and 1950s, but it began in this earlier era. More tourists, more people involved in tourism, and more of a sense that tourism was vital to the town's development all led to an increased tourist consciousness in civic discourse; and this tourist consciousness extended beyond the tourist industry itself. Residents of Niagara were beginning to be convinced—by civic officials, business leaders, and the tourist industry—that tourism was something the whole town ought to be interested in, because, as the story went, the whole town stood to benefit from it. In 1929, for example, a local accounting firm surveyed tourist spending habits and announced the impact of the "tourist dollar." Townspeople were informed not only about what percentage of money was being spent on what service or commodity (hotels, restaurants, retail stores, garages), but also about the more general effects of the "immediate circulation" of all this "new money." Tourism, in other words, was good for everyone, and thus everyone had an interest in being courteous towards, and respectful of, visitors.

This approach represented a significant shift in local thinking. Prosperity-through-tourism was new for Niagara Falls, but it was also a notion that was increasingly taking hold in Canada. Between 1921 and 1929 tourist spending in Canada tripled, and by the end of the decade tourist promoters and government officials across the country were beginning to think about the meaning of this phenomenon for the economic development of the country, and about how the momentum might be maintained.[51] This era also saw the beginnings of the organization of the tourist industry on a provincial and national scale.[52] By the end of the 1920s national facts and figures about the importance of the tourist trade were being issued from various federal departments in Ottawa and picked up eagerly by Niagara-area media. Tourism was the "new giant of Canadian business," second only to wheat exports. In 1928 its revenue was comparable to that of pulp and mineral production. According to Theodore Morgan, president of the Montreal Tourist and Convention Bureau, writing in 1930, the nation's tourist trade had "no limits on the possibilities of growth"—a prediction that was, in the short term, proven quite wrong.[53]

The boosterish talk quickly silenced any public airing of the inconvenience of tourism to local communities. The great thing about tourism, according to almost all who weighed in on the topic, was that it was a beneficent source of good for all. International bodies such as the League of Nations began to notice and study the economic impact of international tourism. Judged solely in terms of its monetary value in international exchanges, international tourism, by the mid-1930s, gained the status of a branch of import/export trade and was endorsed by almost all commentators as "a good thing."[54] Debating the state of the tourist industry in 1934, Canadian senators were more than enthusiastic. "Depletion of tourist assets," proclaimed Senator J.W. Regan of Halifax, "does not take place." Tourism was an "Aladdin's Lamp which every section of the Dominion may invoke and obtain advantages." Another senator agreed, noting proudly that no one was hostile to the tourist industry.[55]

Niagara's own changing sense of the place of tourism in its civic and economic culture was taking place, then, in a context of a nationally, even internationally, increasing profile for the tourist industry. Ironically, to paraphrase Joni Mitchell, they didn't know what they had till it collapsed.

Bust in the 1930s

At the Niagara Falls, Ontario, City Council meeting in November 1930, H.E. Goddard, the city manager, rose to deliver his annual report. This time, however, alongside his regular news of budgets and building statistics, he had a sombre message for the Council. "I would like to draw your attention to the most serious problem confronting the City at the present time," Mr. Goddard declared. "That of unemployment."[56] Over the next eight years this polite notification became a grim reality, because, as it did in many small industrialized towns across Canada, the Depression hit Niagara severely.

In 1924 sixty factories were located at Niagara Falls; by 1937 only half that number remained, and most of those had dramatically reduced production and hence their labour force.[57] The resulting unemployment created social and financial chaos for the town. In the winter of 1935, the worst point, almost six thousand of Niagara's eighteen thousand residents were on relief. Many hundreds more—single men who were, by municipal rules, ineligible for assistance—had been shipped out of town to cut lumber and make highways in Northern Ontario. With one-third of the residents on relief, city finances staggered and finally toppled. The city defaulted on its debentures in 1934, and for a time municipal finances were controlled by the provincial government.[58] A "Municipal Dining Room" was opened at the relief depot to feed the hungry, and two of the town's old hotels, the Drummond and the Savoy, were converted into temporary shelters for the homeless.

Although industrial activity creaked almost to a standstill, the effects of the Depression on tourism were more mixed. The tourist trade didn't come to a halt, but it did slow down. Certainly, across the country many in the tourist industry were alarmed by decreasing numbers of visitors, and in response to this decline the government convened its first investigation of tourism, the 1934 Senate Committee on the Tourist Trade. The number of tourists entering Ontario from the United States each year more than halved between 1930 and 1933, from thirteen to seven million. Nationally, revenue from tourism plummeted from $300 million in 1929 to $120 million in 1933.[59]

In Niagara Falls the press stopped reporting the total number of tourists locally, becoming much more general in its discussion of visitors. Instead of seasonal forecasts and reports, and optimistic talk of the prosperity brought by tourism, the news of the 1930s offered up accounts of the occasional "good weekend" when a "pre-Depression crowd" might be found admiring the view from Queen Victoria Park. The birth of the Dionne Quintuplets in 1934 and the subsequent frenzy of interest when they were put on display brought hordes of people to their home in Caladar, Ontario, but even though many visitors entered Ontario at Niagara Falls, the Quints were a bigger draw than the waterfall and few travellers lingered at the border.[60]

Even on "good weekends," most agreed that tourist spending had plummeted. Niagara Parks Commission police kept a vigilant eye out for tourists camping out in their cars in the park—an illegal but popular way to economize on accommodation—and souvenir vendors sighed about the miserliness of Depression-era tourists. In 1938 a store owner told a typical story about a woman from Detroit who looked "longingly" at a one-dollar china plate but said to the clerk that she only had a dollar and a half with her, and that was just enough to pay for her gas back home.[61]

The 1920s trend towards expansion of the tourist industry was quickly halted. The General Brock, which had fallen out of even nominally local hands in 1932, went into receivership in 1934, though it was soon purchased by Vernon Cardy and its doors remained opened throughout the decade. The Clifton, the only grand hotel from the nineteenth century that had continued as a first-class tourist hotel in the tourist boom of the 1920s, burned to the ground on New Year's Eve 1932 in what the local fire chief described as a "mysterious" fire. It never reopened.[62] The Drummond and the Savoy had been given over to relief recipients, and two other long-standing establishments, the New Windsor and the Queen's, also went out of business. Another hotel, the Orchard Inn, which had opened at the height of the 1920s boom, was razed by fire—intentionally, according to the liquor inspector—in 1933. Provincial inspectors reported through the 1930s that "Niagara Falls has more hotels than they need," proprietors were making only a "bare living," and several other hotels had been "torn down or standing vacant because they cannot be operated at a profit."[63]

The only new tourist attraction that opened in the 1930s was a gift from Niagara's favourite son and millionaire, Sir Harry Oakes, who purchased the land that had been the site of the Clifton Inn and donated it to the Niagara

The view from the top of the General Brock Hotel, 1937. The bus terminal is directly below, with Oakes Garden to the right.

Parks Commission. The lovely Oakes Garden Theatre—built largely by the sweated labour of almost six hundred relief workers contracted to the NPC—opened in 1937.[64] Another (potentially free) proposal, put forward in 1938 by the Chamber of Commerce, that the federal government locate an Indian reserve and an RCMP detachment at the Falls, since "nearly every tourist entering Canada asks where are the Mounties and where can we see an Indian Village," was not implemented.[65]

The main effect of the tourism slowdown was to intensify the various social divisions that had begun to emerge among local tourist entrepreneurs. Given the rivalries of the boom years of the 1920s—when hotel owners, autocamp operators, and tourist-home proprietors squared off against each other (all of them appealing to municipal authorities for assistance), when jazz club establishments pushed the boundaries of respectable amusements and the Niagara Parks Commission attempted at once to cash in on, and control, the boisterous crowd—during the Depression the level of nastiness could only rise commensurately with the level of desperation. Niagara, declared an angry citizen in 1931, had lost its former glory and had become "one of the cheapest and poorest tourist cities from coast to coast."[66] Old conflicts between public-sector and private-sector tourism resurfaced, particularly after the scandalous findings of an inquiry into the NPC instigated by Hepburn's newly elected provincial Liberal government in 1934. In 1937, for example, Niagara City Council endorsed a movement to try to tax the NPC for its property and businesses on the grounds that the Commission's restaurants and souvenir stores were "sabotaging" local businesses. The Council had perhaps been alerted to private complaints from local hotel owners that the NPC information booths were only recommending their own restaurants to tourists looking for an evening meal and, worse still, that they were considering keeping their restaurants open through the winter months. The city also threatened to suspend fire protection for the parks.[67]

In this climate of massive unemployment and increased competition in a far smaller and poorer tourist market, the level of hostility between employers and employees also increased. The service industry, which had been declining before 1921, increased during the tourist boom of the 1920s, and by 1931 it accounted for 40 per cent of the Canadian workforce. For women the service industry was by far the major employer; twice as many women worked in this sector as in clerical work or the professions.[68] But—then as now—service industry jobs were extremely low paying. Indeed, some workers didn't get "paid" at all. Through the 1930s hotel bellhops drew no wages, depending entirely on tips for their incomes. One angry, anonymous bellhop estimated to Ontario's Minister of Labour Arthur Roebuck in 1934 that he and his "partners in slavery" throughout Ontario drew only $7.50 per week in gratuities.[69] At the top of the heap were beverage-room waiters, who, according to a 1935 government study, drew salaries ranging from $10 to $15 per week. Hotel and restaurant workers at unionized establishments were little better off. The highest-paid in Toronto were cooks, at $15 per week, while waiters and waitresses earned between $8 and $10. Bus boys and kitchen help earned $7 to $8 weekly.[70]

Even hotel owners themselves recognized that low wages were the single greatest cause of employee discontent, particularly when the staffs could see all around them, as one hotel manager put it, "guests who are able to indulge in

Information booth and souvenir stand, Queen Victoria Park, c.1940.

every sort of luxury and who obviously have only a passing acquaintance with work." Yet in the end hotel owners like this one could only offer platitudes, suggesting that employees strive for "ideals, a protective outlook on life and an unwavering self-assurance." Large salaries were simply out of the question.[71]

Stories from Niagara Falls in the 1930s indicate that pay and working conditions were even worse than in other Ontario centres. Waitresses and bus boys at Niagara Parks Commission restaurants were paid $25 per month in 1934, wages that even the government called "very low." In the private sector, the proprietor of the Naples Cafe, A. Sorrentino, was fined by the provincial Minimum Wage

Board in 1934 when he admitted to paying his waitresses $3 and $4 per week, well below the 22 cent per hour minimum wage for women. Andy Melbourne, the controversial proprietor of the Prince of Wales Club, developed what he probably considered an inventive system for dodging minimum-wage legislation: he paid his waitresses in cash and kept no personnel records.[72]

At the high end of the spectrum, conditions were no better. Katie Petrullo (now Agar) was hired as a "pantry girl" at the grand General Brock Hotel in 1931, when she was fourteen years old. For five years she made salads, whipping cream, and salad dressing—from scratch—for ninety cents a day. While she resented the low pay and still angrily remembers the long hours—from seven in the morning until after midnight, in peak times—she felt extremely lucky to have found a job in the midst of the Depression. She was also aware that, as the daughter of working-class Italian immigrants, she had secured a rare foot in the door. At the time few hotel industry jobs were open to Italians, and the limited entry was strictly through the back door. "The foreign people would do the hard work" behind the scenes, in the kitchens and laundry, she recalled. It took Katie Petrullo five years in the kitchen—and, perhaps not coincidentally, marriage to an Anglo waiter, a transplanted Maritimer named Myles Agar—to secure better work in the Brock's coffee shop.[73]

First-generation Italian women were not the only ones who had complaints about the service industry. In 1935 Phil Tongler, a waiter at the General Brock, thought he might use his acquaintance with newly elected premier Mitchell Hepburn—Tongler had once been Hepburn's "cabana boy" in Miami Beach—to help him out with his employers. Tongler informed Hepburn about the "terrible" conditions at the General Brock. Waiters and waitresses alike, he said, worked from ten to fourteen hours a day for eleven-day stretches without overtime or time off. Their salaries, under the minimum-wage laws, should have been $30 a month, but they were receiving only $27. Sanitary conditions were also a problem. As well, it was customary for waiters and waitresses to receive meals, for which a small portion of their pay was deducted, but the only food he and his co-workers received was stale leftovers.[74] Tongler's association with Hepburn may well have paid off, for the labour ministry did send an inspector

The General Brock Hotel restaurant staff, 1936. Katie Agar is second row, third from left.

to the General Brock. Unfortunately, she chose to interview the hotel manager rather than the employees and found "no cause for complaint."[75]

Similar stories about long hours, low pay, and poor working conditions for waiters, waitresses, and other hotel staff emerged in cities and towns throughout the province in the 1930s, particularly in the resort areas of the Muskokas and Northern Ontario. In the North, because of low population figures, even the miserly provisions of the minimum-wage act did not apply.[76]

Most of these stories and complaints took place in private, and most of the service industry personnel who voiced their grievances to labour ministry officials did so anonymously, or, like Phil Tongler, they urgently requested that their names not be divulged to their employers. It was only in the remarkably changed labour climate of World War II that General Brock employees, for example, felt confident enough to move from individual letter-writing to collective, public action. In September 1941 they went on strike, successfully, for union recognition. "I cherished the union when it came in," remembers Katie Agar, for it was

Myles Agar (on the right) started as a waiter and worked himself up to bell captain at the General Brock Hotel. He is with an unidentified bell boy, c.1930.

only after the strike that hours of work were regulated and limited.[77]

Rather than the desperate tales of workers, another more familiar tug-of-war within the tourist industry got most of the public limelight in this era: the solicitation of tourists. Again tourist-home operators came in for the brunt of criticism. In 1931 Niagara Falls received special permission from the Ontario provincial government to strengthen its anti-soliciting bylaws, and tourist-home operators were regularly taken to court. The city also passed an equally controversial law requiring the inspection and licensing of tourist homes, which also provided them with a handy weapon against soliciting: those found guilty of soliciting would lose their licences. Some clever tourist-home operators tried to circumvent these new regulations by applying to the provincial liquor board to be classified as "standard hotels." In making this application Mrs. Marion Manette, for example, seemed less interested in serving liquor than in being able to advertise her rates and solicit tourists—in other words, in escaping the category of tourist home.

That ploy didn't work, for Mrs. Manette or any of the others seeking hotel licences in the 1930s.[78] Instead, pandemonium reigned, as neighbours regularly brought each other to court, usually for stealing tourist business from one another by yelling out, during curbside negotiations with customers, that cheaper prices were to be had next door. Sign wars also broke out, with neighbours enlarging their "room for rent" signs or positioning them to obscure their neighbours' signs. After several years of mass meetings, city council discussions, and criminal charges, some tourist-home operators found it prudent to retreat to their front porches, where they stood and yelled out to passing motorists, waving signs advertising their accommodations. But this too was cause for alarm. One alderman complained of hearing about two male New Jersey tourists who expressed amazement at finding "women on the main street, beckoning them into their homes." The gender politics of "soliciting," which had simmered as subtext in these debates since the 1920s, came to the boiling point. Soliciting was, as the alderman put it, an "indecent practice." Profiting from the waterfall was one thing, but pimping—or prostituting—for Niagara was quite another.[79]

But it was not as though male tourist entrepreneurs were behaving with any more decorum. One summer evening in 1930 two male tourist-home solicitors joined the throngs awaiting the arrival of Americans on the Falls View Bridge. One knocked the hat off of the other, who responded by throwing a stone. "The two zealous solicitors let tempers get the best of them," chided the newspaper, and they both ended up in jail.[80]

The dangerous hackman resurfaced in the 1930s, though this time the "problems" of race and ethnicity were eclipsed by competitiveness. The city had regulated taxi drivers some years earlier, positioning them in specific locations throughout tourist areas. But in the dog-eat-dog climate of the 1930s few drivers were content to remain in their designated places, and several among them devised inventive schemes to drum up business. Dressing themselves in generic "uniforms"—white shirts, dark pants, and a police or army-style cap (complete with a maple leaf in the centre)—taxi drivers stood by the highways or bridges on the way into the city, flagging tourists down. Some even jumped on the running boards of tourists' cars that were leaving customs stops near the bridges. Most tourists, understandably, thought a police officer was requesting them to stop and dutifully pulled their cars over.[81]

The battles of the 1930s were a mess of tangled-up threads: of economic self-interest, business rivalry, sexism, and wounded civic pride. Certainly hotel owners continued their campaign against tourist-home operators with the same vengeance displayed in the 1920s. When representatives of the General Brock Hotel went before Niagara's City Council in the fall of 1930 to seek tax relief, they blamed their 40 per cent reduction in business that summer solely on the city's lack of protection from "people soliciting for tourists from our own doorsteps."[82] The *Canadian Hotel Review* singled out Niagara Falls tourist-camp operators for "unethical practices," such as informing tourists that major conventions had filled all the local hotels. But the campaign against tourist homes was not only a local phenomenon.[83] In 1929 the New York state Hotel Association urged its members to "go on the offensive" against tourist homes by sprucing up their grounds, having their employees wear "smart uniforms," and posting what amounted to "warning" signs in hotel rooms urging guests to "Stop at Recognized Hotels." The signs listed such reasons as "good beds and fresh linens," as well as "provides safeguards for maintenance of moral standards."

By 1933 this campaign had taken to the highways, as hotel associations in a number of states began an aggressive billboard campaign against their rivals. Headlined "wayside or safe side?" the billboards featured several different scenes, all of them designed to scare travellers into submission. One depicted an isolated farmhouse at night, with a single window lit. It was labelled "sudden illness." The other half of the billboard depicted a "modern" hotel bedroom, where "a competent looking doctor is examining a sick child, while mother and father look anxiously on." Another told the same story via an isolated farm house erupting in flames.[84]

The Ontario Hotel Association's billboard campaign was, by contrast, oddly subtle. Its billboards, erected though the province in the summer of 1939, featured a uniformed white male bellboy and encouraged drivers that a hotel would provide safety, cleanliness and "a good night's sleep."

But in the 1930s hotel owners were not the only tourist entrepreneurs worrying about soliciting. The Niagara Parks Commission—which was not in the accommodation business and thus had little self-interest at stake—also began a ruthless clampdown of soliciting on its premises. Both tourist-home operators and taxi drivers made a practice of leafleting cars in the Queen Victoria Park parking lot, and some of the more forthright among them also approached tourists in the park directly. NPC officials, incensed by this practice, used their not inconsiderable powers to try to stop it. Constables were instructed to take down the licence plates of importuning taxi drivers or tourist-home operators, and—without the benefit of charges, trial, or appeal—the names of these offenders were passed on to the Highway Department and the vehicle licences revoked. The Commission also forbade taxis the right to drive through the park without a special licence.[85] While the occasional tourist entrepreneur complained—in private—that the parks were a "miniature fascist community," and once the St. Catharines *Standard* editorialized against such "Hitlerian" tactics by the NPC, others, such as the Chamber of Commerce, welcomed the move.[86]

The existence of business rivalry in the 1930s does not completely explain why soliciting became defined and treated as a huge social problem. Indeed, soliciting may not have been quite the "problem" that its detractors declared it to be. There were, certainly, visitors who complained about soliciting to the mayor, the press, the Chamber of Commerce, or the Niagara Parks Commission. Most of them told personal tales of being ambushed or harassed by solicitors. One said he had been "tagged" eight times in two blocks. Another told about paying for a sightseeing ride because the driver "inferred" that he would be able to take him on special routes. Later the tourist realized that he could easily have driven his own car on the same tour. A man from Bridgewater, Massachusetts, warned the mayor that the "pests" on the Canadian side of the International Bridge "make one think that he or she is almost to enter the Chicago Ghetto or the New York Bowery instead of a peaceful law abiding community."[87] Clearly some visitors—I have seen reference to about ten such letters through the 1930s—did take offence.

But visitors of that time also took offence at the price of tea at NPC concession booths and at promotional brochures not being printed in French. In an indignant letter to Prime Minister Mackenzie King, one U.S. visitor voiced her displeasure about a tourist attraction failing to live up to its promise. Racial and ethnic discrimination was also commonplace in Canadian tourism. When discussing the possibilities of expanding the international tourist market in Canada, participants on the 1934 Senate Committee accepted as given that they were only interested in recruiting "white traffic" from India and "eliminating Negroes" in their calculation of possible U.S. visitors.[88] An American tourist visiting Niagara jokingly complained to his NPC guide about the cost of the hike up the Brock monument and was stung when the guide retorted, "What part of Jerusalem do you come from, damn you, you are all alike."[89] Yet none of these stories stirred the same kind of community ferment as soliciting did.

Soliciting—however much it actually occurred, and however tourists actually felt about it—triggered a massive reaction because it touched a deeply felt sore spot at Niagara Falls: its reputation, almost a century old, as a clip joint. Throughout the 1920s and 1930s the debates on the "soliciting menace," the future of tourism, and the place of tourism in the economic development of the town were always underscored by a warning: be nice to tourists, or else. Niagara still had some apologizing to do, because the "bad old days" narrative of the town's past continued to cast a shadow.

In 1926, at the beginning of the boom years, the *Review* gently raised the spectre of this history by editorializing optimistically that "a different spirit is abroad nowadays to a great extent regarding the tourists. The day has gone when the tourists were regarded as just so many chances for exploitation." Yet a few years later, at the height of the legislative debate about banning soliciting in 1930, Mayor Charles Swayze drew the obvious parallel: "When I came to this city thirty or forty years ago you couldn't get off the train but somebody solicited you for a hotel. They did it for hotels only, but now everybody is soliciting."[90]

As the middle class hit the highways in their automobiles, tourist towns like Niagara Falls still had a few things to work out. What had to be done to achieve the proper care, feeding, and amusement of tourists? Who had the authority to offer commercial hospitality? No one, however, disputed that the tourist industry was there to stay. The element of tourist consciousness—the perception that tourism is an undisputed source of economic good for all—was taking root locally, nationally, and internationally in these years. This meant that tourism was becoming a powerful force; it might cause coloured lights to beam on a waterfall or determine the location and direction of a new highway. Then again, when combined with some of the modern era's dramatic changes in heterosexuality, tourism would also profoundly alter the honeymoon.

6

A Laboratory for the Study of Young Love:
Honeymoons and Travel to World War II

In 1926 an American travel writer, accompanied by the assistant manager of the Hotel Statler in nearby Buffalo, visited the Falls. Sitting in their automobile in downtown Niagara Falls, New York, the two watched an "apparently endless" stream of tourists promenade down the main street. "Did you ever see so many B-and-G's in all your life?" asked the hotel manager. The travel writer, after learning that "B-and-G" was hotel industry vernacular for bride and groom, was puzzled. "But I thought Niagara Falls had gone out of fashion as a haunt of the newly wedded," he said.

"Don't you believe it," exclaimed the hotelman, who went on to explain the social dynamics of honeymooning in this era. The place was flooded with honeymooners, he said, especially in the two big "marriage months," June and October. Some were "trippers," couples from nearby towns who could not afford to travel very far and stayed only a day or two. But the rich and fashionable still came. They were just more circumspect about announcing their newly married status. Rather than holding hands and "frankly advertising their state of bliss," wealthy honeymooners preferred to enjoy the scenery, and each other's company, from the seclusion of their "expensive motor-cars." This interpretation was made that much more plausible when the hotelman added that "dozens" of these wealthy "B-and-Gs" were registered at his hotel in Buffalo.

Once alerted to the presence of honeymooners in his midst, the travel writer was intrigued and set off to explore Niagara Falls "as a sort of laboratory for the study of Young Love." He wandered about the town, "watching, listening and

"You are a plucky little woman," he said, fondly. "We'll have another honeymoon and we won't shorten it, either." Illustration from "The Bride," a story by Ella O. Burroughs, *Metropolitan* magazine, December 1913.

drawing conclusions," and later wrote a long, upbeat story about the happy state of heterosexual romance in his day.[1]

This is a remarkable piece of journalism, for it foreshadowed similar stories that would appear in dozens of North American mass circulation magazines after World War II. The notion that the wealthy and refined still made Niagara their honeymoon destination, though from the discreet distance of their cars and Buffalo hotel rooms, may or may not have been wishful thinking—or advertising—on the part of the Statler hotel chain. But the identification of Niagara Falls as a "laboratory" in which the outsider—armed with the specialized knowledge acquired by tourist industry insiders—could observe the rituals of honeymooning couples, and from there offer happy pronouncements on the state of women, men, marriage, and the family, was exactly the same story that dozens of journalists would write about Niagara Falls over the next fifty years. If, following Foucault, we understand the honeymoon as a forbidden or restricted area, certainly many people through the twentieth century expressed a strong desire to peer inside.

This particular journalist, though, had his eyes not on the future but on the past. After roaming the streets of Niagara and talking to tourist industry personnel, he came to what he considered a startling conclusion: this generation of young people had, apparently, shed the shame of honeymooning. A guide explained the tricks he used to identify newlyweds: they wore new clothing, the men were overly protective of the women, and the women looked at the men in starry-eyed wonder. He also declared that couples had no objection to being thus "spotted." "Object!" he exclaimed. "Give 'em one kind look and they'll tell you the whole story! Young people nowadays ain't ashamed of being married!"[2]

Not everyone in this era would have agreed that public heterosexuality wasn't still a bit embarrassing. Yet while the notion of a stark line existing between the social and sexual mores of the old-fashioned Victorian generation and the freer, modern one is overdone, in several important respects the honeymoon in the interwar period had changed. For one thing, more people were watching. In the nineteenth century the only people who gave honeymoons much attention were the writers of advice manuals, who explained how to have

A LABORATORY

FOR THE STUDY

OF YOUNG LOVE:

HONEYMOONS

AND TRAVEL TO

WORLD WAR II

154

them, and the writers of pornography, who lampooned them. In the twentieth century more and different kinds of people got involved in the project of defining the event: along with sex experts came filmmakers and novelists, journalists, advertisers, tourist promoters, and especially doctors, whose attempts to medicalize the ritual—to place it under their scrutiny—were astonishingly successful. By the early twentieth century, according to medical historians, marriage had become too important to be left to the bride and groom alone.[3] So, even though it was still a bit shameful, the honeymoon was becoming increasingly visible and culturally interesting.

The change in the public face of the honeymoon took place in the context of broader changes in the sexual culture of early twentieth-century North America. The 1920s, as Jonathan Katz puts it, was when the heterosexual "came out." Previously understood as a pathological condition—"oversexed," we might say now—heterosexuality had by the end of the 1920s acquired the positive, "normal" meanings still held today. This transformation had much to do with a changing sexual culture. As Katz explains, eroticism was increasingly placed "at the core of modern personality."[4] As sexuality was invested not solely in acts but also in identities such as heterosexual and homosexual, male/female couples were increasingly, and publicly, understood as sexual units. While they were also economic and reproductive units, what became new was the value placed on sexuality in the formation of identity and personality, which made sexual attraction much more central to male/female coupling. The increased importance of sexual expression in turn reshaped the institution of marriage, as couples began to expect that erotic fulfilment was an integral part of a successful alliance.

So as the *sexual* in heterosexuality was emphasized, the honeymoon would also acquire more obvious sexual connotations. The process was gradual, and sometimes the sexual meanings emerged in reverse, as it were, as newlywed couples suffered extreme public embarrassment in their futile search for privacy. Honeymoon-themed fiction, for example, still played with the desirability, but ultimate impossibility, of "passing" as an old married couple. John Ryder and Ruth Mont, protagonists of *Some Honeymoon!* (1918), discover on the train, to their dismay, "a 'newness' sticking to bridal couples that no amount

of deception can hide—from the eagle eye of the railroad porter least of all. The colored functionary on their car hovered about them as though they had been especially placed in his care."[5] Crafty black railroad porters foiled such deceptions in several honeymoon stories of this era. Compared to the menacing black men who populated travellers' imaginations in the nineteenth century, twentieth-century railroad porters had been tamed. They acted, in these stories, as a masculine version of a mammy. Like mammies, they combined folk wisdom ("he knew newlyweds when he saw them!") with caretaking. But they were also, like the mammy, comic figures, often played for laughs.[6] A couple interviewed by the *Ladies Home Journal* in 1929 told their story of being spotted and stared at by fellow railroad passengers, despite bribing the porter to keep their newlywed status quiet. Furious, they accused him of betraying them, to which he responded, "Ah, no sah. Folks ast me if you-all was a bride an' groom, but I said no, you was jest pals, tha's all."[7]

One significant difference between the 1920s and the nineteenth century was that the "G" was now just as likely to feel the bemused scrutiny of outsiders as the "B." To observers, honeymooners behaved in ways that were both innocent and silly, and both of these tendencies were classically female characteristics. The man who blanched at the hotel desk, suddenly assailed by doubts about whether or not his new bride was also supposed to sign the register, or the man who, when asked by the desk clerk if he had a reservation, proudly produced his marriage licence, was hardly acting with the public self-assurance most men were supposed to take for granted. The nineteenth-century groom was a "brute"—so sexually driven the experts fretted he might cause his timid bride irreparable harm. A few decades later, the "bungling" groom seemed as skittish as the bride; more likely to be laughed at than feared.

A wonderful example of masculine anxiety and ineptitude on a honeymoon occurs in King Vidor's classic 1928 silent film, *The Crowd*. This film about the alienation of urban life centres on John Sims, an "everyman" character. Everything about him, including his amusements, reflects his solidly middle-of-the-road existence, including taking his date to Coney Island and his bride to Niagara Falls. On the train to Niagara, newlyweds John and Mary Sims sit nervously together while night falls, and the black porter paces anxiously around them. Finally the porter asks, "Did I hear you-all speakin 'bout havin' yo' bed made up?" Reluctantly they leave the sitting car, and we watch John prepare himself for bed. Following the instructions of the sex experts to the letter, John and Mary prepare for bed separately. He changes, washes his face, and preens in the mirror, as two older gentlemen watch him through the open dressing-room door, nudging each other. He proceeds to brush his hair, and the men smile indulgently as they see rice dropping to the floor. Something falls out of the pocket of his dressing gown, and one of the men retrieves it for him. It's a popular sex manual, Sylvanus Stall's *What a Young Husband Ought to Know*. The two older men dissolve into raucous laughter as they return it to him, and he, of course, is mortified.[8]

Marriage seemed to invite men to step into a world that was, initially at least, foreign and embarrassing. Male ambivalence about entering this humiliating culture resonated in several stories of the era, which portrayed men who chose to remain secure in the familiar routine of commerce rather than taking their brides on honeymoons. This was always, absolutely, the wrong choice. In one such story, the bride dies waiting for her man to return from his business trip. In another, love conquers capital when a new bride forgives her overly ambitious husband, who has delayed their honeymoon, only when he admits his mistake. In the end he agrees with her: it's better to have a honeymoon than motor-cars, sailboats, and a country house.[9] Given the stark choice, however, between going to the office and bungling through the apparently endless mortifications experienced by "B-and-G's," we are meant to understand that honeymoons both confirmed and diminished the groom's manhood. Indeed, one writer thought he had found the answer to Niagara's honeymoon popularity in this exact paradox: the thundering waterfall aroused in women a "primitive feminine appeal," fear, and in men the "primitive masculine response," protection. Thus as generations of women stand before the falls and "instinctively press closer" to their husbands, and men "instinctively put their arms around them, as if to hold them safe," the natural order of heterosexuality is sustained.[10]

A LABORATORY

FOR THE STUDY

OF YOUNG LOVE:

HONEYMOONS

AND TRAVEL TO

WORLD WAR II

158

The Honeymoon Companions

Sex experts of the day placed new expectations on both brides and groom. Faded away was the old notion that men should keep their brutish instincts in check while their dainty brides recovered from the ordeal of wedding planning and travel. It was assumed that newlyweds would go on honeymoon trips.

Couples were merely cautioned not to overextend themselves financially. Automobile travel was endorsed, since "it permits a honeymoon schedule that can be easily changed so as to avoid the fatigue that used to result when the first days of the honeymoon meant long, distant journeys on boats or trains."[11] Delaying sex, though only for one evening, was an option still offered by some experts, but this message was no longer front and centre. Some experts believed that waiting could pose dire problems: "Too much impetuosity or brutality during the first night is apt to have just as disastrous results as complete failure to attempt sexual relations." So the bumbler or "ninny" who, acting either from chivalry or his own insecurity, ignored his wife on their wedding night was just as problematic as "the brute."[12] Even though many brides were "more fit for a rest home than for a honeymoon" after the flurry of pre-wedding entertainment, it was "not such a bad idea to start having intercourse right away."

Most women, declared two marriage counsellors, "have an innate feeling that they are really not married until they have intercourse. They are glad to get it over with."[13]

This (probably unintentionally) ironic description of the bride's relationship to sex highlights the main problem of heterosexuality in this era. When sexual happiness came to the fore as a primary purpose of marriage, women and men were faced with the challenge of harmonizing their vastly different erotic rhythms. Gender difference, the absolute oppositeness of the sexes, was one of the pillars of early twentieth-century heterosexuality.[14] Sex experts, for example, took as their starting point what one called the "natural discordance" of male and female sexual "moods." Men's "sex instinct" was "practically continuous." Nature, declared one doctor, "means him to take the initiative, and has endowed him with imperious needs." Women were "sex-stingy."[15]

Yet despite the presentation of such differences as essential elements of human nature, a basic socialization lurked close by. Most critics agreed that women had been taught their "morbid" fears of sex, usually blaming overprotective mothers and the cultural climate of sexual ignorance. One forward-looking writer located the problem in male domination, the "ages-old discipline of self-denial, [in which] duty . . . bred frigidity," and credited the women's movement with heralding a "sexual awakening of woman."[16] So, however the issue was explained, culture *could* confound nature, and experts were optimistic that, with what one of them called "proper cultivation," women could overcome their sexual reticence. Proper cultivation was to come from two types of male authorities: husbands and doctors.

Sex manuals of the first half of the twentieth century were much more detailed and explicit about lovemaking techniques than an earlier generation of writers had been. Most agreed that orgasms for women were possible; they just took a long time (one book estimated an hour or more was necessary). The problem was more a matter of the "bungling bridegroom"—the crude, or even cruel, male lacking the patience and the skills to help his wife achieve what one writer called a "sexual personality." Some manuals recommended using lubricants, varying positions, manual stimulation, and even oral sex (termed "genital kisses"). One book assured husbands that there was "nothing immoral or obscene" in caressing the breasts or lips of a woman.[17]

Yet, for all the insistence on privacy, couples were not to be left alone on their honeymoons, for doctors—according to their own pronouncements, at least—played almost as important a role as the groom in arousing the bride. Doctors succeeded in creating a new medical condition, "marital maladjustment," and in finding its cure, the premarital medical examination. A widely recognized pioneer of this procedure was U.S. gynecologist Robert Dickinson, who reasoned that the lack of "very simple knowledge nearly every wedding night leaves blind fear to blundering ignorance." Dr. Dickinson firmly believed that only doctors were in a position to rectify this problem. Books, he declared, could not be explicit enough to deal with the issues, for they may "pander to pruriency." Unmarried priests were obviously disqualified, and the subject was far too embarrassing for parents to broach. Relatives, friends, and teachers were too "impersonal." Enter the doctor, "the only proper, qualified and impersonal instructor," who could "save his people from their ignorance." In separate interviews with bride and groom, Dickinson imparted his version of sex education, which included a lecture on the ideal of mutual sexual pleasure as well as information about birth control and other practical wedding-night tips. Overturning conventional wisdom on the topic, he also told couples that an intact hymen was not an accurate or necessary sign of virginity.[18]

By 1913 seven U.S. states required premarital medical examinations, though only the prospective groom was tested; to examine a bride would have been considered an affront. By the late 1930s the U.S. laws had become more detailed and more extensive, with brides subject to examinations along with grooms. Slowly marriage was becoming understood not only as a romantic event, but also as an issue of public health. What caused this connection was not a concern for sexual fulfilment but a fear of disease. Premarital medical examinations were legislated because of growing fears of venereal disease.[19] While, as doctors and sex experts stressed, the VD exam and the premarital exam were not exactly the same, they did spring from the same source. As popular sex educator Ernest Groves put it, such examinations were the "application of science in the realm

A LABORATORY
FOR THE STUDY
OF YOUNG LOVE:
HONEYMOONS
AND TRAVEL TO
WORLD WAR II

160

of matrimony." By the 1930s almost all sex experts—doctors and laypeople alike—were recommending the premarital exam, and women's magazines were attempting to convince their readers that for a respectable woman there was nothing untoward about the procedure. Groves likened it to the long-standing practice of requiring physical examinations for soldiers, sailors, firemen, and policemen: "It is just as reasonable that those commencing marriage should receive the same sort of service from competent scientists."[20] Gladys Groves and Robert Ross warned women that the doctor was the only reliable source of information, because "the 'facts' a woman picks up over the cardtable and elsewhere from her woman-friends are mostly misinformation that proves exceedingly troublesome until corrected."[21]

In their crusade against sexual ignorance, and especially in their frank (sometimes even adventurous) discussion of sexual acts and birth control, sex experts did help to disseminate useful information, little of which was discussed in the educational institutions of the day. But as helpful as these doctors and sex experts may have been, they were clearly products of the prevailing culture when it came to relations between women and men. The assumptions about gender shared by most of the writers—that women and men had vastly differing sexual appetites, and that it was the job of men to learn how to properly coax recalcitrant, terrified brides—reproduced cultural stereotypes of the passionate man and passionless woman (not to mention her evil twin, the harlot), which scarcely differed from earlier, old-fashioned conceptions of male and female roles. The sexual transformation of husbands from Victorian "brutes" to early twentieth-century "blunderers" did little to change cultural norms concerning male power.

The new, healthy ideal was a man who skilfully initiated his bride and offered her pleasure and respect, but, as historian Christina Simmons succinctly puts it, "He was still in charge."[22] Sexual imbalance was fundamental to definitions of both gender and heterosexuality. The sexually voracious—or even simply desiring—female was confined to pornographic and/or imperialist fantasy and to popular humour or burlesque. An English play of the 1930s, *Mrs Brown's First Honeymoon*, features a strong, feisty Cockney woman reminiscing about her honeymoon in Cardiff. "Eh!" she declares, "I did enjoy that honeymoon!

Pink [her first husband] sez I wor a different creature at the end of it. In fact, 'e sez ter me, 'A sailor's supposed to 'ave a wife in ev'ry port, but if all the women in the world wor like you one would be enough fer any man!'"[23] Almost everyone in this era would have agreed, however, that Mrs. Brown was most definitely *not* like all the other women.

In their attempts to medicalize marriage, some doctors were probably offering at least some good advice. A frank discussion about sex in a doctor's office may well have allayed fears and eased communication between husband and wife. But as historians of motherhood have ably demonstrated, the rise of the medical expert also served to diminish the value of conversations and information-sharing on the same topic between friends or within the family. In this era, only the doctor knew for sure.[24]

Furthermore, lurking behind the apparently liberal, sexually modern exterior of at least some medical experts lay a rather more sinister agenda. In Canada, eugenic concerns—the belief that "like would produce like"—motivated doctors, politicians, and women's groups to advocate the strict regulation of marriage. Those judged "feebleminded" or insane and those infected with venereal disease bore the brunt of these concerns, but some doctors also maintained that "potential psychotics" and people with dissimilar height, blood groups, and even eye colour should be discouraged from marriage because of the risk of congenital mental ailments.[25] Dickinson, the pioneer of premarital medical examinations, was also a confirmed believer in eugenics (even after World War II, when it was no longer fashionable for North Americans). Indeed, he extended eugenics into the realm of sexual identity. He headed up the Committee for the Study of Sex Variants, a research group that attempted to find anatomical explanations—such as an elongated clitoris—for lesbianism.

Premarital medical examinations, therefore, had an added benefit: they allowed the doctor to separate the adjustable, and reproductive, heterosexual from the unadjustable homosexual—a bodily distinction that could easily be identified on an examining table.[26] Doctors such as Dickinson were beginning to define heterosexuality by contrasting it to its evil twin, homosexuality. Heterosexuality had begun to speak, but its voice was hesitant, at first, and

A LABORATORY
FOR THE STUDY
OF YOUNG LOVE:
HONEYMOONS
AND TRAVEL TO
WORLD WAR II

162

Early honeymoon merchandising at Niagara Falls: The "Honeymoon Cottages," Clifton Hill, C.I. Burland, proprietor. Postcard published by F.H. Leslie, Limited, Niagara Falls, Ont., c.1920s.

certainly *not* spontaneous. Alone in a sea of dangerous sexual possibilities, it required expert protection and proper cultivation, beginning with the right kind of honeymoon.

The Niagara Trip in the 1930s

For the travelling middle class, the honeymoon had become an established fact. Travel, sex, and privacy were taken for granted as essential elements of the honeymoon; so much so, for example, that the humour of another 1930s play, *The Road to Niagara*, turns on the absurdity of a mother accompanying her newlywed daughter and husband on their automobile trip to Niagara Falls.[27] Similarly, a 1933 Busby Berkeley musical, *Footlight Parade*, features a dance number, "Honeymoon Hotel," which a year later was wonderfully parodied in a Merry Melodies cartoon of the same name. Both feature a bevy of hotel staff, graciously, if somewhat slyly, welcoming the bride and groom. The bellhop in the cartoon version, for example, sings:

I'm the guy that carries all the luggage,
I work in the honeymoon hotel,
I see all the kissage and the huggage
And many other things as well![28]

In the film version, the telephone operator winks as she sings:

A LABORATORY
FOR THE STUDY
OF YOUNG LOVE:
HONEYMOONS
AND TRAVEL TO
WORLD WAR II

164

I'm the girl in charge of conversation,
I hear things I wouldn't dare to tell![29]

The honeymoon couple was never, strictly speaking, alone. Newlyweds brought along medical experts—sometimes, as John Sims did, in their pockets. But they were met at their destinations by an array of others who eased their transitions into wedded life. The single, shuffling black porter—a stereotype who makes a brief appearance in *Footlight Parade*—was slowly replaced by an army of smiling, white hotel personnel. In the fantasy world of Depression-era musicals, the workers are all happy workers, not underpaid people who have just put in thirteen-hour shifts. They delight in fluttering over the hesitant bride and groom; and this is exactly the source of the humour in these sketches, for the staff is *so* gracious, *so* eager to serve that they complicate the main goal of the honeymooning couple: privacy. In *Footlight Parade* the newlyweds clear out singing chambermaids and visiting family and firmly place the "do not disturb" sign on the door. Both the film and the cartoon versions end with the same scene, which illustrates how the honeymoon was at once risqué and permissible: we see the couple in bed together, which fades into an image of a smiling baby.

By the 1930s advertisers had also begun to treat the honeymooning couple as a stock character, which not only suggests a level of cultural visibility but also indicates the ties between honeymooning, travel, and consumption. The *Canadian Hotel Review*, for example, ran a series of ads for Procter & Gamble's Camay soap, which makes the case for both—visibility and consumption—quite plainly. "Lucky the hotel that gets the patronage of this happy, free-spending

Honeymooners as consumers: soap ads attempting to convince hotel owners that newlyweds—and other guests—would like nothing better than to see their rooms supplied with Camay. The ads ran in the hotel industry magazine *Canadian Hotel Review* in 1938.

couple!" declared one ad. An early indication of what would become commonplace in post-World War II popular culture, the ads identify honeymooners as travellers and (in this case, unashamed) hotel visitors, but they were also something more. To hotel owners and soap manufacturers, they were, even more importantly, shoppers.

Before World War II this version of the honeymoon was a cultural norm only among the middle class. If working-class couples travelled on honeymoons at all, they were likely to visit family, in a sort of working-class version of the upper-class wedding tour of the nineteenth century. In Nova Scotia, for example, high levels of outmigration meant that the tradition of reaffirming family ties through post-wedding travel was an important feature of working-class culture; this was also the only sort of vacation they could afford. Most British working-class couples did not take honeymoon trips at all until after World War II. Time and money were part of the story here as well, but the standard customs of the honeymoon—privacy and consumption, especially—were irrelevant to most British newlyweds. Until well after World War II, many couples began their married lives by living with one or the other set of parents. The honeymoon's emphasis on separation and privacy as a prelude to the establishment of autonomous, nuclear families made little cultural sense.[30]

Newlywed Esther Clarke sets out a roadside picnic on the way to Niagara, 1936. Photo by Ganton Clarke.

Many North American working-class couples, armed with a little luck and ingenuity, did make the Niagara excursion in the 1920s and 1930s. Gerald and Janet Zoerhof, for example, had to wait until the day after their wedding in June 1927 to take their trip from Wisconsin to Niagara Falls, because they needed to collect their pay envelopes, which were due that day from their employers, a shoe factory. They spent a full day on the road and stayed two nights at the Falls until their money ran out. With only enough money for gas and a couple of ten-cent hot dogs, they prayed that their car would survive the trip back without a breakdown. Another couple, May and Bill Lindlaw, honeymooned at the Falls in 1938, compromised by avoiding the more expensive hotels in favour of a one-room cabin, but they did treat themselves to dinner one evening at the General Brock. Omar and Frances Stangland, farmers from Albion, Indiana, borrowed the family car in 1935 and spent two days of their three-day honeymoon getting to and from the Falls. They left with forty-one dollars in their pockets and returned with two.

The most ingenious of all, perhaps, was Charles Bredd and his new bride, who took the train to Niagara from the Northern Ontario mining town of Timmins in 1938. Once there they realized they could not afford the accommodation prices, but happily they ran into someone they recognized, an Indian from Timmins. He offered them what Bredd called a "teepee" if they could find some land to set it down on. So they spent a night in a makeshift campground in a vacant lot, until the neighbours complained about "the Indians moving in."[31]

Even when a trip to Niagara was out of the question, there were ways of faking it. Nova Scotia writer Frank Parker Day was completing his first year as an English professor at the University of New Brunswick when he got married, in June 1910. "My wife and I had neither money nor inclination to make the right and proper trip to Niagara Falls," he recalled, but he did appreciate the metaphoric importance of such a journey. "I suppose Niagara, with its swift, smooth waters, gathered slyly together and hurled over a sheer precipice to roar through miles of whirlpool and rapid, is a kind of symbol of newly married life." So Parker Day and his wife opted for a Maritime version of the experience. They purchased an old canoe, fashioned a tent out of canvas, and set out for Grand Falls on the Saint John River, where they spent their wedding night camped on a rocky ledge at the foot of the waterfall.[32]

A trip to Niagara complete with a luxurious stay at a fabled honeymoon hotel was financially beyond the reach of most people. But that does not settle the question of its place, or popularity, in the social imagination. Some might wonder why couples without much money would scrape together a makeshift, low-budget version of the classic Niagara honeymoon, or perhaps some might see this as a pathetic case of working-class mimicry or "wannabes." British feminist writer Carolyn Steedman has cautions against such a rudimentary or instrumental analysis of working-class consumer desire, noting the tendency of analysts from all political persuasions to attribute "psychological simplicity to working-class people." I would rather turn the question around; instead of asking about the misplaced desires (or false consciousness) of working-class people, perhaps we should, as Steedman has, question the "structures of political thought that have labelled this wanting as wrong."[33]

The more popular the Niagara honeymoon became, the more people tried to claim Niagara's fame and hospitality for themselves, even when then they could not quite match the script. Two years before Oscar Wilde's 1882 visit, the U.S. writer

Walt Whitman arrived at Niagara for a short holiday with his ex-lover Peter Doyle. Whitman and Doyle inverted the honeymoon ritual almost completely; their visit came at the end, not the beginning, of their relationship. They had, by Whitman's account, a "first rate time," and in an act stunning in its symbolism Whitman sent a Niagara postcard to another of history's famous homosexuals, England's Edward Carpenter, who was then in Brighton.[34] Oscar Wilde, Walt Whitman, and Edward Carpenter all chuckling over Niagara Falls: the mind boggles.

A LABORATORY

FOR THE STUDY

OF YOUNG LOVE:

HONEYMOONS

AND TRAVEL TO

WORLD WAR II

168

But it certainly wasn't only the gay literati who got the joke. In the late 1920s, Niagara was the destination for another gay male couple, Jeb, a Washington, D.C., civil servant, and his lover Dash. On the train they were delighted to meet "a pair of well-dressed fellows," whom they quickly spotted as another gay couple ("Raging Flames," as Jeb called them), also bound for Niagara. After spending a day "gorging ourselves with natural beauties," including a trip behind the waterfall at Table Rock, the foursome met up in the evening while gazing at the illuminated cataract, after which they headed to a bar to "drink more weak Canadian beer." As Jeb reported, "We got into a gleeful mood, and laughed uncontrollably over trifles."[35]

In public, a single, coherent honeymoon script was emerging. Travel, privacy, service industry hospitality, consumption, romance, and sex were all becoming an integral part of the honeymoon, and these were exactly the ingredients that tourist entrepreneurs began to commodify and promote in the 1930s and 1940s. Those who could not afford this package, or whose sex lives placed them outside it, were not invited, but they could, and did, crash the party. The Northern Ontario couple spending their wedding night at Niagara in a tent in a vacant lot or the four gay men laughing together over a beer reminds us of the often uneasy fit between representation and practice.

Purchasing Romance: The Niagara Honeymoon as Consumption

Despite, or perhaps because of, the tourist boom of the 1920s, few tourist entrepreneurs at Niagara considered honeymooners to be distinct from regular tourists. One campground owner of the 1920s called his cabins "honeymoon huts," and the occasional reference to newlyweds appeared in Niagara Parks Commission literature, but for the most part sustained honeymoon promotion was absent. No mention was made, for example, of honeymoon suites in the flurry of hotel building at Niagara in the 1920s, and as the Chamber of Commerce and other local associations began to place tourist promotion at the centre of their efforts, they came up with no special gimmicks to lure honeymooners. Still, although massive promotion of honeymoon tourism, at Niagara and elsewhere, would be a product of the post-World War II travel boom, glimmers of such promotion did begin to appear in the 1930s and 1940s.

A specific, though informal, pitch to honeymooners began creeping into Niagara publicity. During the annual "Goodwill Tour" through the United States undertaken by Niagara Falls Chamber of Commerce representatives from both sides of the border in 1930, promoters distributed Canadian pennies, which, as they told the women they met, were meant specifically for their honeymoon trips to the Falls.[36] Both the Toronto-Niagara and the New York City-Niagara railway routes were dubbed the "Honeymoon Special" in the early 1930s. Hoping to attract some of the legions of tourists expected to visit New York for the World's Fair in 1939, Niagara Falls hotel owners had all the telephone poles between Syracuse, Rochester, and Niagara Falls stamped "the Honeymoon Trail." New York hotels co-operated with this promotional scheme and placed ads in their rooms stating, "You took her to the World's Fair. Now take her to Niagara Falls by the Honeymoon Trail."[37]

In 1935 the NPC also decided to adopt a more formal, elaborate honeymoon promotion scheme by announcing its plans (the details of which were not clearly spelled out) to revitalize the sagging tourist industry in mid-Depression by creating the Falls as a mecca not only for honeymooners, but also for "second honeymooners"—a newly invented category.[38] Two royal couples visiting in the 1930s, Prince and Princess Takamatsu of Japan and the Prince and Princess Asturias of Spain, both received an enthusiastic local welcome as "royal honeymooners," as did another unique couple, Mr. and Mrs. John Wood, aged eighty-four and seventy-nine respectively.[39]

Such ploys served to raise Niagara's profile and, just as importantly, reinvent the Niagara Falls honeymoon as a modern, fun, and desirable feature of consumer culture. It became obligatory, in that era and seemingly forever after, for travel writers doing any sort of Niagara story to mention its honeymoon fame. A *New York Times* feature on the Falls in 1935, for example, asserted that "no other place in America attracts so many newly married couples as Niagara Falls" and, for the first time, included numerical estimates of honeymooners. Plucking its figures from unnamed "hotelmen," the *Times* suggested that one-quarter of Niagara visitors were honeymooners. The Canadian press followed suit. The *Toronto Telegram* of May 21, 1937, for example, featured a photo of a man and woman standing together on the deck of the *Maid of the Mist* with the caption, "1937 Honeymoon Season Opens!"[40]

A LABORATORY
FOR THE STUDY
OF YOUNG LOVE:
HONEYMOONS
AND TRAVEL TO
WORLD WAR II

170

The Second World War continued the trend. The tourist industry at Niagara Falls faced unique hardships during the war. While tourism in Niagara was not as hurt as the trade in other parts of the country—the Canadian Pacific Railway closed its hotels at Banff, Lake Louise, and several Maritime resorts—the war did cause disruption.[41] Portions of the hydro facilities on the Canadian side were fenced off due to security concerns, marring the view and access to parts of Queen Victoria Park and the tunnels at Table Rock. In 1941 park authorities discontinued the illumination of the waterfall, much to the chagrin of hotel owners, who regularly complained about the setback this represented for their businesses. The tourist industry, at Niagara and elsewhere, also had to contend with the perceived unseemliness of tourism during wartime. As one Ottawa journalist observed, travel restrictions and gasoline rationing forced travellers to consider whether their journeys were really necessary—and "a journey to Niagara Falls of all other places in the world hardly ever seems necessary."[42] Thus the travel industry directed a good deal of its advertising towards convincing people that, as Leo Dolan, head of the Canadian Travel Bureau, explained in 1943, "There is nothing unpatriotic about taking a vacation this year."[43]

As was the case during World War I, tourist promoters also had to combat rumours circulating in the United States that American visitors would face new and restricted rules in Canada, particularly before the U.S. entry into the war.

The Maple Leaf Bazaar, a popular souvenir shop in Niagara Falls, Ont., 1941. Owned by Herb Hands, the store was located between the General Brock Hotel and Foxhead Inn.

It was a testament to both the growing importance of tourism, as well as the climate of wartime Canada, that media commentators reported in all earnestness that German agents had been planted in the United States as hotel clerks and travel agents and were telling prospective visitors to Canada that their cars would be impounded and their money drastically devalued once they crossed the border.[44] As during the First World War, the reverse was true; wartime helped to reinvent tourism as patriotism. As Ontario Provincial Treasurer Leslie Frost told a conference of tourist entrepreneurs in 1944, if the tourist industry was treated as "non-essential" and ignored during the war, Canada would "run the grave risk of seriously impairing international relations."[45]

So tourists continued to be welcomed at the Falls during World War II, and no one more than honeymooners. The increase in marriage rates surely encouraged this tendency. In Canada, for example, the marriage rate increased by fully one-third in the early years of the war, 1938 to 1940.[46] Specific honeymoon

The Spanish Aerocar glides over the Whirlpool, c.1950.

promotion, through fanciful stories of famous or unusual honeymooners, contests, and national media exposure, was a staple of the tourist industry throughout the war. The General Brock Hotel combed the engagement announcements in nearby newspapers and sent personalized letters to brides-to-be, inviting them to consider Niagara (and, of course, the General Brock) for their honeymoons. By this time the longevity of the Niagara honeymoon tradition itself had become a selling point. The General Brock told brides that a trip to the Falls was "akin to wearing grandmother's lace in the bridal veil."[47]

Honeymoon promotion became more systematic, perhaps because the increasing marriage rate expanded the market and perhaps as well because of rumours about the place (again) becoming passé. In January 1940, for example, Niagara Falls, Ontario, mayor George Inglis announced a new joint honeymoon publicity campaign, which also included the Chamber of Commerce and the NPC, to counter the ill effects of a story in an unnamed "morning paper movie column" that heralded the death of the Niagara honeymoon. Fuming, the mayor noted that Dick Powell had recently visited the Falls, as had many other Hollywood stars.[48]

A year later the Chamber of Commerce on the U.S side initiated exactly the sort of campaign the Canadians had promised: they sponsored a contest to find the oldest living Niagara Falls honeymooners and pledged to bring the winners back for a second honeymoon. Over four hundred people replied. The winners, Mr. and Mrs. Albert Praul of Philadelphia, had first visited in 1876 and were now ages eighty-seven and eighty-nine. The Prauls were an enormous hit at Niagara, and their return visit in 1941 generated more publicity than any visiting celebrity of the era. Despite their lack of involvement in the contest, Canadian tourist promoters quickly got involved in entertaining the Prauls, and their visit was a five-day whirl of tours, honorary dinners, and gifts.[49]

The Niagara Falls, New York, Chamber of Commerce was thrilled with the results. The couple had been interviewed by all of the major newsreel companies. An estimated fifteen hundred newspapers carried the story, representing advertising that would have cost tens of thousands of dollars to purchase. Tourist promoters on the U.S. side became quickly convinced of the market value and newsworthiness of the Niagara honeymoon, and they expanded their promotional efforts. The four hundred contestants became members of a hastily organized "Honeymooners Club" and were sent special certificates. Newlyweds could join the "club" by registering at Niagara during their honeymoons, and they too would receive special certificates. This promotional gimmick would be copied after the war on the Canadian side, with great success.[50]

Media commentary during the war continued to present the Niagara honeymoon in lighthearted, jaunty stories. The place, so the story went, was becoming increasingly popular among armed forces personnel, and thus journalists sometimes spoke in coy terms of the "veritable army of honeymooners" or the "honeymoon blitz" that Niagara experienced during spring and summer weekends. According to Toronto travel agents in 1943, "When the buck private takes his new wife on a honeymoon, it's dollars to doughnuts they go to Niagara

Falls." Wartime honeymoons were, of necessity, brief and cheap. One agent estimated, "You could have a really good weekend honeymoon there for $35 to $40."[51]

One travel agent hinted at a wartime phenomenon that would later also be an important feature of postwar travel: a new mobility. As an alarmed United Church of Canada reported in 1943, the "demands of war-time industry have necessitated the greatest migration in Canadian history," which was, from the perspective of the clergy, wreaking havoc on family life.[52] From the perspective of the travel industry, this migration was a plus. Formerly, according to travel agents, a honeymooning couple might venture no further than the hotel in the neighbouring town, but now, "The soldiers are marrying girls from cities far away from their homes. They want to really step out."[53] Thus Niagara was becoming a destination both exotic and affordable. Even the young movie star Shirley Temple, who visited in 1944, said she was torn between Niagara Falls and Hawaii for her honeymoon.

But although the war helped to create the combination of financial stability and mobility that was so important to the further expansion of the tourist industry, Niagara's boosters were convinced that the patriotic sensibilities of North Americans in wartime would not take them *too* far from home. As True Hewitt of the Niagara Falls, New York, Visitors and Convention Service explained, the nine thousand honeymooners who visited the Falls in 1945, most of them GIs and their brides, were on the male side "boys who have seen many distant parts of the world but find sights in their homeland more interesting."[54]

Ronald Ede would probably have agreed. A few days before he was scheduled to go overseas in 1944, he received a leave of absence to get married. "Because I was going overseas; because it was wartime; because of the myriad of uncertainties," Ronald said, he and his new bride decided to mark the occasion with something special, so he cashed in his War Bonds and the two of them left their families in Hamilton to spend three nights at the Foxhead Inn at Niagara Falls.

Even those not in the armed forces, such as Fred Probst, who worked at a shipbuilding yard in Camden, New Jersey, could expect little time off during

A LABORATORY

FOR THE STUDY

OF YOUNG LOVE:

HONEYMOONS

AND TRAVEL TO

WORLD WAR II

174

wartime. Fred and Ella shared their honeymoon with Fred's recently married brother and sister-in-law; this was the condition their father imposed before he'd lend his car. The group spent most of their three-day honeymoon travelling, passing only a few hours at the Falls in 1942. But, as Ella recalled triumphantly in 1992, "We have always said we went to Niagara Falls for our honeymoon, but we can't remember exactly how long we were there."[55]

Compared to what came before—the 1920s boom—and what came after—the postwar explosion—the 1930s and early 1940s were lean years for the tourist industry. They were also years of intense hardship for many of Niagara's residents. Nevertheless, this era witnessed significant changes in the public culture of heterosexuality, resulting in new meanings for the honeymoon. Niagara Falls was well poised to be the beneficiary of such changes, for it had the "franchise"—the history and tradition of the wedding tour—and an energetic tourist industry ready to adapt itself to the popular, modern version of the honeymoon.

When elderly contest winners Mr. and Mrs. Albert Praul were met on the international bridge by a welcoming delegation of Canadian tourist authorities, the local paper noted an "irony" of the happy occasion: four of the eight members of the Niagara Falls Bridge Commission on hand to greet the couple were bachelors.[56] This fact may well have been noted only as an amusing side issue to the main story, but it also reflects something of the changes in heterosexuality and its rituals that had occurred in the previous decades. There was a make-believe, theatrical quality to the contest, which was only a slightly more extreme version of the theatricality of the honeymoon in general as it became a more visible institution.

In this instance the staginess was front and centre because the major players were so wildly miscast: the blushing bride and bungling groom were an octogenarian couple who had been married for sixty-five years, and half of the hosts stood completely outside of the institution that conferred legitimacy on heterosexuality: marriage. Only at Niagara Falls would this group of people have been able to carry off such a performance.

7

Honky-Tonk City:
Niagara and the Postwar Travel Boom

"There are insane places on the earth, and at one of them I grew up."

– Tom Marshall, *Voices on the Brink* (1988)

By the mid-twentieth-century it had become clear that Niagara Falls was endowed with not one but two distinct geographical advantages. One was the spectacular waterfall, but just as important for the tourist industry and the subsequent development of the community was the Falls' position within North America's industrial heartland: Southern Ontario and the Northeastern United States. By 1967 Niagara Falls lay within 500 miles of 75 per cent of the total population of North America, and it had thus welcomed the postwar travel boom like no place else.

Between 1947 and 1966, according to town historians, the tourist business began to "grow and blossom out" to "a multi-million dollar business." Between 1950 and 1960 alone, over a billion dollars was spent developing tourism and recreation facilities on both sides of the Canada/U.S. border.[1] What happens to a small Ontario industrial town when up to thirteen million visitors come to call every summer? Canadian novelist Tom Marshall's fictionalized memoirs of growing up in the Niagara Falls of the 1950s provide a clue. To visitors, he makes clear in *Voices on the Brink*, postwar Niagara was a lark, a landmark of affordable pleasure, travel, consumption, and, to newlyweds especially, sex. To residents, it was prosperous bedlam.

The *Maid of the Mist*, edging towards the base of the waterfalls, c.1950.

Mass tourism truly took flight in North America after World War II, and vacations—now formally mandated in labour laws and collective agreements in most jurisdictions—came to represent almost everything good about North American culture. In Canada mushrooming government tourist bureaucracies, politicians, and entrepreneurs fashioned themselves into an effective cultural and political force dedicated to a simple philosophy: that tourism—usually defined narrowly as Americans visiting Canada—was wholly and unquestionably a good thing; and, therefore, the more of it, the better. An especially zealous Arthur Welsh, Ontario's minister of travel and publicity, had no trouble convincing entrepreneurs at a 1946 tourist industry conference to think of Canada as "a gigantic department store, purveying travel and recreation."[2]

The growth of mass tourism after the war was remarkable. Out of nowhere appeared mass circulation travel magazines such as *Holiday*, published in Philadelphia, as well as regular travel features in newspapers and magazines. In Canada a huge amount of money and effort was spent sprucing up the "tourist plant," as Arthur Welsh termed his country, to make the place more attractive to U.S. visitors. Training programs for service industry staff and management, such as the University of Toronto's program in institutional management, were quickly instituted, and between 1946 and 1960 the service industry in Canada doubled.[3] Motels, more accessible and affordable than the downtown hotel for working-class or middle-class families, appeared almost overnight. In Ontario the number of motels jumped from 150 in 1951 to almost 500 in 1954 to over 2,000 in 1962.[4]

The rapid growth of the tourist industry had startling implications for national identity, especially in Canada. Canadian tourist boosters were concerned about what they called the "travel deficit," with many more Canadians visiting the United States than vice versa. At one especially low point, in 1954, every dollar spent by U.S. tourists in Canada was being multiplied eleven times by Canadians in the United States. There was no particular reason to pair Canadian and U.S. vacation habits, and it is certainly arguable that these two variables have little to do with each other. Despite owning three-fourths of the world's automobiles, Americans were homebodies; fewer than 7 per cent of them crossed

HONKY-TONK
CITY: NIAGARA
AND THE
POSTWAR
TRAVEL BOOM

178

their borders when they travelled. Canada inherited the lion's share of these visitors, 80 per cent. But when up to 60 per cent of Canadian vacationers crossed into the United States, the Canadian tourist industry panicked.[5] Rather than attempt to make Canadians stay home, through the 1950s and early 1960s the Canadian industry undertook countless promotional and educational campaigns to, as one journalist put it, "make Canada more attractive to Mr. and Mrs. U.S. Tourist."[6] References to Canadian vacations were "planted" in Hollywood films. Nationally distinctive souvenirs and food were invented and popularized, and Canadians themselves were constantly harangued by the tourist industry to extend a cordial welcome to visitors. For example, Canadians were encouraged to notice licence plates on cars, and when they spotted Americans they were to approach them with a special welcome. They were also invited to learn all they could about local attractions in order to advertise those features, and they were asked to greet excursion steamers with a band and welcoming committee.

The tourist industry tried to convince all Canadians, not just those employed in the tourist or service industry, that U.S. tourist dollars, and hence the courteous treatment of U.S. visitors, were a national as opposed to commercial concern. The industry had a remarkable ability to blur boundaries; imagine General Motors trying to convince anyone other than its own employees that they should sell their cars for them. When the nation had become a gigantic department store or a tourist plant, what was the difference between employment and citizenship, or between citizen and worker? So when the Ontario provincial government asked its employees to become "salesmen of Ontario" by sending its annual tourist promotion book to friends and family outside the province, those who complied most likely thought they were doing their friends, and perhaps themselves, a favour, rather than acting as unpaid shills for the tourist industry. The tourist industry was able to generate a great deal of enthusiasm for itself precisely because of this ability to recast national goodwill and community spirit into promotion for private industry.

The tourist industry in Niagara Falls was reshaped by these boom years, which in itself helps to explain why the average teacher, autoworker, or housewife became willing, in some ways, to take on double duty as tourist booster.

Shopping at the Niagara
Parks Commission
China Store, 1950.

But as we move away from the patriotic pronouncements of the national tourist industry to the experience of life on the front lines, as it were, in a tourist town, the story becomes more complicated. Certainly no one at the Falls required introductory tutorials on the impact or economic potential of tourism. But the relationship of the tourist industry, other kinds of industrial growth, and civic discourse at Niagara Falls was constantly shifting. Sometimes tourism enjoyed favoured status; sometimes manufacturing or hydroelectric development did. Sometimes residents basked in the glory of living at the "world's most famous address," and at other times the tourist industry embarrassed them. While the region's serendipitous combination of geography and political economy—not to mention its history—guaranteed that the pent-up urge to travel would be unleashed with particular force within its confines, we cannot assume that visitors would always be universally welcomed, or that they would return.

Tourism was hardly a plot foisted upon a pliant or unwilling public. Indeed, it was the apparent democracy and openness of the tourist industry that gave it its appeal. At the same time as travel boosters were proclaiming that anybody could be a tourist, it also seemed as though anybody could be a tourist entrepreneur. From the farmer selling fruit and soft drinks on the roadside to the immigrant mom-and-pop motel operation to the swanky hotel corporation, it appeared that anyone could move into this marketplace and prosper. Yet the long shadow of Niagara's tawdry tourist history still partially crept over this era, and tourist industry rivalries, rocky relations between private and public entrepreneurs, and different ideas about the proper way to care for guests all lingered on.

Tourism was not the only game in town; it had not been so since the nineteenth century. Niagara's manufacturing industries leapt from Depression-era

One of many new postwar tourist attractions: Glen Baechler's Antique Auto Museum, March 1960. Photo by George Butt.

I'm going to join my daddy AT THE **ANTIQUE AUTO MUSEUM** NIAGARA FALLS, ONT.

dormancy to wartime production, and after the war the frenzied pace continued. One commentator dubbed the Niagara Peninsula "the Ruhr of Canada." In 1950, 25 per cent of the region's population was steadily employed in more than fifty manufacturing enterprises. By 1962 the region had seventy-one such enterprises, the second-highest concentration of manufacturing in the province. Manufacturing provided 49 per cent of the total employment in the Niagara region in 1951, declining to 39 per cent in 1961. The growth of the service industry in the 1950s, rather than a loss of industrial jobs, accounts for much of this decline, and even in the 1960s manufacturing remained the single largest employment category in the region.[7]

Despite this, the explosion of tourism after the war seemed to eclipse all else. While at the turn of the century an earlier generation of local entrepreneurs had to contend with misapprehensions of Niagara as "merely" a tourist resort, the same problem now surfaced, though from the opposite direction. Throughout the 1950s the Chamber of Commerce waged an enthusiastic campaign to attract

Dressed up for a trip
behind the Falls, Table
Rock House, c.1950.

new industries to the area but found that the glare of tourist publicity had an unfortunate side-effect. One of the main difficulties facing this campaign was, according to the Industrial Committee of the Chamber in 1954, that "Niagara is so widely known as a tourist centre that industrialists don't generally consider it as an industrial location." The problem was, the committee said, "Many admire our area so much that they tend to build up a resistance in establishing an industry here which might destroy the beauty of the area." This was a fear that local industrial boosters quickly, and successfully, tried to allay.[8]

Factories were not considered to be scenic in the 1950s, or at least they were not as novel and interesting as they had been in the early part of the century. Obviously, it was not as though nobody was aware that tourism and industrial development could at times run at cross-purposes. When Deputy Minister of Travel and Publicity T. C. McCall penned a memo to Ontario tourist entrepreneurs in 1948, giving them tips on how to advertise their establishments and their communities, he suggested that they avoid discussing the industrial activities of their area, because tourism and industrial promotion were "mutually conflicting."[9]

But in the upbeat climate of the postwar era everything—with a little finessing—was possible. No longer did town boosters have to apologize for or hide Niagara's tourist face in order to establish its credentials as a progressive, forward-looking town. As the tourist industry established a national profile as a respectable, even vital, Canadian resource, Niagara Falls proudly embraced its status as one of the leading tourist destinations in the country.

In 1950, when Mayor William Houck welcomed delegates to the Second Annual Ontario Tourist Conference, held, as it had been the first time, at Niagara's General Brock Hotel, and boasted that Niagara was the "most tourist conscious spot on the continent," this claim was, very likely, both true and enviable.[10]

The Town That Was Also a Theme Park

The growth of tourist services—or the "tourist plant"—at Niagara was staggering. On the Canadian side the number of restaurants, for example, increased

Ontario Hydro's Floral
Clock, opened in 1950.

from 40 in 1945 to 79 in 1955 to 115 in 1965. Motels appeared almost out of thin air; there were none in 1945, 79 ten years later, and 115 in 1965. By the early 1960s Ontario's Niagara region, with one-eighth of the province's population, contained 20 per cent, or one-fifth, of the province's motels. The local Chamber of Commerce estimated in 1958 that 80 per cent of the overnight accommodation in town had not existed ten years previously. Across the river in Niagara Falls, New York, the story was the same: the town boasted the United States' highest concentration of motels outside Miami Beach.[11]

When tourists were not eating or sleeping, they could find plenty of other things to do. Certainly, playing with the waterfall remained an important item on the tourist agenda, and the old standbys—the Cave of the Winds and Table Rock tours, the *Maid of the Mist* boat ride, and the Spanish Aerocar over the Whirlpool—remained popular. But postwar Niagara also featured a catalogue of other amusements that would have made nineteenth-century entrepreneurs like Saul Davis and Thomas Barnett green with envy. By the early 1960s tourist

attractions on both sides of the river included two golf courses, replicas of an Indian village and the English crown jewels, an antique auto museum (inexplicably proud of its main attraction, Mussolini's limousine), two children's amusement theme parks, two wax museums, Marine Wonderland and Animal Park, and Niagarama (an "animated historical funhouse"). Then too there was Davis's Niagara Falls Museum (back on the Canadian side of the river in the old Spirella Corset factory), a second museum operated by the Niagara Parks Commission (which also operated a restored eighteenth-century fort at Niagara-on-the-Lake), Ontario Hydro's Floral Clock, a planetarium, and three massive observation towers.[12] The resulting landscape must have been reminiscent of that other great postwar amusement park, Disneyland, which had opened its doors in 1955 in Anaheim, California.

North American entrepreneurs were uncharacteristically slow to recognize and successfully copy the Disney formula. Theme parks did not really proliferate until the 1970s—including Disney World, which opened in Florida in 1971.[13] But in the 1950s and 1960s other popular tourist destinations became

Visitors pose outside Brown's Gift Shop on River Road, 1948. "Heroism Thrilling Daring in Beautiful Terrible Niagara. See The Story in Pictures of Men and Women Who Have Challenged Niagara's Might. It's Free!"

fractured versions of Disneyland, offering many of the same sorts of attractions. At Niagara, Storybook Park, for example, invited children to play with Mother Goose characters, and at the Indian Village visitors could stroll through longhouses and teepees and watch what the brochures called "Real Indians" (from the Six Nations reserve near Brantford) perform dances and manufacture souvenirs. Such attractions were low-budget derivatives of Disneyland's "Fantasy Land" and "Frontier Land," but with important differences. Disney's park operated as a miniature state. Disneyland was (and remains) one of the most highly scripted playgrounds in human history, with centralized control entrenched in its design and day-to-day operations. Park designers worked hard to establish a "coherent, orderly, sequenced layout within which elements would complement each other rather than compete for attention."[14]

But the attractions of Niagara Falls, which was, after all, a community, were not centrally planned or owned. The diffused and hodgepodge nature of Niagara's amusements made for unique problems and neighbourly difficulties. The

Hotel magnate Vernon G. Cardy, the dashing owner of the General Brock Hotel.

Niagara Parks Commission and the New York State Reservation waged a war of words, which eventually ended up in court, with Alice Langmuir, owner of the Burning Springs Wax Museum, located just up the river from both parks. The Wax Museum used a loudspeaker to attract visitors, and park officials complained bitterly of the loudspeaker's "intensive bombardment," audible to park visitors as well as passersby.[15] Similarly, in 1960, motel owners began to complain to city council about their new neighbour, the Indian Village (owned not by Indians but by Murray Ruta, a local real estate broker). Anthony Solose, owner of the Horseshoe Falls Cottages, complained about the "continuous smell and smoke of the bonfire" and the "beating of tom-toms, yelping and hollering." There was more. "Tourists with families have always favoured our cottages," he continued, "but with Indians peeping over fences the younger children get frightened."[16]

Things had changed considerably since the days when travellers eagerly sought a glimpse of their "first Indian." In mimicking—on a smaller and more fragmented scale—the sort of amusements that had drawn 10 million visitors to Disneyland within its first two years of business, postwar Niagara stands as a perfect example of the increasing cultural uniformity—what people today call "McWorld" or "McDisney"—that was beginning to characterize North America.[17]

From Mom-and-Pop to Multinational:
The Postwar Tourist Industry

Niagara defied the sort of rigid control exercised at places such as Disneyland because its tourist industry contained an extremely wide range of players. Ownership of various aspects of the industry—accommodations, restaurants, and attractions—extended from housewives renting rooms and mom-and-pop cabins, motels, or small hotels to the provincial government via the Niagara Parks Commission and multinational corporations that owned larger hotels and observation towers.

Niagara's finest hotel, the General Brock, was perched at the high end of the spectrum. After the hotel opened with much fanfare in 1929 and promptly went

A coveted place to work. The staff of the Rainbow Room, General Brock Hotel, c.1950. Katie Agar is last row, third from right. Ruth Stoner is on her right.

bankrupt, it was eventually purchased, in 1934, by Vernon G. Cardy, a man who retains a legendary aura in Niagara Falls to this day. Cardy had risen through the ranks of the Canadian hotel industry in the 1920s. He had managed Niagara's Clifton, Hamilton's Royal Connaught, and Montreal's Mount Royal through the 1920s and 1930s. In the Depression decade he amassed a string of Canadian hotels and resorts, including the three that had employed him. Niagara claimed him as a kind of local hero, perhaps partly because of his previous association with the local hotel industry and partly because he owned the town's first radio station (CKVC— with the call letters based on his own initials). But his was neither a local nor a rags-to-riches story. He came from Galt, Ontario, and while it seemed to some that he was "barely more than a bellboy" when he began to purchase Canadian hotels, he was in truth the son of a successful Galt hotel owner.[18] He proved an adept hotel-man himself. Some two years after purchasing the ailing General Brock, Cardy added on a sumptuous open-air rooftop dining area, the Rainbow Room, which quickly became the prime nightspot at Niagara through the 1940s and 1950s.

HONKY-TONK

CITY: NIAGARA

AND THE

POSTWAR

TRAVEL BOOM

188

The Rainbow Room was a coveted place to work. The Brock had been unionized during the war, and the days of fourteen-hour shifts were over. Ruth Stoner, who started at the Rainbow Room as a seventeen-year-old waitress in 1947, was intensely proud of the service she provided to her customers. The Rainbow Room featured "French service," which meant the waitress served everything—meat, vegetables, soup—at the table. To top it off the place was run by what Stoner approvingly calls "hotel people," in contrast to the franchise operations of the present day. ("They could be selling real estate," she complains.) Waitresses at the Rainbow Room, Stoner recalls, had no more than three tables to serve per evening, so the service they could provide was excellent. So too were the tips, usually almost double the two-dollar daily wages. The Rainbow Room was also, sometimes, an exciting workplace. Waitress Katie (Petrullo) Agar got autographs from celebrities such as Eddie Cantor, Jackie Gleason, and Melvyn Douglas, and both Agar and Stoner remember Vern Cardy as a dashing, handsome, and respectful employer.[19]

Yet quietly and with little publicity, early in 1950 Cardy sold his hotel empire, which by then included Toronto's King Edward and Windsor's Prince Edward as well as a resort in Quebec, to the Sheraton Corporation of America. This was the largest transaction in the history of the hotel industry in Canada, and certainly a feather in the cap of the Sheraton Corporation, which could now boast thirty-one hotels in its North American chain, including two others (Montreal's Laurentian and Toronto's Ford) in Canada. The reason for this move, and perhaps the reason for the relative silence about it, was revealed in March 1950, when Cardy entered a plea of guilty in a Montreal courtroom to the charge of violating foreign-exchange control-board regulations. Cardy had apparently used undisclosed U.S. funds to advertise his hotel system in the United States and had furthermore "laundered" this money by funnelling it through his racing horse interests—next to hotels, his other passion. In an astonishing example of the power of postwar tourism, Cardy's lawyers attempted to turn his financial crimes into acts of patriotism. The lawyers based their arguments for leniency in sentencing on the grounds that "the money involved had been used for publicity purposes which brought United States tourists to

Canada." The maximum sentence was $400,000 plus a twelve-month jail term. Cardy was fined $40,000 with no jail term.[20]

Cardy was an anomaly, especially compared to most Niagara tourist entrepreneurs. He was fortunate to enter the market in the 1930s, when many hotel owners were being driven out of it, and he must have purchased his empire for something like fire-sale prices. Indeed, that he had an "empire" at all made him stand apart from the rest; most people in the tourist business at the time owned no more than one establishment, and especially not outside their home base. Nor did they sell their businesses to multinational corporations or breed racehorses on a North Carolina estate, as Cardy did. But Cardy was revered and looked up to as a local golden boy—one of the only times the Niagara press identified him as a "Galt native" was when his legal troubles were aired—and he most likely served as an inspiration for the hundreds of tourist entrepreneurs of more humble circumstances.

Detailed biographical data on the typical tourist operator—the owners and managers of the independent small hotels, cabins, motels, restaurants, and roadside attractions—is more difficult to come by. While well-established local businessmen such as Howard Fox (owner, since the 1920s, of the Foxhead Inn) became high-profile lobbyists in the hotel industry province-wide, most did not lead flamboyant or even public lives. For most, the simple fact of owning a small business did not necessarily confer status or authority within the community. Only one-third of motel owners in the mid-1950s, for example, were members of the local Chamber of Commerce, and most likely none of them made it into the ranks of the Niagara Riding and Driving Club, a businessmen's clubhouse that counted among its members Fox, mayor and MPP William Houck, and NPC official Thomas McQueston.[21]

Most participants in the postwar tourist trade were first-generation entrepreneurs, running retail or service industry establishments that required enormous investments of time. Civic affairs and social climbing were probably not high on their agendas. But many of them were also first-generation Canadians and thus culturally in rather a different universe than the business and political elite of small-town Southern Ontario. Immigrants owned a sizeable portion of the accommodation and restaurant market after World War II.[22]

HONKY-TONK

CITY: NIAGARA

AND THE

POSTWAR

TRAVEL BOOM

190

Emil Badovanic was one such immigrant. In 1940 Badovanic, born in Yugoslavia, left South Porcupine in Northern Ontario, where he had been the proprietor of the Goldfields Hotel, to take over the Caverly Hotel, a former Public House dating back to the 1860s. Badovanic was joined in this venture by Stojan Demic, a Porcupine miner. The partnership did not work out, so Badovanic and his wife ran the Caverly alone as a "workingman's hotel" through the 1940s. Although Mrs. Badovanic was invisible in the written record of business transactions and liquor licence applications, her labour contributed substantially to the hotel's success. Liquor board inspectors noted through the 1940s that the Caverly's restaurant—which Mrs. Badovanic operated—was the hotel's biggest and most popular draw. But the place was a hotel in name only. The travelling public did not patronize the place, perhaps because it was located just beyond the main tourist area, and at most four or five workingmen roomed there. The Badovanics's fortunes improved as the postwar tourist boom hit the Falls. They renovated the hotel in 1950, adding twenty-four new bedrooms, expanding the dining room, and refurnishing the two bars, which were even given names: "The Cataract Room" and "The Pine Room." Through the 1950s the Caverly remained, according to provincial liquor inspectors, a "clean and well-operated hotel."

The Badovanics were—at least financially—a classic immigrant success story. They sent their son to university, from whence he returned to take over from his father, and all the while they expanded their real estate holdings.[23] In 1946 they, along with George Sainovich and his wife, purchased another rundown hotel, the historic Prospect House. Allegedly the oldest building in the Niagara Peninsula and, according to local legend, either the headquarters of English War of 1812 hero Sir Isaac Brock or a prison that housed the rebels during the Upper Canada Rebellion of 1837, the Prospect House had, since the 1920s, fallen into disrepair and catered only to long-term boarders. Sainovich and Badovanic quickly turned the place around, "using history to sell beer," as one commentator put it. By 1955, when Sainovich bought Badovanic out, the place boasted a huge new dining room, two beverage rooms, a coffee shop, and twenty new guest rooms. "Today," noted one reviewer approvingly in 1955,

"Americans invade the hotel by the score to revel in its history."[24] If anyone thought it odd that one of the landmarks of old Tory Ontario was now making Eastern European immigrants rich by catering to U.S. tourists, they kept it to themselves.

Frank Podhorn, a Russian immigrant, was another hotel owner who was able to parlay a good location and prosperous times into a sizeable tourist establishment. Podhorn purchased the Falls View Hotel, located on a hill overlooking the waterfall, in 1940, when it was a simple three-storey, eight-bedroom structure. Like the Caverly it had been more a bar than a hotel. Over the next fifteen years Podhorn expanded the dining room and increased the number of rooms from eight to sixty-five, adding first cabins and later a sleek motel complex. Inspectors noted that the place's clientele was "almost 100 per cent American," music to the ears of any tourist entrepreneur of the era. By the end of the 1950s Podhorn had started exhibiting some of the public symbols of small-business success: he became president of the local Hotel Association and started getting his picture in the newspaper.[25]

All of these success stories became so due to a combination of factors, among them hard work, good timing, and good luck. But these establishments also possessed another important and valuable asset—a liquor licence—though a licence alone was not an iron-clad guarantee of financial success. Niagara Falls included plenty of licensed establishments that did not cash in on the postwar tourist boom, remaining instead working-class bars or even, according to the liquor board inspectors who tried to put them out of business, clubhouses for prostitutes, drug smugglers, and gamblers. But for anyone with dreams of entering the tourist market, a liquor licence certainly helped, particularly since on the Ontario side, of all the accommodation possibilities—motels, cabins, tourist homes, and autocamps—hotels alone could qualify for them.

This necessity led to regular definitional skirmishes. As we've seen, in the early 1930s, when local authorities began regulating tourist homes, some clever tourist-home owners attempted—unsuccessfully, as it turned out—to get themselves classified as hotels to avoid the regulations. Other entrepreneurs followed suit, and from the late 1930s on the Liquor Licensing Board received

scores of applications for hotel liquor licences, most of them with the same success as tourist homes had earlier. Sometimes they were rejected because it
seemed obvious to the inspector that the application was little more than a
clumsy attempt to purvey liquor: a grocery store or a tailor shop with a couple
of bedrooms upstairs, for example, stood no chance of convincing anyone that
it was a hotel.

But while the category covered a certain material reality—hotels had to
conform to regulations concerning fire safety and number of bedrooms, for
example—it also evidenced a great degree of subjectivity, and political, class,
and ethnic prejudices held great force. Applications from Italians, for example,
were often rejected on the grounds that the proposed hotel would serve only an
Italian clientele or that the working-class neighbourhood already had sufficient
hotel bars. The Women's Christian Temperance Union occasionally lobbied
against applications, particularly those that intended to serve the "foreign element," and a woman from nearby Fort Erie urged the Liquor Licensing Board
in 1946 to "consider the racial background and character" of permit holders
more closely, because "a great portion of these privileges are finding their way
into the hands of foreigners."[26]

But the most powerful prejudice was politics. Local members of the provincial Parliament intervened for and against would-be hotel owners openly, regularly, and in brazenly partisan ways. One of the most interventionist was
William Houck, a former coal merchant who was, for a time, both mayor and
Liberal MPP. A cheerful note from Houck would often accompany applications,
citing the sterling qualities of the applicant and also mentioning his many
years of service and dedication to the Liberal Party. Houck also attempted to use
patronage against his opponents. In the late 1930s, Louis Sacco tried to get
his licence for the Victoria Inn reinstated. Inspectors had pulled it because, in
their view, "a few cheap beds and mattresses" above his restaurant did not con-
stitute a hotel. (One wonders how it qualified to begin with.) Sacco was furious,
but he knew how the game was played. In his many letters of protest to the
Licensing Board he expressed indignation that he was "being put out of my
property by the Liberal Party, for which I have worked and supported all my

HONKY-TONK
CITY: NIAGARA
AND THE
POSTWAR
TRAVEL BOOM

192

life." Houck supported Sacco's reinstatement, but perhaps not for the reasons the businessman expected. As Houck explained to the commissioners evaluating the case, "The Niagara Hotel is practically next door but the owner of that is quite a decided opponent of mine and naturally I am not inclined to favour him."[27]

As Louis Sacco discovered, keeping a licence could be just as difficult as acquiring one, particularly if one was burdened with an unpopular ethnic background or political affiliation. The vigilance of Liquor Licensing Board inspectors was awesome, and during their regular spot visits to establishments they were positively eagle-eyed. The condition of the toilets, whether women had to walk through the men's tavern to get to their washroom, the amount of liquor and food consumed monthly, the question of single women residing in the rooms or, worse still, white women in the company of black men, the condition of the register, women (even wives or daughters of the owner) waiting tables in the men's beverage rooms, loud music playing or people dancing in the dining room, the alcohol consumption of owners or employees and whether waiters were engaged in the nefarious practice of "double serving" (serving another glass before the patron had fully consumed the first): all of these issues and more came to the attention of the inspectors, and infractions were quickly pounced on. Possessing a liquor licence was a rare and valuable asset in the accommodation business, because only seventeen licensed premises existed in Niagara Falls, Ontario, in 1947, and this number included places offering no accommodation, such as the Canadian Legion. As might have been expected, the inspectors' reports for the swanky General Brock and the Foxhead Inn tended to be brief, perfunctory, and seemingly objective.

Even without liquor licences, however, mom-and-pop motel operations prospered—or at least some of them did. Olga and Mac Ricci, for example, opened the Oakes Drive Motel at the Falls in 1949. Mac was a plumber and had worked on a number of new motels and cabins around the city and decided he wanted to get into the tourist business himself. Olga was less than enthusiastic about this move. As she recalls, the tourist business was risky and she had no idea of how to run a motel. She had young children to worry about and, she says, "I was afraid of my own shadow." Mac had grown up in a hotel-owning family in nearby Merritton and was determined to see if the postwar tourist boom could work for him as well as the others he saw around him. He borrowed $500 from Olga's mother and opened a twenty-one unit motel. Through a combination of hard work and good luck—the town bus station relocated in the area of their motel shortly after it opened—the Riccis built a substantial enterprise. The Oakes Inn—which became a twelve-storey hotel—remained in the 1990s one of the few locally owned, non-chain hotels in the city, and was worth an estimated $5 million.[28]

Tourist homes also flourished after the war, despite the expansion of small hotels and the boom in motels. In 1949 almost five hundred licensed tourist homes operated on the Canadian side alone. Some, at least, were doing very well, reporting annual incomes of $4,000.[29] The federal government certainly believed that tourist homes were making a substantial, and unreported, income, because it organized a massive clampdown on tourist-home operators in 1950, demanding that they begin to pay taxes on their earnings. Tax department officials, tracking down tourist-home operators with the assistance of municipal licensing regulations, declared that the establishments were bringing in from $2,000 to $6,000 of undeclared revenue annually.[30]

While they may have been annoying the tax department, tourist-home operators were enjoying a moment of unusually cordial relations with municipal authorities and other tourist businesses. In Ontario the provincially run tourist information bureau provided listings of local tourist homes alongside information about motels and hotels, and Niagara's Chamber of Commerce was even courting tourist-home operators, trying to convince them to join forces. No longer, it seemed, were entrepreneurs trying to steal business from each other and fighting out turf wars in the city council and media.

These apparently congenial relations owed more to the tourist boom than anything else. Different factions in the industry embraced each other because times were good and there was plenty to go around. The times were indeed so good that they created their own problems. For the first few years after World War II the town could not cope with the deluge of visitors. In 1947 the city

HONKY-TONK
CITY: NIAGARA
AND THE
POSTWAR
TRAVEL BOOM

194

Clifton Hill, the heart of the tourists' Niagara, 1964.

council on the Canadian side issued a desperate plea, "in light of the acute shortage of accommodation in this city," to the Liquor Licensing Board, asking it to soften its rigid categorizations of what was and was not a hotel. Particularly irksome was the requirement that establishments with fewer than twenty rooms were "public houses" rather than "hotels" and could therefore only rent their rooms by the week, rather than the day.

Through the 1940s and 1950s, Niagara Falls residents, particularly those who lived near the waterfall, created tourist accommodations from virtually anything they could get their hands on. Backyard garages became "cabins," and empty lots were quickly transformed into motels. One particularly enterprising soul tried to turn his auto-wrecking yard into a motel. Still the accommodation crises continued, so much so that before Labour Day weekend in 1949 the Chamber of Commerce issued a stirring appeal, requesting that citizens "do

Looking up Clifton Hill, 1964. On the corner, next to the Foxhead Inn, is Tussaud's Wax Museum. A replica of the tightrope walker Blondin crosses the street on a cable above the traffic.

their community a great service" by "opening all available facilities" for weekend visitors.[31]

Yet not everyone in town would have agreed that creating comfortable accommodations for tourists constituted a full-fledged crisis, particularly when the Ontario side was, like most Canadian communities immediately after World War II, experiencing an acute housing shortage. Tourist accommodation problems arose during summer long weekends and special events, but for the rest of the year many Niagara residents considered that they had an overabundance of motels, hotels, and cabins. In January 1949, fifty-seven citizens expressed exactly that sentiment to the city council, presenting them with a petition urging them to halt any future tourist accommodation construction in the city on the grounds that the current building boom was "lowering the prestige and high standards which have been built up over a period of many years." Opponents of motel development also argued that unrestrained growth was not only ugly but would also glut the market, creating what one man predicted would be "a condition comparable to the worst slum conditions ever found in any part of the world." Their opponents had free-market ideology on their side and did not hesitate to use it, terming any attempts at regulation a "dictatorship" and making eloquent speeches about the sanctity of property rights in the free world. This battle did not pit motel owners against residents, for people involved in the tourist industry could be found on both sides of the debate. Eventually the opponents of accommodation development won the day, and council voted, by a large majority, to put a halt to new development. The ban was officially lifted in 1958.[32]

Niagara Falls city council, of course, only controlled Niagara Falls. The town of Stamford had its own municipal infrastructure until the two communities were officially amalgamated in 1963. Several months after the anti-development initiative at Niagara Falls, thirty-one Stamford residents attempted to get their council to pass the same legislation, to no avail. With Niagara Falls proper no longer an option, the building boom in Stamford continued, especially in the areas closest to the waterfall, such as Fall View and Lundy's Lane. Soon the issue began to raise the ire of the Niagara Parks Commission, which complained about the number of tourist accommodations springing up adjacent to its property, threatening the "natural scenic beauty of the area." By 1951 the winds, even in free-enterprise Stamford, had shifted, and the council voted to halt accommodation expansion there as well.[33]

To add insult to injury, early in 1952 Stamford council also raised its motel licensing rates (up $10 per unit), an action revealing that prosperity had not erased community/tourist industry tensions. Tourist entrepreneurs protested this increase vigorously, complaining that they could not afford it and that their enterprises were not nearly as lucrative as those on the main tourist strip of Clifton Hill. Finally, at one meeting, Township Solicitor W.C. LaMarsh (father of Judy LaMarsh, a future Canadian cabinet minister) had heard enough. He began to lecture the assembled motel owners, claiming that they were so well off they worked only one hundred days a year and spent their winters in Florida.

"Wintering in Florida," of course, was (and remains) an emblem of working-class and middle-class success in Canada. The charge that Niagara-area tourist entrepreneurs can afford such indulgence is still made by local people outside the tourist industry; I heard this often during the 1990s in area libraries as I was doing my research. It denotes a combination of envy and contempt, as though running a summer operation such as a motel or souvenir store is not really "work." Certainly this is how the charge was understood in the 1950s, for motel owner Frank Clement responded to LaMarsh's charge as though labour was an issue of masculine physical prowess. According to a newspaper report, Clement argued that "he puts in more working time in six months in his motel than the solicitor does in his law office in two years."[34]

The issue eventually resulted in a compromise—a three-dollar per unit increase rather than ten—and quickly disappeared. But it did represent one of the few times in the postwar era that tourism or the tourist industry was discussed publicly in anything less than reverential terms, and the occasion suggested that, amidst the joyful welcome of visitors, tempers were fraying. The next month the Niagara Police Commission voted against a tourist promotion gimmick that was quite common in the era: extending a policy of leniency to visitors who committed parking or traffic infractions.

Hollywood's arrival at Niagara Falls in June 1952 could not have come at a better time. Beyond what its content said about heterosexuality and honeymooners (see chapter 8), the film *Niagara*, starring Marilyn Monroe and Joseph Cotten and filmed on location, had a profound and immediate impact on the local tourist industry. In the summer after *Niagara* was released, in 1953, between ten and thirteen million people visited Niagara Falls, smashing previous records to smithereens.

The film did not invent the postwar tourist and honeymoon boom, any more than William Howells's popular novel *Their Wedding Journey* caused upper-class honeymoon tourism in the 1870s or King Vidor's movie *The Crowd* created middle-class tourism in the 1920s. Art imitated life, in all three cases, in the sense that the experience represented in these portraits—going to Niagara Falls for a honeymoon—was something large numbers of people were doing in reality. What sets *Niagara* apart from other representations of a holiday at the Falls was that it was produced at a historical moment in which huge numbers of people had the means of undertaking such an outing. A mass-market film about a holiday at a mass-market destination, released at the height of the postwar travel boom, starring Marilyn Monroe, just then at the beginning of her major stardom: the Chamber of Commerce itself could never, not even in its wildest fantasies, have imagined better advertising.

The filming itself created a frenzy of excitement, locally and within the Ontario government's Travel and Publicity bureau. Along with trying to convincing Monroe to pose wearing the uniforms of provincial information hostesses, and along with generally wining and dining film stars and studio executives, Travel and Publicity staff poured carefully over the film script, ensuring accuracy and a favourable portrait of Ontario. Perhaps their vigilance was spurred on by the numerous public complaints of MPP Houck, who was worried that

HONKY-TONK
CITY: NIAGARA
AND THE
POSTWAR
TRAVEL BOOM

198

Gender, heterosexuality, and waterfalls: all out of control. The publicity poster for *Niagara*, released in 1953.

the film, a suspenseful drama of sexual intrigue and murder, would sully what he considered the good reputation of the town. He thought it might scare off tourists because they would think the place unsafe. "We certainly do not want to convey the impression that murders are on the rampage here," he declared when the project was announced.[35]

Houck, it seems, was the only dissenting voice. The most significant problem that Travel and Publicity staff could locate in the script involved a scene outside the motel where the protagonists are staying. The proposed shot would show ice-cold soft drink and beer bottles floating in a tub, for sale. "Can't sell in Ontario," was the terse comment of the deputy minister.[36] No casual flouting of Ontario's byzantine liquor law was allowed; in the film, the characters drink Coke. (Though when offered one Monroe asks daringly, "Is this just Coke or is it spiked?")

The filming of *Niagara* became a major attraction for tourists and locals alike. Local contractors were hired to construct the main set: a five-unit motel court located right beside the waterfall. This fictional motel setting was in the midst of Queen Victoria Park, and no private-sector enterprise had been that close to the waterfall since the 1880s. After the film was released the Chamber of Commerce was swamped with requests from visitors who wanted to spend a night or two at the place. About five hundred area residents got work as extras, and crowds gathered regularly to watch the filming. The filmmakers clearly knew how to purchase local goodwill, for they co-operated easily with the Chamber of Commerce, feting the ten-thousandth couple to register for a "honeymoon certificate"—a popular local promotional gimmick—with a tour of the set and a chance to meet the actors.

Once the filmmakers and their entourage left town it was a different story. Upon their departure, 20th Century-Fox spokespeople had made vague promises of returning for a premiere at the Falls. Several months later it was announced that there would indeed be a local premiere—complete with "leading Hollywood stars and principals of the 20th Century-Fox studio"—in Niagara Falls, New York. Ontario civic officials did not take this brush-off lightly. Noting angrily that the majority of the filming had taken place on the Canadian side,

HONKY-TONK
CITY: NIAGARA
AND THE
POSTWAR
TRAVEL BOOM

200

and that all the extras employed by the film were Canadian, Ernest Hawkins, mayor of Niagara Falls, Ontario, launched a strong protest, which was ultimately successful. And so, on January 28, 1953, the Seneca Theatre at Niagara Falls, Ontario, and the Cataract Theatre at Niagara Falls, New York, both, at the same moment, dimmed their lights and "premiered" *Niagara*.

No one seemed upset that the film had opened in New York City a week previously. Indeed, even the fact that the "leading Hollywood stars" promised by Fox turned out to be one young actor, Dale Robertson, who had no previous involvement whatsoever with *Niagara*, did not dampen local enthusiasm. Niagara Falls was determined to celebrate this event, and celebrate it did. For days leading up to the premiere, local businesses sponsored ads reminding people of their contributions to the film. Sam Gold, of Gold's Men's Wear, was especially proud to announce that actor Joseph Cotten wore Sam's own hat while filming. The General Brock Hotel bragged that it had been home to Monroe and Cotten, and Eaton's department store devoted its windows to a display of some of the stills from the film. The Seneca Theatre was packed that night, and many more potential viewers had to be turned away.[37]

While film reviewers were less than enthused about *Niagara*'s plot—*Variety* described it as "clichéd" and *The New York Times* chose "transparent"—everyone agreed that the scenes of the waterfall were magnificent. Contrary to the fears of William Houck—who continued to criticize the film after its release—*Niagara* acted like a magnet for tourists that season. While different authorities came up with different figures—ranging from ten to thirteen million—everyone agreed that tourist attendance at the Falls in 1953 was record-breaking, and that *Niagara* deserved much of the credit.[38]

The movie proved a tough act to follow. There was a flurry of excitement a couple of years later when comedian Jackie Gleason arrived in town, declaring that he wanted to make a feature film of his popular *Honeymooners* television show at the Falls, but this plan came to nought. The Chamber of Commerce became instant converts to the strategy of using celebrity and film as tourist promotion and tried to woo famous people to the Falls through the rest of the decade. They also made their own film, a dull and wooden documentary, *Location*

Niagara, which received some U.S. television exposure. Jolie Gabor, mother of the more famous Zsa Zsa and Eva, arrived for her (third) honeymoon in 1959, the mayors from both sides appeared together on the TV quiz show *I've Got a Secret*, and stories of Niagara honeymoons appeared in almost every mass circulation magazine through the 1950s.[39] But none of this approached the excitement of a Hollywood film, and never again was Niagara Falls to feel the media spotlight quite so intensely.

HONKY-TONK
CITY: NIAGARA
AND THE
POSTWAR
TRAVEL BOOM

202

Niagara the Tacky: Ripoffs and Racism

Certainly not all media attention was welcome. Complaints that had been lodged by travellers for about one hundred years—that it was, in the parlance of the mid-twentieth century, "tacky," and a giant confidence game—came back to haunt Niagara Falls in the postwar era. The perception of the Falls as an overpriced, overbuilt tourist trap gained a renewed prominence. The fact that the place was now absolutely, unambiguously a mass tourist destination accounted for some of the criticism. As Canadian journalist Larry Krotz observes, modern tourism has a "flavour-of-the-month" quality, but being "hot" can be just as much a problem as being "not."[40] The distance between new discovery and passé tourist trap is tiny in the modern era, and fame begets disdain with amazing speed. While hardly an undiscovered tourist destination, postwar Niagara exhibited elements of faddishness: intense media exposure, an absurd assortment of tourist attractions, and huge numbers of newly enfranchised working-class tourists swarming the place every summer. Naysayers were bound to emerge.

But it was not only the class snobbery of spoilsports that fuelled complaints, for, in this era as in the past, the tourist industry itself had a good deal to answer for. As tourism became more commonplace it also became, from the perspective of the tourist, easier: standardized, routine, and predictable. But still the hint of corruptibility lingered around tourist towns, as did the insecurities of being what was called in the nineteenth century a "stranger." The travel columns of magazines were filled with advice aimed at helping the uninitiated negotiate their way through unfamiliar situations, and especially, confront the apparently rapacious tourist industry. *Holiday* magazine, for example, suggested that travellers wanting to walk around unfamiliar cities "without being annoyed by street urchins, vendors and others who prey on tourists" should purchase a local newspaper and "tuck it prominently under your arm." This trick would instantly recast the stranger as local, allowing "full freedom to gather local color at will."[41]

While mistrust was—and remains—a feature of the host/guest relationship, certainly some critics continued to believe that Niagara Falls had cornered the market on fraud. Niagara was regularly lambasted, publicly and privately, for being "backward," full of fast-buck operators who had fallen out of step with the service-oriented, professional tenor of postwar tourism.

The factional rivalries within Niagara's tourist industry made cheating relatively simple. Canadians blamed crooked Americans, who, they claimed, told lies about Canada in order to keep U.S. visitors to themselves. At different times U.S. tourists came forward with familiar tales told by taxi drivers and motel owners in Niagara Falls, New York: that accommodations on the Canadian side were fully booked due to conventions, that Americans were not allowed to bring their automobiles into the country, that naturalized Americans could lose their citizenship by visiting a foreign country, that the *Maid of the Mist* boat tour was physically dangerous. Officials on the Canadian side, furious at this slur campaign, retaliated by advertising Canadian attractions more aggressively in the United States.

Niagara Falls, New York, also had to deal with an epidemic of fake "information booths" that set up shop on the highways into the city. Official-looking uniformed staff at these establishments would not only attempt to keep tourists on the U.S. side by lying about Canada, but also steer them towards particular motels, tour buses, and attractions—the ones that paid them kickbacks. When city officials attempted to crack down on these operations, the entrepreneurs simply moved further and further out of town; one such enterprise was discovered 200 miles from the Falls.[42]

HONKY-TONK

CITY: NIAGARA

AND THE

POSTWAR

TRAVEL BOOM

204

National rivalries and the complexity of crossing a border—even one as permeable as the border at Niagara Falls—could provide just enough confusion to hoodwink strangers. But Canadians were as adept at trickery as their American counterparts. "Officially" dressed taxi and tour-bus operators continued to flag down motorists to attempt to sell them their services, and some motel owners hit on an inventive way to raise their rates: they left "No Vacancy" signs on until after dark, and then opened up again, charging desperate travellers higher prices. At peak times some motels would only rent rooms for two or more evenings or would rent rooms on the condition that patrons signed up for a sightseeing tour as well. The fluctuations of the dollar also provided plenty of opportunities to skim a few pennies here and there. Provincial officials constantly warned tourist entrepreneurs that the primary complaint they received from U.S. tourists was being cheated on exchange rates.[43] Tourists also had to contend with garden-variety crime, occasionally aimed specifically at travellers, such as a string of robberies at motels or cabins or the theft of cars with out-of-town plates.

One *Niagara Falls Review* reporter was so concerned about his town's lingering reputation as a clip joint that he did some investigative reporting. In August 1967, Georgs Kolesnikovs says, he "slung a camera" around his neck, "stuffed some tourist brochures in a pocket, asked a blonde friend to come along and played the innocent honeymooner role." While in general Kolesnikovs found that "tourists need not worry about being swindled or robbed in Niagara Falls today," he did find what he called "isolated cases" of tourists being bamboozled, especially in area restaurants. One Lundy's Lane pizzeria no doubt gained a loyal local clientele by charging tourists slightly more than locals for a pizza, and another restaurant added twenty-five cents to the bill for every visit a tourist made to its washroom.[44]

Black Americans visiting Canada faced an additional problem: Canadian hotels and restaurants did not always confirm Canada's smug sense of itself as an open and racially tolerant society. Openly discriminatory ads from summer resorts—directed against Jews and blacks—were commonplace in Ontario newspapers, especially during the 1930s.[45] Historian Alan MacEachern has discovered that discriminatory practices in the country as a whole continued many decades later, with one especially ironic example: Martin Luther King Jr. and his wife Coretta were refused accommodation at a private resort in New Brunswick's Fundy National Park in summer 1960 on the grounds that their presence might prove an "embarrassment" given the large numbers of white visitors from the U.S. South.[46]

Niagara was, then, hardly alone in using racial criteria to select guests, despite its surprisingly enlightened history. In 1905, for instance, a leading African-American intellectual, W.E. Du Bois, had gathered with twenty-nine other black leaders to organize an alternative to the accommodationist leadership of Booker T. Washington. They had intended to have this meeting in Buffalo, but could not find a hotel willing to rent rooms to them. Thus they moved the event across the river and registered, without incident, at the popular Erie Beach Hotel in Fort Erie, just down the road from the Falls. The Niagara region's unprejudiced hospitality was entrenched in the name given to the newly born organization: the Niagara Movement.[47]

Some forty years later Du Bois and his group would probably have had trouble finding a hotel, or even a restaurant, open to them in the area. Ontario passed legislation in 1944 prohibiting any business from advertising that it catered to "restricted clientele," the euphemism previously used by whites-only and/or Gentiles-only establishments. Ontario's Travel and Publicity Department monitored tourist industry advertising for such language, though Deputy Minister T.C. McCall did suggest to a resort owner who claimed he wanted to restrict "drunken parties" that he should use the phrase "we reserve the right to refuse any reservation" on his advertising. This phrase was perfectly legal and, as McCall pointed out, "much broader in its effect."[48]

Some Niagara establishments did not even attempt to play such semantic games. In 1948 a racially mixed group was refused service at a Niagara Parks Commission restaurant in Queenston. "You met us like we were tigers," said Mrs. E. Whitecotton of New Rochelle, New York, in an indignant letter to Parks Commission authorities. "I hate to think you are like the Dixie crackers."[49]

In 1949 the manager of the General Brock declared at a Chamber of Commerce meeting that his hotel made it a policy not to accept reservations from "large groups" of blacks, although some tourist homes, and two other local hotels, would. The next year the prize-winning four-thousandth couple to register for a honeymoon certificate were African-Americans from Kansas, and they received all the customary honours: guided tours, a welcome from the mayor, and their photo in the local paper. They did not, unlike other prize-winners, get a night, or even a meal, at the General Brock.[50]

By then Niagara Falls was again becoming known as a bawdy, working-class carnival. Extensive and overtly sexual honeymoon promotion was part of this, and so too was the town's resolutely working-class image; not a product of this era, but certainly intensified by postwar changes in leisure and travel. While mass travel after World War II was celebrated as one more example of the good life delivered by North American consumer capitalism, at close range democratized vacation spots looked, to some, rather unappealing. In the original script for *Niagara*, Mr. Qua, the kindly motel operator, delivered a stout, populist defence of Niagara Falls when he welcomed two of the protagonists to his establishment. "We sure get folks from everywhere," he said. "Just catch the license plates: Vancouver, Texas, Mexico City, Iceland. Not the stylish crowd, of course. No sir. To get those folks, them falls there would have to fall up!" But this kind of public tribute to the grassroots tourist was rare; it only happened in the movies.[51] Much more common were complaints.

Some tourists, such as a self-described member of "the better class" from Toronto, took pen to paper, this one complaining to authorities that Queen Victoria Park was being ruined by ballplayers and beer drinkers. Travel writers also gave the place mixed reviews. A visiting British journalist declared Niagara "one of the most highly commercialized tourist traps in the world" in 1960, though, like others before him, he softened when he saw the "awe-inspiring" waterfall, which made it "all worthwhile." The U.S. magazine *Saturday Evening Post* concurred, encouraging readers in 1965 to ignore the "fringe excitement" and "souvenir stores selling Japanese-made American Indian artifacts." "When you stand there on the promontory," wrote journalist Anne Chamberlain, "you realize that the falls themselves are still the best show in town."[52]

Canadian travel writers were much harder on the place. A special travel issue of *Canadian Homes and Gardens* in 1959 created a local controversy when

HONKY-TONK
CITY: NIAGARA
AND THE
POSTWAR
TRAVEL BOOM

206

Queenston Heights Park
Restaurant staff, 1943.

it dismissed the town as "strictly a tourist place" and warned readers, "You'll be bombarded by hawkers peddling plastic replicas of the Falls, gaudy ash trays and pennants." The mayor was especially annoyed that the magazine neglected to place Niagara on its map, which included places like the Northern Ontario mining town of Timmins. Even the house organ of the hotel industry, the *Canadian Hotel Review*, usually a relentlessly upbeat booster of tourism, could not resist taking a swipe at the Falls. A favourable story on a new motor hotel and restaurant that opened in 1967 declared, "It proves that interesting decor and Niagara Falls do go together, an idea many who know the city will find hard to believe."[53]

Did the problem lie with the poor taste and low standards of the working-class holidaymaker or with the scheming, quick-buck tourist operator? Did tourists get the holidays they deserved (or desired) or were they being manipulated by greedy entrepreneurs? These questions were posed bluntly and answered easily by different players. While provincial tourist department officials could not be as candid as they probably would have liked to be, their collective

Make Every Tourist A Royal Visitor

Editorial cartoon from the
Niagara Falls Review, 1959.
Rolling out the "Red Carpet
of Courtesy" for visitors
are "Hotels and Motels,"
"Service Stations,"
"Restaurants," "Local
Police," and "You `n' Me."

answer was clear enough. In the eyes of the provincial government, the Niagara tourist industry had borne an atrocious reputation for about a century, and civic authorities at the Falls were not interested in changing a thing. As one official declared in a private 1950 memo, "There is nothing wrong with Niagara Falls that their Council could not clean up if they chose."[54]

In a rare public address on the issue, newly appointed Minister of Tourism James Auld spoke to the Niagara Falls Visitors and Convention Bureau in 1964 about what he called the "two-sided image" of the Falls. A curious dichotomy of Niagara's tourist industry, which seems, he said, "as old as history," was the juxtaposition of two Niagaras: the grand waterfall and the "tawdry, slightly down at the heels image of the publicity stunt—over the falls in a barrel, sleazy honeymoon hotels, the bride's second biggest disappointment and the like." Even if these images were no longer true, he declared, "What matters is that people believe them to be true," and he urged tourist entrepreneurs to cease gouging U.S. visitors by shortchanging them on exchange and accommodation rates. His words had little effect. A few years later the Ministry of Tourism was still receiving more complaints from tourists about the Niagara region than any other area in the province.[55]

Some local citizens took these complaints to heart and tried to clean up their image. Niagara's tourist industry implemented many of the national ideas and campaigns initiated after World War II, all designed to remind townspeople that tourism was good for them and thus they should behave politely, even obsequiously, to visitors. As John Fisher, chairman of the Canadian Tourist Association, explained during a visit to the Falls, all of the many attractions of Niagara "can be wiped out in the shrug of the shoulders of indifference." The city always commemorated "Tourist Service Week" in May with newspaper editorials and public lectures on the importance of courtesy to tourists. The Chamber of Commerce and the Niagara Parks Commission sponsored regular "courtesy schools" for tourist industry staff and the public alike, and in 1961 the city opened the "Niagara School of Hospitality." Niagara Falls residents— whether or not directly connected with the tourist industry—were urged to answer a questionnaire designed to test their knowledge of local attractions.

Winners received a certificate, free admission to the attractions, and a strong hint that their participation could be the first step to employment in the tourist industry. Even for those without any designs on such employment it became an article of faith that, as one editorialist put it, the "magic of tourist dollars" was making the whole community prosperous, and thus overcrowded stores, streets, and parks were opportunities, not frustrations.[56]

Along with the stick of continued employment and community prosperity, Niagara residents also enjoyed the carrot of fame and (aside from the occasional trashing by a travel writer) flattery. After all, no other small Ontario towns were visited regularly by movie stars and royalty. In no other place could children amuse themselves by spotting licence plates from all over North America—and indeed, probably see all of them in one summer. Canadian journalist Barbara

Frum recalled that growing up in the Falls gave a person an unusual international perspective, because "Everyone in the world came to Niagara Falls."[57] Through the 1950s and early 1960s the *Niagara Falls Review* ran a regular summer column in which reporters gathered comments—almost always folksy and positive—from visitors, who were almost always Americans.

Along with self-congratulations, such encounters with tourists also allowed residents to let off steam by laughing at them, for another popular summer pastime was to swap stories of the silly things tourists said and did. They chuckled at the Americans—again, almost always Americans—who marched into the tourist bureau seeking directions to "Ontario" or "Canada," people who expected Niagara Falls residents to speak French, who thought they could drive to Montreal and back before dinner, who were disappointed that the *Maid of the Mist* steamboat did not go over the Falls, who thought they had to get their money changed before they travelled from Ontario to Nova Scotia, or who left their false teeth behind in public washrooms. Such stories may have gone some way towards evening out the host/guest relationship.

Whether Niagara Falls had become, in local parlance, "honky-tonk" was on the minds of some members of the community, and the question drew on the same issues that had haunted Niagara since the nineteenth century. Had the place become "too" commercial or raucous? Were human-built attractions interfering with the scenic beauty of the waterfall? Were local people acting as responsible custodians? J.R. Matthews, a gift-store owner, took his concerns about the "general move towards honky-tonk establishments" at Niagara to the minister of tourism in 1963. The last straw, for Matthews as well as several members of the city council, had come when a tourist entrepreneur hoisted a gigantic balloon over his establishment, which lay dangerously close to—as the *Review* put it, "at the very edge of"—Queen Victoria Park.[58] Memories of Thomas Barnett and Saul Davis lingered, and to be pushing the limits of good taste that close to the waterfall was to invite controversy.

When the *Review* asked them, "Is Niagara Falls Honky Tonk?" a number of local residents balked at the phrase, but worried that the place was becoming "more like Coney Island." Too much tourist development, according one

HONKY-TONK
CITY: NIAGARA
AND THE
POSTWAR
TRAVEL BOOM

210

resident, was going to "wreck it for everyone," and another wondered why honeymooners continued to flock to such an unromantic atmosphere. For their part, tourist industry spokespeople claimed they were simply providing what their customers demanded. Ross Kenzie, manager of the Visitors and Convention Bureau, said simply, "Honky tonk, if it must be called that, is there for those who demand it."[59]

As it had for the previous century, the Niagara Parks Commission offered everyone the comforting illusion that capital "N" Nature was being protected where it mattered most. As a Canadian journalist explained, perhaps a bit defensively, because the Parks Commission controlled most of the land around the waterfall, "There is not much danger of Niagara Falls degenerating into a false-fronted sideshow."[60]

If Canada was a "gigantic department store" of travel, Niagara was the bargain basement: cheap and widely accessible, a little bit tawdry, and a lot of fun. Through a happy convergence of geography and history, Niagara was destined to take centre stage as newly enfranchised working-class travellers enjoyed a frantic week or two of paid leisure. The postwar travel boom reinvented Niagara as a fun-filled, populist carnival, and the honeymoon trade—above all else, and as always—gave the place a shady but cheerful tinge.

8

Heterosexuality Goes Public:
The Postwar Honeymoon

"Leave It To Beaver was not a documentary."

– Stephanie Coontz, *The Way We Never Were:*
American Families and the Nostalgia Trap

It is tempting to think of the 1950s as a time of conformity, conservatism, and silliness. One of the first feminist histories of that era, a book that helped to convince me I was fortunate not to have come of age then, was U.S. historian Elaine May's *Homeward Bound*, published in 1988. Beginning her study with a powerful 1959 *Life* magazine photograph of a newlywed couple who spent their honeymoon in a backyard bomb shelter, May tells the story of the domestic Cold War, which was based on the containment of threats to home and family. Lurking beyond this heavily fortified haven were not only the nefarious Russians but also a host of sinister home-grown dangers, spawned in what another historian has termed "the other Fifties"—tough butch lesbians, juvenile delinquents, rebellious "Beats," and pregnant teenagers.[1] The reds were under the bed, the queers were bunked down on top of it, and the normal people, so it seemed, were surrounded.

If we remember only those who obeyed the rules—the people of the white, suburban, middle-class fifties—we miss out on how the normal and the abnormal helped to create each other. To the normal went considerable spoils. Postwar North America was a place of prosperity and upward mobility, and a young

Can this marriage be saved? Wedding postcard, outside a motel, New Hampshire, 1958. Photo by Elliott Erwitt.

married couple had good reason to expect a life of relative financial security. The abnormal—the sexual and gender non-conformists of the day such as homosexuals, promiscuous women, or disobedient teenagers—had an equally reasonable chance of ending up in a doctor's office, an unwed mothers' home, a psychiatric institution, or perhaps even a jail cell. But the creation of appropriate standards of social and sexual conduct invariably relies on a balance of consent and coercion; repression or punishment alone is not always effective (or necessary). The sexual politics of this era were shaped as much by the enthusiastic public emergence of the ideal—the happy heterosexual—as they were by the demonization of the pathological homosexual.

Homosexuality was relegated to the shadowy, unappealing margins of postwar culture. Certainly scenes like the ending of the 1962 film *The Children's Hour*, in which the self-loathing lesbian Shirley MacLaine moans about how dirty and perverted she is before hanging herself from the rafters, offered little in the way of positive advertising. Heterosexuality looked great when contrasted with this dreary Other. But heterosexuality was also transformed by postwar changes in the economy, leisure time, family life, and gender identities. Public, self-conscious, and thoroughly sexualized, heterosexuals became ubiquitous figures in the mid-twentieth century in part because they got around so much. "We are everywhere" remains a popular slogan of the modern gay movement, but in the 1950s it would have made more sense as a heterosexual maxim.

Getting everywhere started with the honeymoon. The travel boom after World War II was organized to take advantage of the disposable income and vacation time of the working class, as well as of the middle and upper classes. Like travel itself, the honeymoon became a popular and—along with the automobile and television set—accessible item of mass consumption. A great many more people could afford a honeymoon, but what was being purchased had also changed. Public discussions of the honeymoon expanded after the war, as did the promotion and advertising efforts of the tourist industry, especially at Niagara Falls.

Immediately after the war it seemed everyone was either getting married and having a honeymoon, or if not they were writing, joking, or singing about those events, advising others on how to plan them properly, or making films or television shows about them. Thus the honeymoon, and Niagara Falls as a honeymoon destination, acquired a much more overtly sexual meaning in the popular imagination. For the first time in history, massive numbers of people were invited to mark their entry into officially sanctioned public sexuality with a visit to an internationally renowned cultural icon, where they would be treated like honoured guests and showered with free gifts, roses, and complementary cocktails. With PR like this, who wouldn't want to be straight?

Performance Anxieties: Experts Debate the Honeymoon

William Wyler's 1946 film *The Best Years of Our Lives* provides a telling illustration of how travel was incorporated into the discourse of working-class consumption after World War II. This populist portrait of the lives of three servicemen returning and readjusting to life in small-town America after the war includes a reunion scene between working-class war hero Fred Derry (Dana Andrews) and his flashy blond wife, Marie (Virginia Mayo), who were married just prior to Fred's departure overseas.

Like many hasty wartime marriages, theirs was a mistake, which Fred begins to realize as soon as he returns home. His attempts at a romantic, emotional reunion with Marie are rebuffed. She is more interested in the presents he brought her from France than she is in him, and she chides him about his unfashionable pre-war civilian wardrobe. Fred capitulates and proudly tells her about his discharge money, "a thousand bucks, right from the U.S. Treasury." Marie is thrilled, and she instantly declares how the money should be spent: "It's so wonderful, I can hardly believe it. Now we can have a real honeymoon, without a care in the world!"[2]

A "real honeymoon" became a standard, routine, and familiar feature of postwar marriages. On one level, a real honeymoon was a simple undertaking. The more visible the honeymoon became, the more people understood what it was supposed to look like: it involved travel, privacy, and plenty of sex. But on another level, as more and more people participated and as the ritual attained wider cultural visibility, the meaning, purpose, and main features of the honeymoon came under serious scrutiny.

As before, doctors, psychiatrists, counsellors, and other marital experts led the debate. The huge growth of mass media determined that their messages would be carried far and wide. No longer did sex experts confine themselves to writing discreet, chastely titled advice manuals. After the war they spread their wisdom far and wide in newspapers and magazines, how-to films, radio shows, and even university courses.

Most postwar experts combined conservative views about gender roles with upbeat and optimistic predictions of heterosexual pleasure in marriage. Sexual compatibility was, as one Canadian manual put it, "the cement . . . that binds a home together." Others voiced the same sentiment in a gloomier manner, claiming, for example, that three-quarters of divorces were caused by sexual "maladjustments."[3] If sexual harmony "cemented" the marriage, the honeymoon was the foundation. A "bad" honeymoon might cause lifelong impotence for the male (particularly for "Mama's boys who fear women," latent homosexuals, or others with "doubts about their own virility"). For the woman, the experts diagnosed a new disease, "honeymoon shock" (*vaginismus*), which had potentially dire and similarly lifelong consequences. Bad honeymoons wrecked three out of five marriages, caused nervous and mental disorders, and, as Canadian sex expert Alfred Tyrer explained, "More psychological damage may be done on the honeymoon than the balance of life can correct."[4]

Here we see something of the dilemma of Cold War culture in North American culture generally: life was good, certainly superior to that of almost everyone else on the planet, but we had to guard what we had zealously, lest it go terribly wrong. This combination of optimism and anxiety was especially ironic when the topic was sex. For at the same time that the honeymoon—defined in explicitly sexual terms—was becoming a mass cultural phenomenon, North American society received some surprising news from Dr. Alfred Kinsey and his research staff. Apparently, about 50 per cent of American women and up to 90 per cent of American men came to their honeymoon as something other than blushing and virginal.

Many postwar magazine stories instructed newlyweds on honeymoon etiquette. This illustration appeared with one such article, in *Coronet*, 1951.

If premarital sex was as widespread as Kinsey's figures suggested, one might think that this news would have taken some of the spotlight off of the wedding night. The reverse was true, and medical experts and honeymoon promoters alike continued to assume that they were addressing the sexually innocent. Experts did begin to caution husbands against attaching too much importance to external signs of virginity, such as the condition of the hymen. According to one writer, this was an "unfortunate hangover from the past centuries of ignorance." But all concerned reminded old-fashioned husbands that hymens could be disrupted accidentally, through sports or doctors' examinations. In the world of advice-giving, rarely was the possibility—much less statistical probability—of premarital sexual activity raised. When it was, it was only to diminish its significance, for, as Maxine Davis declared in 1963, "Prior physical encounters, whatever their extent, are no preview of sexual love at its very best—within marriage."[5]

The honeymoon was not just popular, it was *important*. Like their predecessors in the 1920s and 1930s, postwar sex experts imagined a direct line that began at the honeymoon and extended to the health and well-being of the marriage and, hence, society itself. As historian Mary Louise Adams notes, the

Illustration from "My Wedding Night," a humorous story about a bride who thinks beds are for sleeping, 1950.

influence of psychoanalytic theories in postwar North America determined that heterosexuality meant something much more than relationships between women and men. Rather, "It came to be seen as essential to the expression of 'maturity.'" Yet, as always, heterosexual development was "a fragile process, one open to corruption."[6] Heterosexuality bore the weight of an increasing number of social, cultural, and political virtues: the well-being of the family and nation and the psychological fitness of the individual, to name just a few. A good send-off, in the form of a proper honeymoon, was crucial.

As in other eras, conformity to gender roles was part of the script. The notion that women and men had vastly differing sexual appetites was still widely held. Experts confidently asserted that women possessed a vastly slower libido (desiring sex approximately half as often as men did, one said), were slower to climax, and generally more "repressed" than men. One of the most popular experts of the era, Theodore Van de Velde, likened women to dogs (a comparison, it must be said, he had "hitherto intentionally abstained from drawing"). In both, he argued, "The dread of the beginners is unmistakable, in spite of the visible and ardent instinct to mate; but the already initiated are all eagerness for the male." One team of Canadian writers explained that male physiology gave men both a stronger sex drive *and* a greater interest in their work, whereas women have only one "consuming interest" in life: home and family ("nature's purpose" for women, as another put it). Less crudely, perhaps, Maxine Davis explained that women "are equipped but not conditioned for sexual pleasure."[7]

The consequences of toying with gender boundaries were severe. Psychiatrist Harry Tashman related the sad tale of one couple, Laura and Ralph, who switched roles during their honeymoon. Ralph was seized by a bout of "surprising, shocking" insecurity, and so Laura took over and "attempted to make a success of their nuptial night." This effort proved a disaster. "They separated in bed, each taking a distant edge. Their brooding silence established an abyss between them. That abyss became a gulf they never really spanned" until, some ten years later, Ralph sought psychiatric help. The same logic determined that women should refuse sex only rarely, for "in this," Dr. Paul Scholten noted in 1958, "she is rejecting that which her spouse considers the most valuable and personal thing he has to offer her."[8]

The honeymoon was no picnic for men, either, though they were still clearly in charge. Francis Strain reminded husbands that they were "the leading man" and "this was his hour," and Margaret Sanger urged the husband to "dominate the whole situation." Women, she said, bear the burden of the engagement period, but the honeymoon "is essentially the responsibility of the bridegroom."[9] This was a responsibility men were not to take lightly. The old Victorian figure of the "brute"—rechristened "the caveman"—re-emerged, and postwar experts continued to deplore the "rape" of wives by insecure, overcompensating husbands. But the problem now was not that brutish men ignored women's natural timidity or post-wedding exhaustion. Rather, modern women bore some responsibility for *causing* male brutality. As popular sex expert Lois Pemberton explained, "The bride's reticence leads the husband to act over-aggressively. He feels that he must use force in order to assert his masculinity." After hearing the story of Barbara and Jimmy, separated since their wedding night after Jimmy raped his new bride, Pemberton mused that she didn't know which of the couple she pitied more.[10]

But a greater problem than the emergence of the caveman was the updated, more medicalized version of the bumbling groom: the insecure, impotent husband. Men, argued one doctor, were under much more pressure than women: "She has not to do but merely to be, to exist." Little wonder that several experts cited "marital stage-fright" or "honeymoon impotence" as a serious wedding-night problem for men. They advised brides to "exercise extreme tact" should this situation arise, for "there is probably no subject about which the male is more sensitive." However, unless impotence had deeper psychological causes (such as repressed homosexuality), it could usually be dealt with by that modern panacea: consultation with experts such as doctors or psychiatrists.[11] Not surprisingly, no parallel alarm was raised over women's sexual dysfunctions, despite studies indicating that only 6 to 25 per cent of women achieved orgasms during their honeymoons. Some declared this to be physiological truth—that most women simply did not reach orgasm right away, or at all, or until after their first child was born. Others repeated the same advice that had been dispensed to men since the passionate woman was discovered decades earlier: slow down. "Even a wife," declared marriage counsellor Sidney Goldstein in 1945, "must be wooed in order to be won."[12]

The female wedding-night malady that did alarm physicians was the newly diagnosed condition "honeymoon shock" or *vaginismus*. The condition was first discussed in the 1950s, when doctors tended to blame it on husbands, whose failure to provide the "proper erotic atmosphere" caused their wives painful spasms of the vagina—also described as a "nervous reaction to a severe emotional shock." In the early 1970s doctors identified a similar problem, "honeymoon cystitis," a lower urinary tract infection apparently acquired after the "onset of regular coital activity."[13] The attempt to medicalize the wedding night—which, as we have seen, had begun much earlier in the twentieth century—reached its zenith in the early 1970s, when a Niagara Falls, New York, physician conducted a study of the various honeymoon-related medical emergencies that twenty-one of his colleagues at the Falls had handled. Dr. Boris Golden's predictably jocular study of honeymoon problems centred almost solely on the bride—imperforate hymens, cystitis, ectopic pregnancies, vaginal tears—and offered up a long discourse on various items—tampons, condoms, even Saran Wrap—"lost" in the vagina.[14]

Such are some of the ways that the wedding night was, by mid-century, colonized by the helping professions. The premarital medical examination was taken for granted as part of wedding planning; almost everyone writing about the honeymoon recommended it. And lots of people, it seemed, were reading expert advice: according to a 1947 U.S. study, 70 per cent of men and 50 per cent of women had acquired a "book-knowledge of sex-life" and the "art of love" that helped their honeymoons considerably. Indeed, the proliferation of advice, and the ubiquity of the expert, spawned a backlash. As early as 1948 *Cosmopolitan* magazine wondered "Are Those Marriage Manuals Any Good?" and worried that the huge influx of "Baedekers to wedlock" was taking the mystery out of sex. In the late 1950s one pair of writers fashioned their claims to authority on a deft combination of anti-expert sentiment and heterosexuality, noting that they were "not physicians, but a married couple."[15]

In some quarters the backlash extended beyond the role of expertise to the honeymoon itself. There were those who believed the honeymoon craze had gone too far, that the ritual was outdated, overdone, and a "barbaric" introduction to married life. The most outspoken critic was British psychiatrist and Member of Parliament Reginald Bennett, whose anti-honeymoon views made quite a splash in North America. The honeymoon, Bennett declared in 1955, was simply an "ordeal," and wedding-night sex was too often "a hopeless, fumbling effort." Like Victorian commentators before him, Bennett opposed the honeymoon because it was exhausting and embarrassing. He was especially perturbed by "the lore of the honeymoon, the vast repertory of awful jokes." Other commentators argued that, as a vacation, the honeymoon "constitutes an unreal introduction to life together." Still others adopted a more self-consciously "modern" perspective, maintaining that the ritual was simply out of step with the experience of the travel and sex-savvy postwar generation. Two such modern writers, the husband and wife team of Jerome and Julia Rainer, scorned the "doleful warnings" of other experts, arguing instead: "Only in the rarest instance is there a possibility of some deeply disturbing result from coital awkwardness during the honeymoon. Most modern

"Back Bench," a comic strip by Graham Harrop, suggests another reading of Niagara. The Globe and Mail, 1995.

couples are so keenly absorbed in the experience of total emotional surrender that they easily surmount even bungling and apprehension."[16]

A more breezy approach was taken by *Cosmopolitan* writer Caroline Bird, who praised "nature's merciful amnesia" for allowing most women to forget how horrible their honeymoons were. Fortunately for "the preservation of the race," she said, most women couldn't remember any more about their honeymoons than they could about "the pangs of childbirth."[17]

For it or against it, the honeymoon, it seemed, was everywhere. That the modern honeymoon had travelled far from the nineteenth-century wedding tour was clear from the story—which surfaced several different times in the 1940s and 1950s—of the mother-in-law who attempted to register in the same hotel as her honeymooning daughter and son-in-law.[18] That this situation was exactly what a honeymoon had been several generations earlier would have been lost on contemporary readers, who were expected to chuckle at the absurdity of the scenario.

Heterosexuality Off-camera:
Hollywood Discovers the Honeymoon

While the advice of medical and marital experts on the honeymoon—as on many other matters—cast a long shadow, those counsellors were certainly not

"Give us a good suite, Johnny and get Bobby to fix us something nice for breakfast and have Steve serve it!"

" . . . and now tell me everything you did on your honeymoon!"

From a 1956 joke book: H.T. Elmo, *Honeymoon Humour*.

alone in their depiction of the wedding night as a thoroughly reclusive, sexualized ritual. In the pop culture of the postwar era, the honeymoon quickly became a dirty joke—a sort of shorthand, indirect way of talking about what one was not supposed to talk about: sex. The only culturally permissible sex possible—between two married, adult heterosexuals—could be addressed *on-camera* only through innuendo, hints, and veiled, risqué humour, all reliant on social meanings and knowledge acquired *off-camera*.

The honeymoon could be used to say almost anything naughty, as long as it was said indirectly. The entire plot of RKO's 1940 film *Lucky Partners*, for example, turns on the impossibility of two people taking an "impersonal," non-romantic trip together to Niagara Falls. Actor Ronald Colman is horrified when he hears that Ginger Rogers plans to postpone her honeymoon after marrying her boyfriend, played by Jack Carson. "A honeymoon isn't something you can put away in cold storage like a mink coat," he says. "It just isn't the same moon. And it certainly isn't the same honey." Colman hatches a plot to escort Rogers to Niagara himself, but the absurdity of their attempt at an asexual visit to the Falls is illustrated the moment they arrive. They meet another couple in the elevator at their hotel. The woman asks Rogers, "Did you just get here, honey?" and declares, snuggling into her husband, that they had been there

GETTING MARRIED IS LIKE BUYING A CAR ONCE YOU GET THE LICENSE

YOU CAN GO AS FAR AS YOU LIKE!

The honeymoon as a dirty joke: postcard, undated, c.1940s.

a week. "How are the Falls?" asks Colman. "We're seeing them tomorrow," says the man.[19]

This particular horse was flogged often, with Niagara Falls and other popular honeymoon destinations being used to make the joke. "Let's go again to Niagara," sang Frank Sinatra in "Let's Get Away from It All," adding, "This time we'll look at the Falls." Similarly Joan Davis, star of the domestic television sitcom *I Married Joan*, was surprised to learn, many years after her honeymoon in Las Vegas, that "they have gambling there?"[20]

Honeymoon humour generally turned on three sorts of jokes or scenarios: sexual potency, sexual anxieties, and disruptions to the traditional honeymoon script. Jokes about the honeymoon as the zenith of sexual passion were cheap and plentiful. In Alfred Hitchcock's *Rear Window*, among the neighbours Jimmy Stewart spies on through his window is a newlywed couple. We see them enter an apartment in the building across the way. The husband carries his bride over the threshold, and they embrace passionately. They draw the blind, and the closed window becomes a running visual joke through the film, especially when contrasted to the hive of activity visible in the other apartments. Occasionally the husband, clad only in underwear, pops his head out the window. He is exhausted and taking time to smoke a cigarette, and we can hear his wife calling to him from behind. By the final scene the various melodramas across the courtyard have been resolved, and so too have things changed for the newlyweds. The blinds are open, they are fully clothed, and we can hear the nagging voice of the wife: "If you'd told me you quit your job we wouldn't have gotten married!"[21]

A guest challenger on a 1955 episode of the TV quiz show *What's My Line?* stumped the panellists and provided much hilarity for the audience when he revealed that his occupation was "social director for a honeymoon resort." Panellist Fred Allen's question, "Do you teach people to do things better?" was met with especially raucous laughter. The premier episode of the popular sitcom *Bewitched* featured a surprise appearance by Samantha's mother Endora at her daughter's honeymoon hotel suite. Endora is furious that her daughter has chosen to marry Darren, who is not possessed with witchcraft. She argues with Samantha and plays a series of tricks on Darren, who is impatiently waiting (in a dressing gown) in the other room. "Mother," declares Samantha, "you've got to get out. Even witchcraft won't keep him out all night. It's our honeymoon!"[22]

The flip side of potency is anxiety, and here too honeymoon humour played on some of the tensions identified by marital experts. Anxious brides were funnier. Ginger Rogers did a wonderful parody of a blushing bride in a hotel suite in Howard Hawks's 1952 film *Monkey Business*. She is alternately modest (changing into a prim nightgown in the bathroom), jealous (reminding her husband, Cary Grant, of all his former girlfriends), and terrified (bursting into tears and calling loudly for her mother). What makes this a parody is the premise: she is regressing under the spell of an anti-aging drug concocted by her chemist husband, to whom she's been married for several years. Doris Day films are always a great source of sexual innuendo. In *Lover Come Back* Day wakes up in a hotel suite after a drunken evening and finds she is married to her adversary, a playboy advertising executive (Rock Hudson). She screams, runs out of the room half-dressed, and asks two chambermaids where she can get her marriage annulled. One of them pats her arm reassuringly. "It's only natural to be a little frightened at first." The other woman nods. "It's like olives, dear. It's something you acquire a taste for."[23]

The Long, Long Trailer, starring Lucille Ball and Desi Arnaz, addressed the question of male anxieties. A virtual smorgasbord of popular Freudian sexual clichés, most of the humour in this film derives from Desi's fears of driving the "long, long trailer" they take on their honeymoon.[24] The original *Father of the Bride* (1950) makes great fun of honeymoon anxieties more generally. Kay and Buckley are set to call off their wedding after a huge fight. "I've learned something about Buckley that's unforgivable," declares Kay (Elizabeth Taylor) to her father (Spencer Tracy). "He should have told me before! He shouldn't have kept it from me!" Finally she sobs out the sad truth: "Nova Scotia for our honeymoon!"[25]

Disruptions to the conventional honeymoon narrative were another popular storyline. When Eddy Cantor interviewed Hattie McDaniel on his 1941 radio show *A Time to Smile*, she had just been married. "Did you have a nice honeymoon?" inquired Cantor. In her most robust mammy voice, McDaniel replied, "I don't know. My husband ain't come back from it yet!" Absence was funny, but so was presence. In the pilot episode of TV's *The Brady Bunch*, Mike and Carol Brady begin their honeymoon by checking into a hotel. "Oh yes, Mr. Brady," leers the oily hotel clerk, "You have the honeymoon suite." Mike signs the register "Mr. and Mrs. Brady and family" and then realizes his mistake. "Force of habit," he says, "the kids aren't with us." The clerk glares and says, "But you did ask for the honeymoon suite." (Later the clerk is apoplectic when the parents, having decided they miss their kids, usher all six of them into the hotel.) Similarly, the humour of *My Favorite Wife* (1940, remade as *Move Over, Darling*, with Doris Day, in 1963) arises when Cary Grant's long-disappeared (and presumed dead) first wife turns up at the hotel he has arrived at on honeymoon with his second wife.[26]

Narrative disruptions were popular plot lines in honeymoon-themed fiction as well, and short stories and novels of this era abounded with ex-girlfriends, evil twins, children, or boorish friends tagging along with a newlywed couple. Travel mishaps were another narrative device that brought temporary catastrophe or, sometimes, adventure to newlyweds. Two genres, horror and pornography, have especially favoured this device.[27]

Pop culture, then, helped to establish the mass appeal of the honeymoon, as well as its particular features: travel, privacy, and sex. Niagara Falls was not the only place in which these stories unfolded, but it did come up often enough, especially in Hollywood films, to consolidate its reputation. Just as the honeymoon became a culturally acceptable, if risqué, metaphor for sex, so too did Niagara Falls itself. The connection between the two—Niagara and sex—was pretty obvious, as the imaginary geography of the place became a whole lot less imaginary. "To Niagara in a sleeper, there's no honeymoon that's cheaper, and the train goes slow" wrote Harry Warren and Al Dubin in the 1938 song "Shuffle off to Buffalo." I've already mentioned Cary Grant's uncharacteristically crude remark to Grace Kelly in *To Catch a Thief*: "What you need is ten minutes with a good man at Niagara Falls." Similarly, in the 1940 film *Remember the Night*, written by Preston Sturges, straight arrow Fred MacMurray finally declares his love for bad girl Barbara Stanwyck as they pass through Niagara on their way home to New York. The next day Stanwyck insists that he must have changed his mind about wanting to marry her. "It was all settled," declares MacMurray. "That," says Stanwyck, "was at Niagara Falls. People aren't responsible for what they say in Niagara Falls."[28]

Certainly *Niagara* is the most famous cinematic depiction of the Falls. That the movie was a tremendous boon to the local tourist industry was perhaps more a testament to its fabulous cinematography—it was, on one level, a two-hour travelogue chronicling the main attractions of the Niagara region—than its plot. Yet the film is not without its narrative charms, and it is especially striking how well it straddles two distinct eras of Niagara's sexual culture.

The story—of the awful power of female sexuality for men—echoes nineteenth-century depictions of Niagara as an alluring female icon, seducing and entrapping her male suitors. Indeed, the advertising for the film featured Monroe reclining over the waterfall, her body and the water merging into each other; the caption: "Marilyn Monroe and Niagara—a raging torrent of emotion that even nature can't control!" (See p.199.)

The film opens with Joseph Cotten standing in a raincoat at the base of the waterfall, railing at its power. The script notes that Cotten stares at the Falls, "his eyes filled . . . with an uncomfortable fascination." The next scene depicts his trampy, scheming wife Rose (Monroe, a telling female/nature juxtaposition) naked in bed, smoking a cigarette. The script describes her as a "blonde, beautiful, animal-like girl of twenty-four."[29] The plot has Monroe orchestrating a plan to kill Cotten; in this instance dangerous female sexuality operates metaphorically and literally.

This sexually charged but destructive couple contrasts with the "good" honeymooners, Ray and Polly Cutler. The film introduces us to them as they cross the border from the United States into Canada. A Canadian customs officer instantly spots them as honeymooners, and he inquires if they are carrying liquor in a box in their back seat. "Oh no," Ray answers. "Those are books, I'm going to catch up on my reading." The officer's eyebrows raise. "Reading?" he asks. Polly Cutler glares at her husband. As they drive on she pouts sarcastically that the officer will think she is a "pretty hot article" since her husband is planning to spend his honeymoon reading about Winston Churchill. The confusion is resolved when Ray lets us know they are on a delayed honeymoon. They have been married for three years. Polly nestles in close to Ray and declares it will be just as good as a "real" one, better even, because "I've got my union card now."[30]

Contemporary journalists adopted this same innuendo-laden, jocular script—the point of view so prevalent in Hollywood's honeymoon stories. Lurking between the lines of postwar newspaper and magazine commentary on the Niagara honeymoon was sex. Indeed, by all accounts postwar honeymooners were having so much sex that they forgot to tip their waiters, left their wedding rings in hotel bathrooms, did not emerge from their rooms for days on end, crossed busy streets on red lights, and generally wandered around the town dazed and disoriented.

This public recasting of the honeymoon as a specifically sexual ritual, geared solely to the newlywed couple, occurred at the same time as the postwar travel boom; and the two trends came together at Niagara Falls, the self-styled "Honeymoon Capital of the World." The expanded, reinvented, slightly lewd

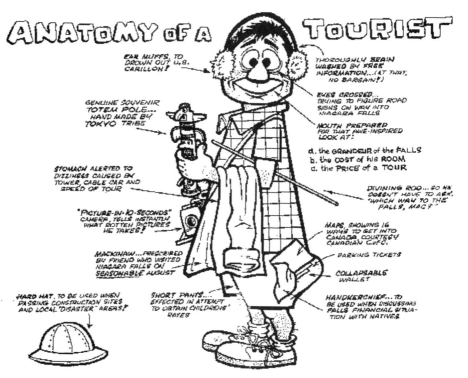

ANATOMY OF A TOURIST

EAR MUFFS, TO DROWN OUT U.S. CARILLON!

THOROUGHLY BRAIN WASHED BY FREE INFORMATION...(AT THAT, NO BARGAIN?)

GENUINE SOUVENIR TOTEM POLE... HAND MADE BY TOKYO TRIBE

EYES CROSSED... TRYING TO FIGURE ROAD SIGNS ON WAY INTO NIAGARA FALLS

MOUTH PREPARED FOR THAT AWE-INSPIRED LOOK AT:

d. the GRANDEUR of the FALLS
b. the COST of his ROOM
c. the PRICE of a TOUR

STOMACH ALERTED TO DIZZINESS CAUSED BY TOWER, CABLE CAR AND SPEED OF TOUR

DIVINING ROD... SO HE DOESN'T HAVE TO ASK "WHICH WAY TO THE FALLS, MAC?"

"PICTURE-IN-10-SECONDS" CAMERA, TELLS INSTANTLY WHAT ROTTEN PICTURES HE TAKES!

MAPS, SHOWING 16 WAYS TO GET INTO CANADA COURTESY CANADIAN C.P.C.

PARKING TICKETS

MACKINAW...PRESCRIBED BY FRIEND WHO VISITED NIAGARA FALLS ON SEASONABLE AUGUST

COLLAPSABLE WALLET

HARD HAT, TO BE USED WHEN PASSING CONSTRUCTION SITES AND LOCAL 'DISASTER' AREAS!

SHORT PANTS... EFFECTED IN ATTEMPT TO OBTAIN CHILDRENS' RATES

HANDKERCHIEF...TO BE USED WHEN DISCUSSING FALLS FINANCIAL SITUA- TION WITH NATIVES

One of the first times the locals ridiculed the tourists, at least in public: cartoon from the *Niagara Falls Gazette*, c.1960.

honeymoon found a congenial physical home in the expanded, reinvented, slightly lewd tourist industry at the Falls. It was a perfect match.

The Niagara Honeymoon: "Magic in the Mist"

When newlyweds Bernie and Virginia Hogan boarded the train at their home in Windsor, Ontario, in September 1946 for a week-long honeymoon at Niagara's Foxhead Inn, they knew they were doing something more than having a nice holiday. They were participating in a ritual that was as important as the wedding itself. As Virginia declared almost fifty years later, "Newlyweds today travel to exotic places around the world," but if they don't go to Niagara Falls, "they may as well have a wedding cake without the icing."[31]

A pavilion called "Ramblers Rest," Queen Victoria Park, 1951.

There were plenty of reasons that people like Bernie and Virginia Hogan were drawn to the Falls for their honeymoons. Tourist entrepreneurs liked to say that Cupid was the city's "best press agent" and in a sense they were right, for by the 1940s the Niagara honeymoon was a century-old staple of North American culture. Legend had it that at least one newspaper, *The Ottawa Citizen*, used to leave permanently in type that famous last line in wedding announcements: "The bride and groom later left on a honeymoon journey to Niagara Falls."[32]

But few postwar tourism boosters were willing to leave their business success up to reputation, even one as powerful or enduring as Niagara's. Honeymoon advertising and promotion skyrocketed, and establishments outdid themselves trying to woo the honeymoon trade. Complementary cocktails, roses, breakfasts, and an array of other specials greeted honeymooners at local motels, hotels, and restaurants. Journalists were popping up everywhere wanting to interview or photograph newlyweds. City fathers on both sides of the river welcomed them warmly, and the entire tourist industry seemed to recognize them the moment they hit town. The attention may have been a bit embarrassing, but it also must have been flattering.

An early, and enduring, honeymoon promotional device was the "honeymoon certificate." The members of the Niagara Falls, Ontario, Chamber of Commerce lifted this idea from their counterparts across the river in June 1949, and they honoured the first winners, a cleverly chosen mixed-nation couple (he was from Ohio, she from Ontario) in a ceremony in the Oakes Garden Theatre. A procession of horse-drawn carriages paraded the winners and local dignitaries through Queen Victoria Park, carillon bells rang out the wedding march, a choir assembled to sing the "Niagara Honeymoon Song," and an airplane flying overhead scattered confetti on the crowd.[33] The ensuing publicity was so great—stories and photos appeared in newspapers across North America and Warner Brothers even sent a cameraman to cover the event for Pathé Newsreels—that tourism entrepreneurs discussed making it an annual contest, a honeymooner's version of the Miss America pageant.

The contest didn't materialize, but the success of the certificates convinced local businessmen that the honeymoon trade was both lucrative and newsworthy. Milestones were quickly manufactured—the one-thousandth couple, the two-thousandth couple, couples on anniversary honeymoons—and "winners" were announced and celebrated. Dozens of local merchants contributed gifts to what the Chamber of Commerce called a "community shower" for the one-thousandth couple, and most winners (at least the white ones) could expect a night or two at the General Brock and, always, their pictures in the paper. Over time the search for couples to commemorate grew wider and more bizarre: the first English couple, the first Alaskan honeymooners, the first Israeli couple, the first couple to arrive on motorcycle, and so on. In 1951 the Chamber of Commerce estimated that it was spending two days a week on honeymoon certificate business, and about four thousand couples were registering annually. So when a honeymooning couple from Ecuador dropped in, and the local press enthused that the certificates were "just about as well known as the Falls themselves," the hyperbole—and the time spent on these affairs—probably seemed justified.[34] Yet despite this self-congratulatory cosmopolitanism, tourist boosters were slower to recognize diversity within their own country. It was not until 1957—and prompted by a study indicating that close to 20 per cent of honeymooners hailed from Quebec—that French-language certificates were issued. Chamber staff reported two years later that French-language certificates were moving at a brisk rate, some days constituting half of the total.[35]

In 1949, just before the honeymoon certificates were officially launched on the Canadian side, Canadian Prime Minister Louis St. Laurent paid a visit to the Falls. His stopover was a working visit; the Canadian Bar Association was having its annual meeting at the General Brock Hotel, and St. Laurent was scheduled to deliver the keynote address. Jeanne St. Laurent accompanied her husband on the trip, and, at Niagara Falls in 1949, this could only mean one thing. "St Laurents to Have Honeymoon" announced the local newspaper, despite the fact that the couple had, by that time, been married forty-one years. As Mayor Houck officially welcomed the couple, he delivered a testimonial to the cozy domesticity of the postwar world and to Niagara's special place within it. The ladies of Niagara, Houck declared, were particularly happy that "at last we have a Prime Minister with a wife."[36]

The postwar travel and honeymoon boom ushered in a flurry of renewed media interest. Locally, Niagara's first radio station, CKVC, began a regular morning program, "Honeymoon in Niagara," in which visiting newlyweds were invited into the studio—conveniently located beside the Rainbow Bridge—interviewed, and showered with gifts. The first television broadcast from the Falls, in 1948, featured—what else?—a honeymooning couple.[37] Beyond the Falls, stories about the Niagara honeymoon experience—usually positive and quite sentimental, and often written by husband and wife teams— appeared over and over in North American popular magazines in the 1940s and 1950s.

Journalists covering this oft-travelled Niagara honeymoon beat filled their pages with sly, but, for the most part, good-humoured insinuation. Writing for *Chatelaine*, Canadian journalist Lotta Dempsey noticed that most tourists at the Falls held hands and wandered around in a "dazed and daffy coma." June Callwood and Trent Frayne, sent by *Maclean's* magazine in 1950 as "undercover honeymooners" (at the time they had been married six years), were delighted to discover the tricks that Niagara residents used to spot the newlyweds: honeymooners

CANADA'S NATIONAL MAGAZINE

MACLEAN'S

August 1, 1950   Ten Cents

NIAGA
By June Callwood and

How Hockey's
Made His First
By J

MAID OF THE MIST

The cover of a 1950 *Maclean's* issue in which journalists June Callwood and Trent Frayne go "undercover" to investigate honeymoon culture.

sported new shoes and haircuts, held hands in public, and, especially, suffered acute embarrassment when registering at hotels.[38]

Others weighed in with a range of special honeymooner traits: they were poor tippers, they never ate breakfast, they constantly stared at each other. According to officers who patrolled Queen Victoria Park, "Love is conducive to forgetfulness," because jewellery, movie cameras, and full wallets were, apparently, regularly mislaid in the park. "I'll wager," declared the local police chief, "eighty percent of these items were left by honeymooners." U.S. journalists Jhan and June Robbins thought they had found the answer to Niagara's popularity as a honeymoon site in the courtesy and discretion of the hotel staffs, because "nowhere else is the 'Do Not Disturb' sign, dangling from a doorknob, held in such sacred respect." A journalist from the rather more frank *Esquire* magazine remarked that hotel staff kept track of newlywed sexual marathons, awarding the "unofficial record" to one couple who did not emerge from their room for nine days.

Writing for the more conventional *Saturday Evening Post*, Henry and Kathleen Pringle were put off by the "honky-tonk, tawdry" character of the town, particularly its "unbelievably vulgar" souvenirs and photographic displays of "happy honeymooners, some of them necking violently" on Main Street. Even an elderly couple, returning to Niagara for their fiftieth anniversary in 1952, were coded in sexual terms: the seventy-three-year-old woman "smiled roguishly" as she explained to reporters that she and her husband didn't tell a soul that they were returning to the Falls for their second honeymoon.[39]

So closely were they identified with heterosexual passion, the Falls became, as they had in previous eras, an easy and obvious target for gay camp parody. This time, though, gay appropriations of the Falls went further than a few men giggling together over a beer. Now there were sequins. At the U.S. gay resort Fire Island, for example, drag shows featured a dance number that had a male/female couple dancing to "Shuffle off to Buffalo" in front of a chorus line of six-foot-tall men draped in glittering strips of silver foil: Niagara Falls. The place was a popular location for self-styled "honeymoons" among working-class lesbians in Toronto in the early 1960s, and a gay male couple even registered for a honeymoon certificate later in the 1970s (which they received with "no giggles," according to the Chamber of Commerce).[40]

The Niagara region's local gay population might have had a less ironic perspective on the place. Regular police harassment was a staple feature of gay life in most North American centres in this era, and the Niagara area was no exception. When the scandal-mongering Toronto tabloid *Hush* reported a massive roundup of men at the Falls on gross indecency charges in 1962, the region's other important commodity, agriculture, inspired an attempt at metaphor: "Police admitted that Niagara Falls is in the Fruit Belt. And they are so right."[41]

As a metaphor for lost sexual innocence, an approved invitation into sexual adulthood, or gaining a "union card," the Niagara honeymoon was never discussed without a nudge, giggle, or wink. But while this cultural script rarely varied, real honeymoons were being taken by real people, who were not living their lives in film scripts or magazine articles. Some of these people have written their own versions of their honeymoons, in the form of responses to a contest held at the Falls in 1992. Over four hundred contestants from across North America accepted the invitation to "relive the magic moments" of their Niagara honeymoons by writing their honeymoon memoirs. A panel headed by Canadian historian Pierre Berton read the entries, and the winner and his or her spouse were flown back to the Falls for a lavish "second honeymoon" weekend.

According to the results of this contest, the popular honeymoon script matched people's experiences—or at least memories—of their Niagara honeymoons surprisingly well. A kind of playful modesty or knowing sense of embarrassment characterizes many of the accounts. Displacing sexual and emotional anxieties, many of them narrate their stories as triumphs over a variety of adversities: botched hotel reservations, missed train connections, automobile breakdowns. The refrain is always the same: the stories serve to highlight the anxiety and absurdity of potentially spending a wedding night in a hotel lobby, a train station, or a garage parking lot. Oblique and humorous sexual references also emerge, from those who recall their lack of interest in the waterfall when they first arrived or persistently missed the complementary breakfast in the mornings or never bothered to view the illuminated waterfall in the evening.

One woman said that her first child was born exactly nine months after their honeymoon. "There is magic in the mist," she concluded. Only a few women were less than coy and less than willing to enjoy the role of blushing bride. "I didn't learn till 20 years later what a woman's parts of her body was made of, I was just a baby machine," declared one woman, who honeymooned at the Falls in 1946 and titled her letter, "Forty Six Years and Eight Kids Later." She wrote, "I didn't know what foreplay was, I thought it related to golf."

Postwar stereotypes took their toll, as couples, especially brides, struggled with the public embarrassment of being a walking sexual cliché. Despite carefully removing corsages and shaking confetti from their hair, newlyweds felt as conspicuous as popular opinion held them to be. As one woman explained, "Everyone knew we were honeymooners, even the elevator boy, from the knowing glances that passed between the others." Yet others were quick to point out that visibility had its benefits. Several recalled noticing other honeymooners—in their hotel, on the dance floor at the Rainbow Room at the General Brock, on the *Maid of the Mist*—and, clearly, for many the presence of other newlyweds was both a comfort and a reassuring sign that they had made the right vacation choice. Adding to such anxieties were the travails of travel in general, especially for this first generation of newly enfranchised working-class and middle-class tourists. The Niagara honeymoon was, for many, a project that required considerable saving and sacrifice. Couples spent their recently acquired wedding money on the trip or compromised on the lavishness of the wedding to afford it—or even, as one woman recalled, chose the Falls over a new living-room set.

The contest responses show that the romantic lure of postwar Niagara was more than matched by what was, for many, a series of "firsts": the first time they travelled out of state or province, the first border crossing, the first train trip or hotel stay, and even, for some, the first restaurant meal, steak, or glass of wine. That all the correspondents expressed fond, even glowing, memories is perhaps not surprising; they were, after all, trying to win a contest. But despite the boosterish rhetoric, the responses reveal the significance of the Niagara experience. Many couples had gone back to the Falls regularly, for anniversaries or with their children. Others had carefully saved their honeymoon certificates, hotel receipts, or motel postcards. Roger and Annette Holloway, who drove their DeSoto from Indiana to the Falls in 1952, had kept their honeymoon certificate, "a real conversation piece," hanging on their household wall ever since.[42]

When the Niagara Falls, Ontario, Chamber of Commerce celebrated honeymoon couple one thousand, local businessmen were, as always, thrilled with the ensuing publicity. The winning couple, declared the Chamber's president, were "naturals," and he congratulated his men on "the outstanding success of their carefully organized 'show.'"[43] Intensive honeymoon promotion, especially in the 1940s and 1950s, had made Niagara's tourist entrepreneurs hardened and cynical social constructionists. Several decades later, scholars of sexuality are busily investigating what Niagara's businessmen had figured out many years earlier: sexuality, like gender, is learned, acquired, ritualized, and performed.

They put on quite a show at the Falls, and it played to a packed house for decades. For millions of North Americans, married life after World War II began with travel, consumption, and plenty of sex. It was a vision of family life that most people, not surprisingly, found appealing, at least for awhile.

9

Conclusion:
The Sublime Becomes Ridiculous

In the past people were afraid of Niagara Falls. Today they are more likely to smile at the thought of it, perhaps even laugh, maybe grimace. The "laboratory for the study of young love" now exists, in the popular imagination, as a laboratory for bad taste, toxic nightmares, and just plain weird goings-on. Niagara Falls is where the Hooker Chemical Company spewed its poison into Love Canal, and then, a decade later, *the neighbourhood was reopened and the houses sold again.* It is where Maharishi Mahesh Yogi and magician Doug Henning want to build a new age theme park, complete with levitating buildings. It is where sadistic Canadian murderer Paul Bernardo proposed to his partner in crime, Karla Homolka. In 1992 the John F. Kennedy Assassination Exhibit, which features autopsy photos and the shooting itself on a continuous loop of film, opened in Niagara Falls, Ontario. Across the river Niagara Falls, New York, is where John Bobbitt is from. If Niagara represented all that was sublime in nineteenth-century North American culture, it now signifies the outlandish, cheesy, over-the-top.

Almost no one who writes about Niagara takes the place seriously any longer. Instead, almost every account of a visit to the Falls since the late 1960s has served to establish the hip, above-the-crowd credentials of the writer. "I hate Niagara Falls. I hate it because of the clutter, the kitsch, those bus tourists from hell, or perhaps just Iowa," declared Toronto journalist Catherine Dunphy in a 1991 rant, quite typical of the general media tone.[1] Features on Niagara appear rarely these days in travel magazines or newspapers, but when they do,

Honeymooners as part of the landscape: "Honeymoon Couple," postcard, Niagara Falls, Ont., c.1950.

they too adopt the same world-weary pose, offering precise instructions to visitors on how to "sidestep the tack."[2] In a surprisingly enthusiastic *New York Times* feature on Niagara in 1996—one of the few Niagara travel narratives of the past thirty years in which the visitor obviously enjoyed herself—the author repeatedly apologized for liking the place so much.[3] Niagara also remains a favourite target for those wishing to hold forth on tourism and mass culture. In the 1940s and 1950s, the "Niagara beat" consisted of watching besotted honeymooners do silly things in public. Now journalists follow tourists around Niagara with pen or camera, catching them saying things like, "There's nothing here but the view."[4]

These days, though, it is not just Niagara Falls that gets this kind of press. The disdain expressed about mass tourist destinations—from waterfalls to historical landmarks to theme parks—is often as much about the "mass" as it is about the destination. The quest for difference and authenticity is written into the fabric of modern Western tourism, as the designation "tourist" becomes increasingly a term of embarrassment, something almost everyone does and no one wishes to be. As Trinh T. Minh-ha notes, "One among some fifty million globe trotters, the traveller maintains his difference mostly by despising others like himself."[5]

But such ambivalence is not only about the complicated feelings of the individual towards the mass. Look carefully at who is being mocked at places such as Niagara Falls, for I think we can still observe some thinly disguised racial and class-based hostilities. Consider, for example, that universal Western comic figure, the Japanese tourist, who now regularly appears at Niagara Falls. That the Falls, along with Prince Edward Island and the Rocky Mountains, has become a popular destination for Japanese tourists is now a cliché in North American culture. Despite the larger number of visitors to Canada from at least two other countries, the United States and Britain, journalists never seem to tire of the tale of the Japanese couple spending thousands of dollars for a week of snapping photographs of Niagara or posing with Anne of Green Gables.[6] Go figure, seems the subtext, they sure are inscrutable. Such stories work to establish North American ironic distance, even superiority; *we* abandoned the place long ago.

Just as Niagara became passé to the European and North American upper class when the middle class arrived in the 1920s, the working-class tourist boom of the 1940s and 1950s had a similar effect. White middle-class or upper-class North Americans have been difficult to spot at Niagara for some time. A Chamber of Commerce survey in 1968 revealed what had been obvious for some time: two-thirds of Niagara's visitors were working-class, and 80 per cent were American.[7]

By the end of the 1960s, the Niagara bubble had burst. One culprit was Expo '67, the World's Fair in Montreal. Expo was expected to provide a major boom to the Canadian tourist industry, but at Niagara Falls it spelled disaster. Niagara motels owners reported as much as a 50 per cent decline in their business in the summer of 1967. As Jack Cairns, owner of a local motor hotel put it, "Everyone is going to or coming from Expo. If they're going they are not spending any money, and they have none on the way back."[8] Tourist industry expansion came to a screeching halt, and to make matters worse some of the town's large industrial employers, such as Kimberly-Clark, the Dominion Chain Company, and International Silver Limited, packed up and moved out.[9]

Tourism experienced a brief resurgence through the 1980s, and the industry again expanded. As in the past, competition brought out the worst. In the mid-1980s the state of New York decided against replacing quickly disappearing traffic signs around Niagara Falls. Tourist entrepreneurs were suspected of destroying them so that visitors would have to stop and ask for directions at the official-looking information booths run by private tour companies. Three of the largest tour companies experienced a rash of violence in 1986: vandalism, death threats, and even firebombs. At the same time Niagara Falls, Ontario, residents blamed the United States for what they called an "invasion" of prostitutes fleeing harsh New York criminal laws. The women, it was claimed, brought with them a rash of drug and robbery offences and tarnished the town's image as a honeymoon capital. A century of rivalry between the U.S. and Canadian tourist industry hit what was arguably its lowest point in 1989, when in its annual tourist map the visitors bureau on the U.S. side omitted any references to Canada or even to the bridges crossing the river.[10]

The ensuing international flap was quieter than it might otherwise have been. Hardly anyone was around to hear it. The region's industrial base, suffering for decades, almost collapsed in the early 1990s, as the mainstays—automobile and chemical plants—closed down or cut production. In 1993 Niagara Falls, Ontario, had Canada's fourth-highest unemployment rate, at 14 per cent. Across the river civic officials in Niagara Falls, New York, taking stock of their declining manufacturing base and downtown core, estimated that more than half the town's housing stock was substandard. It seemed unlikely that tourism was going to pull the place out of the mire, for it was suffering also. In the early 1990s tourism had declined by 40 per cent, three major hotels in Niagara Falls, Ontario, went into receivership, and the city faced huge property tax arrears from other hotel and motel owners. On average tourists spent about six dollars on their Niagara Falls visits, usually lunch at a fast-food franchise.[11]

For Niagara residents, the first and second greatest disappointments might be the failure of tourism to provide a consistent and decent standard of living. Life in the gigantic department store has its moments, to be sure. But it is a life that tends to be lived at two speeds and two speeds only: feast (congested, exhausting, and lucrative) or famine (quiet, eerily still, and broke). As a veteran Niagara Falls, Ontario, reporter exclaimed when I told him I wanted to interview him about the history of the tourist industry, "The tourist industry! They stole our town away from us." This is exactly the downside of tourism that rarely gets any public airing, at Niagara Falls or elsewhere. For many locals, the boom and bust tourist economy offers little more than alienation and annoyance. Optimistic chamber of commerce slogans aside, tourism is *not* everybody's business. Indeed, at Niagara Falls tourism is increasingly big, corporate business. Multinational chains dominate Niagara's hotel and motel industry, and the mom-and-pop restaurant trade has also been eclipsed by franchise operations.

The slow decline of Niagara Falls since the 1960s is exactly the opposite of what's been happening to its next-door neighbour, Niagara-on-the-Lake. The Niagara Parks Commission and local historical societies have been active since the 1920s, but especially since the 1960s, refurbishing forts, old buildings, burial grounds, and historical markers at Niagara-on-the-Lake, quite consciously

How *honeymoons* have changed!

Betty and Bill are honeymooning in far-off Hawaii . . . even though Bill has only a two-week vacation. Flying made it possible—the Islands are now less than a day from either coast. Betty's mother says, "In my time, we couldn't even consider travelling so far!"

Helen and Frank are easterners. They longed to see "foreign" lands—but on a budget. Flying made it possible! They're visiting Spanish-speaking Puerto Rico, Cuba, the Dominican Republic . . . French-speaking Haiti . . . British Jamaica! The West Indies are popular the year round.

Joan and Bob have just returned from a honeymoon in Europe. They've been away only fourteen days . . . but it was plenty of time to visit England, France, Switzerland, Italy and Portugal. Flying made it possible!

Let low-cost help in planning your next trip, ask one of the airlines listed below. Or consult a travel agent—see "Travel Bureaus" in your classified phone book.

WORLD'S MOST MODERN AIRPLANE—Today, 75% of Douglas production is military. But new DC-6's are being built for the airlines, too. The big Douglas DC-6, most modern civilian airplane in the skies today, has carried over 20 million people on these leading airlines of the world!

Twice as many people fly

DOUGLAS
as all other airplanes combined

Niagara got some serious competition for tourists after the Second World War. This ad for Douglas Aircraft, which ran in *Life* magazine in 1952, encourages North American honeymooners to look further afield for adventure.

shaping the tourist gaze around education and history rather than amusement. This work helped to distinguish the place from what historian Cecilia Morgan calls its "disreputable and better-known older sibling," Niagara Falls.[12] The success of the Shaw Festival, a summer theatre featuring the works of George Bernard Shaw, begun in 1962 at Niagara-on-the-Lake, has also provided an upscale contrast to the Falls. The difference between the two towns, ten miles apart, remains jarring and is a testament to the continued significance of class to the tourist gaze.

The 1968 Chamber of Commerce survey revealed one surprising statistic: only 3 per cent of those surveyed were honeymooners. The decline of the Niagara honeymoon had been predicted for decades, but by the late 1960s it seemed the naysayers were correct. While the honeymoon trade experiences the same economic cycles as the tourist trade generally, the industry has historically also been shaped by other forces, and after World War II competition was on the horizon. Niagara lost its exclusive cultural hold on the honeymoon during the 1960s and has never since regained it. As early as 1961, as jet travel and the expansion of the Pocono Mountains resort region in Pennsylvania drew newlyweds away from the Falls, journalists were beginning to ask, "Is the honeymoon over for Niagara Falls?" A U.S. marketing survey undertaken in 1970 placed Niagara fifth among honeymoon destinations, behind the Poconos, California, Florida, and New York City. Newlyweds of the 1980s and 1990s were even more likely to ignore Niagara, as honeymoon features in travel and wedding magazines extolled instead the pleasures of Europe, Caribbean islands, and the Florida Keys.

· A Toronto travel agent put it simply in 1990: "Nobody in their right mind would go to Niagara Falls for their entire honeymoon in this day and age."[13]

But changes in the public culture of heterosexuality have made the honeymoon itself, especially at such a conventional place as Niagara Falls, embarrassingly prosaic. Blushing brides and bungling grooms are, after all, a tad old-fashioned, which is why fantasy-themed hotel rooms and heart-shaped hot tubs—and other images lifted directly from modern soft-core pornography—have become standard honeymoon clichés. No longer is it expected that the honeymoon is the moment in which people must confront their sexual innocence, and instead honeymoon promoters now quite obviously peddle sex. As early as the 1960s Niagara-area motel owners were observing, "Greater casualness about sexual matters has freed brides from embarrassment." By the 1970s and 1980s the joke was truly over. "They all live together already, you know," declared one Niagara woman, a forty-year veteran of the hotel industry.[14]

Changes in marriage patterns and sexual practices have not spelled the end of the honeymoon itself. Image and practice do not always match. After all, even through premarital sex rates were soaring in the 1950s, the honeymoon retained its cultural importance as a rite of sexual passage. Today such paradoxes are everywhere: the divorce rate is increasing, but so too is the amount of money people spend on weddings.[15] According to wedding magazine surveys, the vast majority—98 per cent—of today's newlyweds still take honeymoons.[16] There are travel agencies, magazines, trade shows, and web sites devoted exclusively to honeymoons, yet almost 90 per cent of single adults are sexually active.[17]

Compared to the flood of honeymoon-themed movies and journalism in the 1940s and 1950s, the honeymoon has all but disappeared from popular culture. Travel writing about Niagara scarcely mentions the honeymoon anymore, and newspaper wedding reports (which are themselves increasingly perfunctory) rarely identify Niagara Falls as the destination of newlyweds. Film or television plots rarely feature honeymoon narratives—except for parodies such as Australian Craig Rosenberg's 1996 film *Hotel de Love*, a gentle satire of heterosexual true romance set at a honeymoon hotel near Australia's "Niagara Smalls."

Yet to forecast the end of either the Niagara tourist industry or the honeymoon would be foolish. Days after I first drafted this conclusion, declaring confidently that newspapers "never" report Niagara as the honeymoon destination of today's newlyweds, a friend sent me a wedding announcement from a Nova Scotia newspaper, which informed me that "After a honeymoon in Niagara Falls, Danna and Al will reside in Poulamon, Richmond County."[18] The place has managed to reinvent itself successfully for two centuries; there is no reason to think that it won't survive a third.

And there are some intriguing possibilities. Hoping to stem the economic decline of the 1970s and 1980s, the Niagara Parks Commission hired leading Canadian architect Raymond Moriyama to come up with a vision for Niagara tourism for the next century. Moriyama's report, published in 1988, was a valiant attempt to win the middle class back to the Falls. He argued strongly that tourism at the Falls must "meet the needs of the well-educated and the prosperous," and he urged the NPC to try to attract yuppie tourists by developing green spaces, galleries, and museums.[19]

As it turned out, this vision of Niagara tourism was shelved in favour of that new panacea for economic development, a casino. Casino Niagara in Niagara Falls, Ontario, attracted ten million visitors in 1997, its first year of operation, and practically wiped out the ailing tourist industry across the river, where state laws prohibit gambling. The huge, glitzy casino—so noisy you can barely hear the sound of Frederick Olmsted turning in his grave—provides yet another stark contrast between nature and culture. It sits jarringly close to Queen Victoria Park, which remains an emblem of State High Culture and Tradition, the mirror image of the frenzy of free enterprise that reigns in the casino. It remains to be seen whether gambling contributes to or inhibits the growth of tourism. So far, Marilyn—the name of the bar at the casino—seems to be outdrawing Queen Victoria, and some local tourist boosters believe that gambling and tourism are contradictory, because gamblers tend to stay in the casino. It certainly looks as though the next version of Niagara Falls will owe more to Las Vegas than to Disneyland.

Or maybe something even more peculiar will happen. There is no reference to honeymooners in the 150 pages of Raymond Moriyama's report on Niagara's next century. They have been replaced by what Moriyama called "the new singles," which reads to me, at least in part, as a thinly disguised euphemism for gays and lesbians. "The new singles" are people who have no children, plenty of disposable income, and a hankering for nightlife and good restaurants. They obviously make really great tourists. Perhaps we have arrived where we began. Instead of building a tourist industry on heterosexuality alone, maybe in the next century Niagara Falls will also see the flourishing of a gay and lesbian tourism. The symmetry would be kind of sweet. At Niagara Falls, anything is possible.

Notes

Publication Abbreviations

NFER: *Niagara Falls Evening Review*, Niagara Falls, Ont.

NRF: *Niagara Falls Review*, Niagara Falls, Ont.

NFG: *Niagara Falls Gazette*, Niagara Falls, N.Y.

NPC: Niagara Parks Commission, Niagara Falls, Ont.

PAO: Provincial Archives of Ontario, Toronto.

1 Introduction: Practising Heterosexuality at Niagara Falls

1 John Urry, *The Tourist Gaze: Leisure and Travel in Contemporary Societies* (London: Sage, 1990), pp.1-4.

2 Patrick McGreevy, *Imagining Niagara: The Making and Meaning of Niagara Falls* (Amherst: University of Massachusetts Press, 1994); Patricia Jasen, *Wild Things: Nature, Culture and Tourism in Ontario, 1790-1914* (Toronto: University of Toronto Press, 1995); William Irwin, *The New Niagara: Tourism, Technology and the Landscape of Niagara Falls, 1776-1917* (University Park: Pennsylvania State University Press, 1996); and Elizabeth McKinsey, *Niagara Falls: Icon of the American Sublime* (Cambridge: Cambridge University Press, 1985). In Canada Pierre Berton has written a general history of the Falls, and H.V. Nelles studied the history of hydro development on the Canadian side. Pierre Berton, *Niagara* (Toronto: McClelland and Stewart, 1992); H.V. Nelles, *The Politics of Development* (Toronto: Macmillan, 1974). Ernest Sternberg, in "The Iconography of the Tourism Experience," *Annals of Tourism Research*, vol.24, no.4 (1997), pp.951-69, offers an analysis of contemporary tourism at the Falls.

3   Victoria de Grazia, "Introduction," in *The Sex of Things: Gender and Consumption in Historical Perspective*, ed. Victoria de Grazia with Ellen Furlough (Berkeley: University of California Press, 1996), p.21.

4   *Food for Thought*, June 1954.

5   Patricia Williams, *The Alchemy of Race and Rights* (Cambridge, Mass.: Harvard University Press, 1991), p.148.

6   This phrase has become the popular paraphrase of Wilde's remarks about Niagara, which he visited in 1882. The comment that Wilde actually offered to the British press on his return to England was reportedly: "Every American bride is taken there, and the sight of the stupendous waterfall must be one of the earliest, if not the keenest, disappointments in American married life." Lloyd Lewis and Henry Justin Smith, *Oscar Wilde Discovers America* (New York: Harcourt, Brace, 1936; reprinted New York: Benjamin Blom, 1967), p.163.

7   She, more charitably than most, agreed with the rest of her party that no one would speak of their first impressions for twenty-four hours. When she did speak, she loved it. Harriet Martineau, *Retrospect of Western Travel*, vol. 1 (London: Launders and Otley, 1838), p.96.

8   Frances E. Monck, *My Canadian Leaves: An Account of a Visit to Canada in 1864-1865* (London: Richard Bentley, 1891), p.161.

9   Ian Ousby, *The Englishman's England: Taste, Travel and the Rise of Tourism* (Cambridge: Cambridge University Press, 1990), p.133.

10 Quoted in Richard Ellmann, *Oscar Wilde* (London: Hamilton, 1987), pp.226, 185.

11 Colleen Ballerino Cohen, "Marketing Paradise, Making Nation," David Leheny, "A Political Economy of Asian Sex Tourism," and Deborah Pruitt, "For Love and Money: Romance Tourism in Jamaica," all in *Annals of Tourism Research*, vol.22, no.2 (1995); Cynthia Enloe, *Bananas, Beaches and Bases: Making Feminist Sense of International Politics* (Berkeley: University of California Press, 1990), pp.19-41; Haunani-Kay Trask, "Lovely Hula Lands: Corporate Tourism and the Prostitution of Hawaiian Culture," *Borderlines*, no.23 (Winter 1991/92), pp.22-29; and Polly Pattullo, *Last Resorts: The Cost of Tourism in the Caribbean* (London: Cassell, 1996).

12 Ellen Furlough, "Packaging Pleasures: Club Mediterranee and French Consumer Culture, 1950-1968," *French Historical Studies*, vol.18, no.1 (Spring 1993), pp.65-81; Robert Aldrich, *The Seduction of the Mediterranean: Writing, Art and Homosexual Fantasy* (New York: Routledge, 1993); Brighton Ourstory Project, *Daring Hearts: Lesbian and Gay Lives of the 1950s and 1960s* (Brighton, England: Queen Spark, 1992); Kevin Meethan, "Place, Image and Power: Brighton as a Resort," in *The Tourist Image: Myths and Mythmaking in Tourism*, ed. Tom Selwyn (Chichester, England: John Wiley, 1996), pp.179-96; Rob Shields, *Places on the Margin: Alternative Geographies of Modernity* (London:

Routledge, 1991), pp.73-116; Ester Newton, *Cherry Grove, Fire Island: Sixty Years in America's First Gay and Lesbian Town* (Boston: Beacon Press, 1993); and Ian McKay, *The Quest of the Folk: Antimodernism and Cultural Selection in Twentieth-Century Nova Scotia* (Montreal and Kingston: McGill-Queen's University Press, 1994), pp.251-64.

13 See, for example, Mary Louise Pratt, *Imperial Eyes: Travel Writing and Transculturation* (New York: Routledge, 1992).

14 Mary Louise Adams, *The Trouble with Normal: Postwar Youth and the Making of Heterosexuality* (Toronto: University of Toronto Press, 1997); Jonathan Katz, *The Invention of Heterosexuality* (New York: Dutton, 1995).

15 William Dean Howells, *Their Wedding Journey* (Boston: Houghton Mifflin, 1871), p.2.

16 Urry, *Tourist Gaze*, p.2. See also George Robertson, Melinda Mash, Lisa Tickner, Jon Bird, Barry Curtis, and Tim Putnam, eds., *Travellers' Tales: Narratives of Home and Displacement* (London: Routledge, 1994).

17 John Sears, *Sacred Places: American Tourist Attractions in the Nineteenth Century* (New York: Oxford University Press, 1989), pp.11, 8. See also David Nasaw, *Going Out: The Rise and Fall of Public Amusements* (New York: Basic Books, 1993); and John Jackle, *The Tourist: Travel in Twentieth Century North America* (Lincoln: University of Nebraska Press, 1979).

18 Louis Turner and John Ash, *The Golden Hordes: International Tourism and the Pleasure Periphery* (London: Constable, 1975).

19 Pattullo, *Last Resorts*. See also Larry Krotz, *Tourists: How Our Fastest Growing Industry Is Changing the World* (London: Faber, 1997).

20 Christopher Hope, *Darkest England* (London: Macmillan, 1996), p.162.

21 Daniel J. Boorstin, *The Image: A Guide to Pseudo-Events in America* (New York: Harper and Row, 1961), p.99.

22 Historians who have adopted this approach to popular culture (and have influenced my work considerably) include John F. Kasson, *Amusing the Million: Coney Island at the Turn of the Century* (New York: Hill and Wang, 1978); The Project on Disney, *Inside the Mouse: Work and Play at Disney World* (London: Rivers Oram, 1995); Kathy Peiss, *Hope in a Jar: The Making of America's Beauty Culture* (New York: Metropolitan, 1998); and Keith Walden, *Becoming Modern in Toronto: The Industrial Exhibition and the Shaping of Late Victorian Culture* (Toronto: University of Toronto Press, 1997).

23 Tina Loo, "Tonto's Due: Law, Culture and Colonization in British Columbia," in *Making Western Canada*, ed. Catherine Cavanaugh and Jeremy Mouat (Toronto: Garamond Press, 1996), p.63.

24 Martin Amis, "St. Lucia," in *Visiting Mrs Nabokov and Other Excursions* (London: 1994), quoted in Pattullo, *Last Resorts*, p.83. Another powerful indictment of the impact of tourism in the Caribbean is Jamaica Kincaid, *A Small Place* (London: Virago, 1988).

2 "The Pleasure Is Exquisite but Violent": The Imaginary Geography of the Nineteenth Century

1 Ellen Rothman, *Hands and Hearts: A History of Courtship in America* (New York: Basic Books, 1984) p.175.

2 Stephen Kern, *The Culture of Love: Victorians to Moderns* (Cambridge, Mass.: Harvard University Press, 1992), p.326.

3 Lawrence Stone, *The Family, Sex and Marriage in England, 1500-1800* (Harmondsworth, England: Penguin, 1977), p.223. See also John Gillis, *For Better or Worse: British Marriages, 1600 to Present* (New York: Oxford University Press, 1985), p.138.

4 Peter Stallybrass and Allon White, "Bourgeois Hysteria and the Carnivalesque," in *The Cultural Studies Reader*, ed. Simon During (London: Routledge, 1993), p.288.

5 *Christian Guardian*, Aug. 4, 1886; B.G. Jefferis and J.L. Nichols, *Searchlights on Health* (Toronto: J.L. Nichols, 1900), p.200; Henri Martin, quoted in Andrée Levesque, *Making and Breaking the Rules: Women in Quebec, 1919-1939* (Toronto: McClelland and Stewart, 1994), p.28.

6 Sylvanus Stall, *What a Young Husband Ought to Know* (Philadelphia: Vir, 1897), pp.228-29. See also O.S. Fowler, *Creative and Sexual Science* (n.p., 1875), p.529, who warns that the wedding tour is "especially fatiguing and injurious to the bride; whose commencement of her specific marriage relations must needs all her strength"; and Jefferis and Nichols, *Searchlights*, p.202, who also warn that the bride "is nervous, timid, and exhausted by the duties of preparation for the wedding."

7 George Napheys, *The Physical Life of a Woman: Advice to the Maiden, Wife and Mother* (Toronto: Rose-Belford, 1880), pp.69-70.

8 Jefferis and Nichols, *Searchlights*, p.200.

9 An Old Physician, *The Physiogy of Marriage* (Boston: John Jewett, 1856), p.122; Jefferis and Nichols, *Searchlights*, pp.202, 204. See also Michael Gordon, "The Ideal Husband as Depicted in the Nineteenth Century Marriage Manual," *The Family Coordinator*, July 1969, pp.226-31.

10 Jean Brassey, *My Honeymoon Trip* (New York: F. Berkley, 1897), p.5.

11 *Mysteries of Venus: A Nuptial Interlude* (London: Mary Wilson, 1882), no page numbers; *First Three Nights of Married Life* (Paris: Vie de Boheme, 1900), p.2.

12 *Letters from Laura and Eveline* (London: privately published, 1883).

13 Stall, *What a Young Husband*, p.231.

14 Quoted in Eva-Marie Kroller, *Canadian Travellers in Europe 1951-1900* (Vancouver: University of British Columbia Press, 1987), p.66.

15 Mary Wood-Allen *What a Young Woman Ought to Know* (Philadelphia: Vir Publishing, 1928), p.270.

16 Fowler, *Creative and Sexual Science*, p.530. On the social benefits of nature tourism in this era, see Alexander Wilson, *The Culture of Nature: North American Landscape from Disney to the Exxon Valdez* (Toronto: Between the Lines, 1991); and Jasen, *Wild Things*. On perceptions of the rural and urban life in Western culture, see Raymond Williams's classic study *The Country and the City* (London: Chatto and Windus, 1973).

17 Howells, *Their Wedding Journey*, p.2.

18 Arthur White, *Palaces of the People: A Social History of Commercial Hospitality* (New York: Taplinger, 1970), p.141.

19 *American Magazine*, vol.102 (July 1926), p.92; *Frank Leslie's Illustrated Newspaper* (New York), Oct. 25, 1879; *Daily Graphic* (New York), July 23, 1878.

20 H. Perry Robinson, *Essence of Honeymoon* (London: William Heinemann, 1914), pp.5, 15.

21 Michel Foucault, "Of Other Spaces," *Diacritics: A Review of Contemporary Criticism*, vol.16 (Spring 1986), pp.24-25. My thanks to Eric Darier for passing on this reference.

22 McKinsey, *Niagara*, p.180. McKinsey includes all five verses.

23 Monck, *My Canadian Leaves*, p.161; Captain William Butler, *The Great Lone Land* (London: Sampson, 1872), p.25.

24 Urry, *Tourist Gaze*, pp.16-37; Wilson, *Culture of Nature*, pp.22-33; Jasen, *Wild Things*, pp.105-32.

25 Shields, *Places on the Margin*, pp.11, 29.

26 James Buzard, *The Beaten Track* (London: Oxford University Press, 1993); I.J. Saczkowski, "History of Tourist Accommodation at Niagara Falls," unpublished paper, Niagara Falls Public Library, 1985; Kiwanis Club, *Niagara Falls, Canada: A History of the City and the World Famous Beauty Spot* (Niagara Falls, Ont.: Kiwanis Club, 1967), pp.48-54.

27 Dona Brown, *Inventing New England: Regional Tourism in the Nineteenth Century* (Washington, D.C.: Smithsonian Institute Press, 1995), pp.15-40.

28 Isabella Bird, *The Englishwoman in America* (London, 1856; reprinted, Toronto: University of Toronto Press, 1966), p.217; *Niagara Falls: Nature's Grandest Wonder* (Buffalo, N.Y.: Matthews and Northrup, n.d., c.1890), p.22.

29 Recent writers have treated Taylor with more respect. See Carolyn Fish, "Taking the Plunge: A Gendered Analysis of the Life of Anna Edson Taylor," unpublished paper, Queen's University, Kingston, Ont., 1997. An inventive fictional account of Taylor's feat can be found in Suzette Mayr, *The Widows* (Edmonton: NeWest Publishers, 1998).

30 McKinsey, *Niagara*, p.2. On Niagara in Canadian photography and film, see Patricia Pierce, ed., *Canada: The Missing Years* (Don Mills, Ont.: Stoddart, 1985) p.29; and Peter Morris, *Embattled Shadows: A History of Canadian Cinema, 1895-1939* (Montreal and Kingston: McGill-Queen's University Press, 1992), pp.8-9.

31 The roster of nineteenth-century celebrity visitors is impressive, and includes: Charles Dickens, Frances Trollope, Anthony Trollope, Abraham Lincoln, Rupert Brook, Oscar Wilde, Nathaniel Hawthorne, Mark Twain, Anna Jameson, Daniel Webster, Harriet Martineau, Margaret Fuller, H.G. Wells, Sarah Bernhardt, Jenny Lind, Henry James, Harriet Beecher Stowe, William Morris, and Walt Whitman.

32 Bird, *Englishwoman in America*, p.216; William Morris of Sindon, *Letters Sent Home, Out, and Home Again* (privately published, 1874), p.220; Butler, *Great Lone Land*, p.25; Henry Jones, *Portraits of Plenty* (Boston: Houghton Mifflin, 1883), p.370; Thursty McQuill, *The Hudson River by Daylight* (n.p., 1875), p.97. The concept of "canonical sites" is from William Stowe, *Going Abroad: European Travel in Nineteenth-Century American Culture* (Princeton, N.J.: Princeton University Press, 1994), p.18.

33 Nicholas Woods, *The Prince of Wales in Canada and the United States* (London: Bradbury, 1861), quoted in Charles Mason Dow, *Anthology and Bibliography of Niagara Falls*, vol.1 (Albany, N.Y.: J.B. Lyon, 1921), p.273.

34 Stowe, *Going Abroad*, p.13.

35 McKinsey, *Niagara*, p.101.

36 William Howells, "Niagara First and Last," in William Howells et al., eds., *The Niagara Book: A Complete Souvenir of Niagara Falls* (Buffalo, N.Y.: Underhill and Sons, 1893), p.9; George Menzies, *Album of the Table Rock*, 1846; *A Souvenir of Niagara Falls* (Buffalo, N.Y.: Sage, 1864), p.1.

37 Agnes Machar, *Down the River to the Sea* (New York: Home Book Co., 1894), p.25. A few British visitors stated their preference for the Canadian side, but this was usually because of a perceived different social climate. British visitor William Howard Russell, for example, an abolitionist who hated the United States, found Niagara Falls, New York, "a lanky pretentious town, with big hotels, shops of Indian curiosities, and all the meagre forms of the bazaar life reduced to a minimum of attractiveness which destroy the comfort of a traveller." Russell, *My Diary, North and South* (New York: Harper, 1863), p.237.

That description was echoed in many other travellers' accounts of *both* villages. A U.S. contributor to William Howells's *The Niagara Book* also commented on the different "temperaments" of the two countries evident in the warning signs at the waterfalls. "Canadians," wrote Frederic Almy, "are less considerate of the tender feelings of the dear public than with us. Mark the autocratic barbarity of the British declaration that persons throwing stones over the bank will be prosecuted according to law, as compared with the exquisite delicacy of the placards on Goat Island: 'Do Not Venture in Dangerous Places,' . . . 'Stones Thrown Over the Bank May Fall Upon People Below.' On Goat Island, you always feel as if your mother were with you." Almy, "What to See at Niagara Falls," in Howells, *Niagara Book*, pp.41-42.

38 Menzies, *Album of the Table Rock*; *Table Rock Album and Sketches of the Falls* (Buffalo, N.Y.: Thomas and Lathrop, 1856); John Russell, ed., *Memoirs, Journal and Correspondence of Thomas Moore* (London, 1853), quoted in Ralph Greenhill and Thomas Mahoney, *Niagara* (Toronto: University of Toronto Press, 1969), p.4.

39 "The Mighty Niagara of Souls," *War Cry*, Nov. 9, 1895, quoted in Mariana Valverde, *The Age of Light, Soap and Water: Moral Reform in English Canada* (Toronto: McClelland and Stewart, 1991), p.37.

40 McKinsey, *Niagara*, pp.11, 39.

41 *Niagara Falls Guide, with Full instructions to Direct the Traveller* (Buffalo, N.Y.: J. Faxon, 1850), p.32; George Holley, *Niagara: Its History, Geology, Incidents and Poetry* (Toronto: Hunter Rose, 1872), p.161.

42 A.R.C. Grant and Caroline Combe, *Lord Rosebery's North American Journal—1873* (London: Sedgewick and Jackson, 1967), p.60.

43 Bird, *Englishwoman in America*, p.224.

44 George Curtis, *Lotus Eating—A Summer Book* (New York: Harpers, 1852), reprinted in Dow, *Anthology and Bibliography of Niagara Falls*, p.254. See also Daniel Pidgeon, *An Engineer's Holiday* (London, 1882), quoted in Dow, *Anthology and Bibliography of Niagara Falls*, p.338; Mrs. S.D. Morse, *Greater Niagara* (Niagara Falls, N.Y.: Gazette Printing, 1896), p.12; J. Murray Jordan, *Niagara in Summer and Winter* (Philadelphia, 1904); and Peter Conrad, *Imagining America* (New York: Oxford University Press, 1980), p.16.

45 Jones, *Portraits of Plenty*, p.365; *The Niagara Parks Commission Welcomes You* (n.d., c.1950).

46 George Borrett, "Letters from Canada and the U.S." (London, 1865), in Dow, *Anthology and Bibliography of Niagara Falls*, p.309; Holley, *Niagara*, p.163; Canada Steamship Lines, *Romantic Niagara*, 1940; Niagara Parks Commission, *Niagara Welcomes You* (1920).

47 Menzies, *Album of Table Rock*, p.19; Curtis, quoted in Dow, *Anthology and Bibliography of Niagara Falls*, p.259; Niagara Parks Commission, *Niagara Welcomes You* (1920); Jordan, *Niagara in Summer and Winter*; H.T. Allen, *Tunis Illustrated Guide to Niagara Falls* (Niagara Falls, N.Y.: Gazette Printing, 1877), p.46; Mary McDowell Hardy, *Between Two Oceans* (London: 1884), quoted in Dow, *Anthology and Bibliography of Niagara Falls*, p.342.

48 William Russell, quoted in Dow, *Anthology and Bibliography of Niagara Falls*, p.318; Canada Steamship Lines, *Niagara to the Sea*, 1915. An insightful analysis of the nineteenth-century "tourist Indian" can be found in Daniel Francis, *The Imaginary Indian: The Image of the Indian in Canadian Culture* (Vancouver: Arsenal Pulp Press, 1992).

49 This passage is compiled from Curtis, *Lotus Eaters*, J. Benwell, *An Englishman's Travels in America* (London, 1853), Pidgeon, *Engineer's Holiday*, Edwin Arnold, *Seas and Lands* (New York: 1891): all in Dow, *Anthology and Bibliography of Niagara Falls*, pp.257, 263, 339, 345. Also: A.M. Ferree, *The Falls of Niagara and Scenes around Them* (New York: A.S. Barnes, 1876), p.23; Howells, *Niagara Book*, pp.130, 15; *The Falls of Niagara Depicted by Pen and Camera* (Chicago: Knight and Leonard, 1893); R.R. Bell, *Diary of a Canadian Tour* (Coatbridge, England: Alex Pettigrew, 1927), p.32; and *Niagara Parks Commission Welcomes You* (c.1950).

50 Holley, *Niagara*, p.1.

51 Myron Pritchard, ed., *Poetry of Niagara* (Boston: Lothrop Publishing Company, 1901).

52 Machar, *Down the River*, pp.12-15, 263.

53 Howells, *Their Wedding Journey*, p.103.

54 Woods, *"Prince of Wales,"* in Dow, *Anthology and Bibliography of Niagara Falls*, p.271; F.H. Johnson, *Every Man His Own Guide at Niagara Falls* (Rochester, N.Y.: Dewey, 1852), p.37. Visitors in the mid-nineteenth and late nineteenth century were consumed by the notion that the Falls made people want to kill themselves, but earlier visitors believed the reverse. Travellers in the 1830s were of the opinion that "the agitation of the surrounding air produced by the tremendous Falls, combines with the elevation and dryness of the soil" to produce "the most healthful [place] on the continent of North America." As proof of this, many noted that the "magic neighbourhoods" surrounding the Falls had remained untouched by the cholera epidemics of the 1830s. William Barham, *Descriptions of Niagara* (self-published, 1850); Burke, *Illustrated Guide*, 1856; Menzies, *Album of the Table Rock*. The association of water with curative powers continued through the nineteenth century in other places in Canada; a children's hospital was built on Toronto Island in the 1880s for precisely these reasons. See Sally Gibson, *More than an Island* (Toronto: Irwin, 1984) p.93.

55 Burke, *Illustrated Guide*, p.62; Charles Marshall, *The Canadian Dominion* (London: 1871), in Dow, *Anthology and Bibliography of Niagara Falls*, p.331; Ferree, *Falls of Niagara*, p.72; *Chisholm's Complete Guide to the Grand Cataract* (Portland, Ore.: Chisholm Brothers, 1892), p.14.

56 McGreevy, *Imagining Niagara*, pp.41-70.

57 *Chisholm's Complete Guide*, p.12.

58 *Illustrated Guide to Niagara Falls* (Chicago: Rand McNally, 1897), p.87.

59 *Complete Illustrated Guide to Niagara Falls and Vicinity* (Niagara Falls, N.Y.: Gazette Publishing, c.1880), p.31; Bird, *Englishwoman in America*, p.225.

60 John Edbauer, *New Guide and Key to Niagara Falls, Toronto and Buffalo* (Buffalo, N.Y.: Volksfreund, 1925), p.30.

61 Ernest Jones, *Essays in Applied Psycho-Analysis* (London: The International Psycho-Analytical Press, 1923), p.16.

62 The Stantons are turned into honeymooners first by Lloyd Graham, in *Niagara Country* (New York: Duell Sloan and Pearce, 1949), p.182. See also Raymond Yates, *A Picture History of Niagara* (Buffalo, N.Y.: Henry Stewart, 1953), p.49, and Yates, *The Niagara Story* (Buffalo, N.Y.: Henry Stewart, 1959), p.11; Arnold McAdory, *Niagara's Story of Customs* (self-published, Niagara Falls, Ont., 1960), p.55; Mike Michaelson, "Niagara's Winter Ice Show," *Today's Health*, January 1969, p.59; and Gordon Donaldson, *Niagara! The Eternal Circus* (Toronto: Doubleday, 1979), p.234. See also *Niagara Falls Review* (Niagara Falls, Ont.) (hereafter cited as NFR), Feb.4, 1948, Feb.5, 1964.

63 Frederic Almy, "What to See at Niagara," in Howells, *Niagara Book*, p.32.

64 Borrett, *Letters from Canada and the U.S.*, in Dow, *Anthology and Bibliography of Niagara Falls*, p.311; Cousin George, *Sketches of Niagara Falls and River* (Buffalo, N.Y.: Peck, 1846), p.86; Robert White, *The New Northwest* (Boston: n.p., 1872), p.364.

65 Bird, *Englishwoman in America*, p.232; Conrad, *Imagining America*, p.17.

66 Borrett, *Letters from Canada and the U.S.*, quoted in Dow, *Anthology and Bibliography of Niagara Falls*, p.313.

67 Bird, *Englishwoman in America*, p.232; White, *New Northwest*, p.362.

68 Almy, "What to See at Niagara," p.37.

69 *The Complete Illustrated Guide to Niagara Falls* (Niagara Falls, N.Y.: Gazette, c.1880), p.33; Thomas Hughes, *Vacation Rambles* (London: Macmillan, 1895), p.147.

70 John Tyndal, "Niagara Falls," *Eclectic Magazine of Foreign Literature, Science and Art*, vol.18, no.1 (July 1873), p.28.

71 Edward Roper, *By Track and Train through Canada* (London: Allen, 1891), p.418.

72 The ion story crops up a lot: see McKinsey, *Niagara*, p.183; Donaldson, *Niagara!*, p.226; Dwight Whalen, *Lover's Guide to Niagara Falls* (Niagara Falls, Ont.: Horseshoe Press, 1991); and Conrad, *Imagining America*, p.25.

3 Local Colour in "the Contact Zone": The Spectacle of Race

1 Dean McCannell, *The Tourist: A New Theory of the Leisure Class* (New York: Schocken, 1976), pp.84, 101.

2 David Brown, "Genuine Fakes," in *Tourist Image*, ed. Selwyn, pp.33-34. Brown cites, by way of example, a tree stump in Finland. Once a highly popular tourist site, the tree stump is presented as the place where Lenin sat awaiting the call to return to Russia for the 1917 revolution.

3 Urry, *Tourist Gaze*, p.11. See also Chris Rojek, *Ways of Escape: Modern Transformations in Leisure and Travel* (London: Macmillan, 1993), p.133; and Ousby, *Englishman's England*.

4 Allan MacEachern, "No Island Is an Island: A History of Tourism on PEI, 1870-1939," M.A. thesis, Queen's University, Kingston, Ont., 1991.

5 Roy Rosenzweig and Elizabeth Blackmar, *The Park and the People: A History of Central Park* (Ithaca, N.Y.: Cornell University Press, 1992), p.127. See also John F. Kasson, *Amusing the Million: Coney Island at the Turn of the Century* (New York: Hill and Wang, 1978), pp.11-17.

6 Butler, *Great Lone Land*, p.25.

7 Valene Smith, ed., *Hosts and Guests: The Anthropology of Tourism*, 2nd ed. (Philadelphia: University of Pennsylvania Press, 1989); "Preface," in *International Tourism: Identity and Change*, ed. Marie-Francoise Lanfant, John B. Allcock, and Edward M. Bruner (London: Sage, 1995), p.viii. Interesting contemporary studies of tourist industry employment include Philip Crang, "Performing the Tourist Product," in *Touring Cultures: Transformations of Travel and Theory*, ed. Chris Rojek and John Urry (London: Routledge, 1997), pp.137-54; and Project on Disney, *Inside the Mouse*.

8 Linda K. Richter, "Gender and Class—Neglected Variables in Tourism Research," in *Change in Tourism: People, Places, Processes*, ed. Richard Butler and Douglas Pearce (London: Routledge, 1995), p.74; and Krotz, *Tourists*, pp.10-11.

9 Graham Dann, "The People of Tourist Brochures," in *Tourist Image*, ed. Selwyn, pp.61-81. In only 10 per cent of international tourist advertising are hosts and guests depicted as interacting with each other; usually guests are either gazing or being served.

10 Pratt, *Imperial Eyes*, p.5.

11 Dennison Nash, "Tourism as a Form of Imperialism," in *Hosts and Guests*, ed. Smith, pp.420-45.

12 See, for example, Kay Anderson, *Vancouver's Chinatown: Racial Discourse in Canada, 1875-1980* (Montreal and Kingston: McGill-Queen's University Press, 1991), pp.211-44: Barbara Buntman, "Bushman Images in South African Tourist Advertising: The Case of Kagga Kamma," in *Miscast*, ed. Pippa Skotnes (Cape Town: University of Capetown Press, 1996), pp.271-79; Furlough, "Packaging Pleasures," pp.65-81; Francis, *Imaginary Indian*; Jasen, *Wild Things*; Keith Hollingshead, "White Gaze, 'Red' People—Shadow Visions: The Disidentification of 'Indians' in Cultural Tourism," *Leisure Studies*, vol.11 (1992), pp.43-64; McKay, *Quest of the Folk*; Catherine Palmer, "Tourism and Colonialism: The Experience of the Bahamas," *Annals of Tourism Research*, vol.21, no.4 (1994), pp.792-811; Ruth B. Phillips, "Consuming Identities: Curiosity, Souvenir and Images of Indianness in Nineteenth-Century Canada," David Dunton Lecture, Carleton Univer-

sity, Ottawa, 1991; Ciraj Rassool and Leslie Witz, "South Africa: A World in One Country: Moments in International Tourist Encounters with Wildlife, the Primitive and the Modern," *Cahiers d'Etudes Africaines*, vol.143, 36-3 (1996), pp.335-71; Frank Fonda Taylor, *To Hell with Paradise: A History of the Jamaican Tourist Industry* (Pittsburgh: University of Pittsburgh Press, 1993); and Pierre L. Van Den Berghe, *The Quest for the Other: Ethnic Tourism in San Cristobel, Mexico* (Seattle: University of Washington Press, 1994).

13 James Clifford, *Routes: Travel and Translation in the Late Twentieth Century* (Cambridge, Mass.: Harvard University Press, 1997), p.34.

14 Pratt, *Imperial Eyes*, pp.6-7.

15 See, for example, Annie E. Coombes, *Reinventing Africa: Museums, Material Culture and Popular Imagination in Late Victorian and Edwardian England* (New Haven, Conn.: Yale University Press, 1994); Anne McClintock, *Imperial Leather: Race, Gender and Sexuality in the Colonial Contest* (New York: Routledge, 1994); Robert W. Rydell, *World of Fairs: The Century-of-Progress Expositions* (Chicago: University of Chicago Press, 1993); Catherine A. Lutz and Jane L. Collins, *Reading National Geographic* (Chicago: University of Chicago Press, 1993); R.G. Moyles and Douglas Owram, *Imperial Dreams and Colonial Realities: British Views of Canada, 1880-1914* (Toronto: University of Toronto Press, 1988); Richard Phillips, *Mapping Men and Empire: A Geography of Adventure* (London: Routledge, 1997); June Namais, *White Captives: Gender and Ethnicity on the American Frontier* (Chapel Hill: University of North Carolina Press, 1993); and Janet Davis, "Spectacles of South Asia at the American Circus, 1890-1940," *Visual Anthropology*, vol.6 (1993), pp.121-38.

16 Mariana Torgovnick, *Gone Primitive: Savage Intellects, Modern Lives* (Chicago: University of Chicago Press, 1990), p.11.

17 Influential analyses of travel writing include Catherine Hall, "Going A-trolloping: Imperial Man Travels the Empire," in *Gender and Imperialism*, ed. Clare Midgley (Manchester, England: Manchester University Press, 1998); David Spurr, *The Rhetoric of Empire: Colonial Discourse in Journalism, Travel Writing and Imperial Administration* (Durham, N.C.: Duke University Press, 1993); Sara Mills, *Discourses of Difference: An Analysis of Women's Travel Writing and Colonialism* (London: Routledge, 1991); Billie Melman, *Women's Orients: English Women and the Middle East, 1718-1918* (London: Macmillan, 1992); Shirley Foster, *Across New Worlds: Nineteenth Century Women Travellers and Their Writings* (New York: Harvester, 1990); and Stowe, *Going Abroad*.

18 Jonathan Culler, "Semiotics of Tourism," *American Journal of Semiotics*, vol.1, no.1-2 (1981), pp.127-40; Carol Crawshaw and John Urry, "Tourism and the Photographic Eye," in *Touring Cultures*, ed. Rojek and Urry, pp.176-95.

19 Jasen, *Wild Things*; Bart Robinson, *Banff Springs: The Story of a Hotel* (Banff, Alta.: Summerthought Press, 1973), p.34; Francis, *Imaginary Indian*, pp.176-82.

20 *Handbook of Indians of Canada* (Ottawa: King's Printer, 1913), p.496; David Landy, "Tuscarora among the Iroquois," in *Handbook of North American Indians*, ed. Bruce Trigger, vol.15 (Washington: Smithsonian Institute, 1978), p.522.

21 Jasen, *Wild Things*, pp.42, 70. On how Europeans have represented Native culture in Canada, see Deborah Doxtator, *Fluffs and Feathers: An Exhibit on the Symbols of Indianness* (Brantford, Ont.: Woodland Cultural Centre, 1992).

22 Namais, *White Captives*, p.97.

23 McClintock, *Imperial Leather*, p.46.

24 Lady Duffus Hardy, *Through Cities and Prairie Lands* (London: Chapman and Hall, 1881), pp.26-27.

25 George Sala, *My Diary in America in the Midst of the War* (London: Tinseley Brothers, 1865), p.184; Jacques Offenbach, *America and the Americans* (London: William Reeves, 1875), p.74; William Howard Russell, *My Diary, North and South* (New York: Harper, 1863), p.137.

26 I am using the term "racial panic" in the same sense that Eve Sedgewick has used the term "homosexual panic," to emphasize the permeability of boundaries, a central feature of relations between observer and observed in the contact zone. See Eve Sedgewick, *Epistemology of the Closet* (Berkeley: University of California Press, 1990), pp.19-22.

27 Ida Pfeiffer, *A Lady's Second Journey round the World* (London: Longman Brown, 1855), p.244.

28 Landy, "Tuscarora among the Iroquois," pp.518-24; Clinton Rickard, *Fighting Tuscarora: The Autobiography of Chief Clinton Rickard* (Syracuse, N.Y.: Syracuse University Press, 1973), p.71.

29 Duncan McLeod, "Niagara Falls Was a Hell-Raising Town," *Maclean's*, Nov. 26, 1955; "Reminiscences of an Old Timer, from the Recollections of Colonel Sidney Barnett," *NFR*, Oct. 31, 1919. On the North American popularity of Wild West Shows, see Francis, *Imaginary Indian*, pp.87-96; and Richard Slotkin, "Buffalo Bill's 'Wild West' and the Mythologization of the American Empire," in *Cultures of United States Imperialism*, ed. Amy Kaplan and Donald Peace (Durham, N.C.: Duke University Press, 1993), pp.164-81.

30 *The Humbugs of Niagara Falls Exposed* (Niagara Falls, N.Y.: Suspension Bridge Company, 1884), p.2. See also George Seibel, *Ontario's Niagara Parks—One Hundred Years* (Niagara Falls, Ont.: Niagara Parks Commission, 1985), p.21.

31 Offenbach, *America and the Americans*, p.74; Edward Roper, *By Track and Trail: A Journey through Canada* (London: W.H. Allen, 1891), p.419; Karl Baedeker, *The United States* (1893; reprinted, New York: Da Capo Press, 1971), p.200.

32 Sala, *My Diary*, pp.184-85. In imagining the Indian man as a victim, Sala is himself conforming to a common convention among white writers. Pratt calls this the anti-conquest, when Europeans "secure their innocence in the same moment as they assert European hegemony." Similarly, David Spur calls this the strategy of idealization, which "makes use of the savage in order to expand the territory of the Western imagination, transforming the Other into yet one more term of Western culture's dialogue with itself." Pratt, *Imperial Eyes*, p.7; Spurr, *Rhetoric of Empire* p.128.

33 It is also an exchange with enduring cultural significance in North America. On the legacy of blacks as visual but voiceless icons, from anti-slavery images to Rodney King, see Houston A. Baker, "Scene . . . Not Heard," in *Reading Rodney King, Reading Urban Uprising*, ed. Robert Gooding-Williams (New York: Routledge, 1993), pp.38-48.

34 Rickard, *Fighting Tuscarora*, p.34.

35 *Niagara Falls Gazette* (Niagara Falls, N.Y.) (hereafter cited as NFG), Sept. 6, 1887; Moses Jackson, *To America and Back: A Holiday Run* (London: McQuordale, 1886), p.131.

36 Phillips, "Consuming Identities," p.20. See also Ruth Phillips, "Why Not Tourist Art? Significant Silences in Native American Museum Representations," in *After Colonialism: Imperial Histories and Postcolonial Displacements*, ed. Gyan Prakash (Princeton, N.J.: Princeton University Press, 1995), pp.98-125; and Jasen, *Wild Things*, p.81. For an account of recent campaigns by Canadian Native people to protect their craft production from non-Native mass producers, see Valda Blundell, "Aboriginal Empowerment and the Souvenir Trade in Canada," *Annals of Tourism Research*, vol.20 (1993), pp.64-87.

37 Francis, *Imaginary Indian*, p.23.

38 *Humbugs of Niagara*, p.7.

39 One of many versions of the origins of this story is Lt.-Col. Frederick C. Curry, "The Discovery of the Cave of the Winds," *Ontario Historical Society Papers and Records*, vol.27 (1946), pp.19-22.

40 Terry Goldie, *Fear and Temptation: The Image of the Indigene in Canadian, Australian and New Zealand Literature* (Montreal and Kingston: McGill-Queen's University Press, 1989), pp.71-72; McClintock, *Imperial Leather*, p.22. See also Spurr, *Rhetoric of Empire*, p.171.

41 NFR, Sept. 15, 1910, Sept. 17, 1928; NFG, June 21, 1956; Carl Biemiller, "Wish You Were Here," *Holiday*, June 1946.

42 Quoted in Alfred Runte, "Beyond the Spectacular: The Niagara Falls Preservation Campaign," *New York Historical Society Quarterly*, vol.57, no 1 (January 1973), p.34.

43 Bird, *Englishwoman in America*, p.235; William Ferguson, *America by River and Rail* (London: James Nisbet, 1856), p.445; Jones, *Portraits of Plenty*, p.366; W.S. Caine, M.P., *A Trip round the World in 1887-1888* (London: Routledge, 1888), p.28.

44 Amelia M. Murray, *Letters from the United States, Cuba and Canada* (New York: G.P. Putnam, 1856), p.109; *Table Rock Album and Sketches of the Falls* (Buffalo, N.Y.: Thomas and Lathrop, 1856), p.71; *Canadian Illustrated News*, Oct. 14, 1876.

45 James Carnegie Southesk, "Saskatchewan and the Rocky Mountains" (Edinburgh: Edmonton and Douglas, 1875), in *Anthology and Bibliography of Niagara Falls*, ed. Dow, p.268; Russell, *My Diary*, p.136; Morris of Sindon, *Letters Sent Home*, p.226; W.G. Marshall, *Through America* (London: Sampson, 1881), p.71; Moses Sweetser, *The Middle States: A Handbook for Travellers* (Boston: James R. Osgoode, 1874), p.177; Ferree, *The Falls of Niagara*, p.35.

46 F.H. Johnson, *Every Man His Own Guide at Niagara Falls* (Rochester, N.Y.: D.M. Dewey, 1852), p.1; *Guide to the Great Lakes and Niagara Falls* (Northern Transit Co., 1877); *Humbugs of Niagara Falls Exposed*.

47 *Outing and the Wheelman*, vol.5, no.6 (March 1885), p.458; J.B Harrison, *The Condition of Niagara Falls and the Measures Needed to Improve Them* (New York: University Press, 1882), p.61.

48 While visiting her parents in the south of England, Robyn Penrose, who works in the heart of the industrial north, "wondered whether it was by luck or cunning that the English bourgeoisie had kept the industrial revolution out of their favourite territory." David Lodge, *Nice Work* (London: Penguin, 1988), p.306.

49 A Fellow of the Royal Society of Literature, *Homeward Through America* (Chicago: P. Eustis, 1887), p.29.

50 I was reminded of this paradox during the 1996 Summer Olympics, which, at least in the Ontario media I was reading, took a major beating for their apparently unacceptable level of commercialism. How odd it seemed when—in a political climate in which the free market is being touted as a better system for everything from parks to prisons to health care—international sports competitions are suddenly in need of protection from the greed of speculators. And it was a particular kind of speculator that seemed to be inflaming commentators: journalists reserved most of their scorn for the street vendors peddling T-shirts and other "tacky" souvenirs. Why T-shirt vendors and not the multinational sportswear companies, whose logos were visible on every athlete and every venue?

51 *Niagara Falls: Nature's Grandest Wonder* (Buffalo, N.Y.: Matthews and Northrup, c.1890), p.15.

52 Greenhill and Mahoney, *Niagara*, p.111; Jackson, *To America*, p.126.

53 Harrison, *The Condition*, p.15; *Canadian Illustrated News*, 1872, cited in *NFG*, April 1, 1937; *NFR*, June 13, 1929, Nov. 5, 1929.

54 *NFR*, Nov. 5, 1929; *Chicago Tribune*, Aug. 21, 1872; Robinson, *Banff Springs*, p.21; Morris, *Letters Sent Home*, p.226.

55 "Village of Niagara Falls, New York," clipping, Buffalo and Erie County Historical Society, Vertical Files, Buffalo, N.Y., n.p., n.d., c.1880s.

56 Bird, *Englishwoman in America*, p.219; Sala, *My Diary*, p.169.

57 Jackson, *To America*, p.132.

58 "Taking in the Stranger at Niagara," *Brotherhood of Locomotive Engineers Monthly Journal*, February 1884, p.74.

59 *Humbugs of Niagara Falls Exposed*, pp.3-12; Government of Ontario, *Royal Commission to Enquire into Alleged Abuses Occurring in the Vicinity of Niagara Falls*, Nov. 17, 1873, RG 18, Provincial Archives of Ontario (hereafter cited as PAO), Toronto.

60 Stanley G. Grizzle, with John Cooper, *My Name's Not George: The Story of the Brotherhood of Sleeping Car Porters in Canada* (Toronto: Umbrella Press, 1998), pp.37, 67.

61 Robin Winks, *The Blacks in Canada: A History* (Montreal and Kingston: McGill-Queen's University Press, 1971), p.146. See also Owen Thomas, *Niagara's Freedom Trail: A Guide to African-Canadian History on the Niagara Peninsula* (Thorold, Ont.: Region of Niagara Tourist Council, 1995); and Kiwanis Club of Stamford, *Niagara Falls, Canada: A History of the City and the World Famous Beauty Spot* (Niagara Falls, Ont.: Kiwanis Club, 1967), pp.171-72.

62 *NFR*, May 5, 1921. On R. Nathaniel Dett and the British Methodist Episcopal Church in Niagara Falls, Ontario, see Thomas, *Niagara's Freedom Trail*, pp.17-19. Robert and Charlotte Dett had separated, and Robert left his estate, rumoured to be large, to a white woman, coyly referred to in his obituary as his "friend," and his two sons. On the "mulatto girl," see *Providence, Rhode Island Journal*, n.d., c.1850s.

63 Jasen, *Wild Things*, p.72.

64 John Tyndall, "Niagara Falls," *Eclectic Magazine of Foreign Literature, Science and Art*, vol.18, no.1 (July 1873), p.26.

65 Bird, *Englishwoman in America*, pp.231-32.

66 *NFR*, Jan. 25, 1922; William Howard Russell, "Canada: Its Defences, Condition and Resources" (1865), in Dow, *Anthology and Bibliography of Niagara Falls,*, p.323; Marshall, *Through America*, p.81.

67 Ivan Golovin, *Stars and Stripes, or American Impressions* (London: W. Freeman, 1856), p.15; Monck, *My Canadian Leaves*, p.161; Thomas Hughes, *Vacation Rambles* (London: Macmillan, 1895), p.150; and Samuel Phillips Day, *Life and Society in America* (London: Newman and Co., 1880), p.150. U.S. sources suggest that black men accounted for about one-quarter of the restaurant labour force until the 1930s. See Dorothy Sue Cobble, *Dishing It Out: Waitresses and Their Unions in the Twentieth Century* (Urbana: University of Illinois Press, 1991), p.18.

68 John Sinclair, *Sketches of Old Times and Distant Places* (London: Murray, 1875), p.245.

69 Brassey, *My Honeymoon Trip*, pp.13-19.

70 Walden, *Becoming Modern in Toronto*, p.118.

71 "My Adventure at Niagara," author and magazine unknown, July 29, 1871.

72 Robin D.G. Kelley, *Race Rebels: Culture, Politics and the Black Working Class* (New York: Free Press, 1994), p.177.

73 Rickard, *Fighting Tuscarora*, p.78.

4 The People's Niagara at the Turn of the Century

1 Government of Ontario, *Royal Commission to Enquire into Alleged Abuses Occurring in the Vicinity of Niagara Falls*, Nov. 17, 1873, RG 18, PAO. (The report, cited hereafter as Ontario, *Royal Commission Report*, is unpaginated.) The Royal Commission is also discussed in Gerald Killan, "Mowat and a Park Policy for Niagara Falls," *Ontario History*, vol.70 (June 1975), pp.115-35; and Robert Welsh, "The Early Years of the Queen Victoria Niagara Falls Parks Commission: A Study of the Development of an Ontario Government Park at Niagara Falls, 1873-1893," M.A. thesis, Queen's University, Kingston, Ont., 1977.

2 *Chicago Tribune*, Aug. 21, 1872.

3 Seibel, *Ontario's Niagara Parks*, pp.19-20; *NFG*, June 29, 1870.

4 *Canadian Illustrated News*, June 8, 1872. Barnett also had a better lawyer, Edward Blake, a former provincial premier. Welsh, "Early Years," p.20.

5 There is mixed evidence about Davis's and Barnett's hiring policies. Nicholas Weber, a local constable, told the Royal Commission that "no coloured men" were working for Barnett, only for Davis. Perhaps William Price, the Barnett employee shot by Davis's son three years earlier, had been the only black person working for Barnett. Another Royal Commission witness, a Niagara hack driver, reported that Barnett hired "one or two coloured men to assist him about his establishment, a man and an errand boy." The testimony of witnesses mentioned only Davis's black employees. Davis also hired Jewish employees, which drew attention in the press. During the *Hamilton Times* libel suit, the paper noted that one employee, Lyon Isaacs, "being a Jew," was allowed to keep his "hat" as he testified in court. Ontario, *Royal Commission Report*.

6 Ontario, *Royal Commission Report*.

7 Hailed as "our venerable townsman," Sidney Barnett proposed to the Niagara Parks Commission in 1919 that he would establish another museum, "The Canadian Museum of the Empire," on the grounds of Queen Victoria Park. The plan received the enthusiastic endorsement of the local press: such a proposal could "come from no

other local man so well qualified." The parks commissioners declined the offer. *NFR*, Dec. 23, 1919, Aug. 28, 1920. Saul Davis's son Edward continued in the tourist industry, running a souvenir business, "The River Road House," in Niagara Falls, New York, until his death in 1928. His obituary noted that his early days "were spent in a time when life was rougher than it is now, and when there was a vendetta between the old Davis and Barnett families, in which much blood was spilt." *NFR*, April 18, 1928.

8 *NFG*, Oct. 31, 1877.

9 Ontario, *Royal Commission Report*; *NFR*, Oct. 31, 1919.

10 Quoted in Sears, *Sacred Places*, pp.185-86.

11 Greenhill and Mahoney, *Niagara*, p.117.

12 Jonathan Baxter Harrison, *Certain Dangerous Tendencies in American Life* (Boston: Houghton, Osgood and Company, 1880).

13 Sears, *Sacred Places*, p.189; Alfred Runte, "Beyond the Spectacular: The Niagara Falls Preservation Campaign," *New York Historical Society Quarterly*, vol.57, no.1 (January 1973), pp.30-50. On Olmsted's vision of landscape and social order, see Geoffrey Blodgett, "Frederick Law Olmsted: Landscape Architecture as Conservative Reform," *Journal of American History*, vol.62, no.4 (March 1976); and Elizabeth Blackmar and Roy Rosenzwieg, *The Park and the People: A History of Central Park* (Ithaca, N.Y.: Cornell University Press, 1992). For a chilling look at how this reformist vision of public space has become as "obsolete as Keynesian nostrums of full employment" in contemporary U.S. cities, see Mike Davis, *City of Quartz: Excavating the Future in Los Angeles* (London: Verso, 1990).

14 Jonathan Baxter Harrison, *The Condition of Niagara Falls and the Measures Needed to Improve Them* (New York: privately published, 1882), pp.8-9.

15 Ibid., pp.48, 12, 18, 24, 36, 21.

16 Runte, "Beyond the Spectacular," p.43.

17 *Outing and the Wheelman*, vol.5, no.6 (March 1885), p.458.

18 Runte, "Beyond the Spectacular," p.45; Niagara Parks Commission (NPC), *Annual Report*, Niagara Falls, Ont., 1895.

19 Welsh, "Early Years," pp.210-20. Welsh points out that the Conservative *Toronto Empire* later changed its tune about the park and also condemned the NPC for charging tolls. See also *Toronto Saturday Night*, June 9, 1888.

20 E.A. Meredith, "The Queen Victoria Niagara Falls Park," *Canadian Magazine*, July 1897, p.7.

21 Sears, *Sacred Places*, p.188.

22 NPC, *Annual Report*, 1885, p.2.

23 Welsh, "Early Years," pp.200, 203, 222.

24 Ibid., p.222.

25 Letter from James Foster, Chairman, Executive Committee of Conservative Association, County of Welland, Sept. 18, 1905; and James McClive, Oct. 18, 1905; in Niagara Parks Commission (NPC) correspondence, RG 38, PAO.

26 Letter to Hon. J.P. Whitney, Premier, from R.M. Gonder, May 23, 1905, in NPC correspondence.

27 *Canadian Horticulturalist*, September 1909. Major H.H. Snelgrove, president of the Ontario Horticulturalist Association and author of the editorial, also made his views public in a speech at Toronto City Hall, Nov. 9, 1909, and again in an interview, *Toronto Star*, the same day.

28 Frank Yeigh, "Queen Victoria Niagara Falls Park," *Canadian Magazine*, October 1912.

29 *NPC* correspondence, Feb. 7, 1921.

30 *NFR*, Feb. 11, 1921.

31 Ellis to Drury, Feb. 23, 1921, in NPC correspondence.

32 Memo, Jackson to Ellis, Feb. 12, 1921, in NPC correspondence.

33 "Contemptible Piffle from Niagara Falls," *Saturday Night*, Feb. 19, 1921, reprinted, *NFR*, Feb. 21, 1921.

34 *NFR*, Sept. 7, 1926.

35 *NFR*, July 18, July 24, July 26, 1934.

36 *NFR*, Aug. 3, Aug. 7, Aug. 9, Aug. 18, Aug. 29, Sept. 15, 1934; Niagara Parks Commission Enquiry, Report of Armand Racine and Henry J. Welch, July 17, 1934, NPC Archives, Niagara Falls, Ont.

37 NPC, *Annual Report*, 1885, pp.2-4; and NPC, *Annual Report*, 1887, p.4.

38 Nelles, *Politics of Development*, pp.218-23.

39 Canada Steamship Lines brochure, 1915, p.8; E.T. Williams, *Niagara, Queen of Wonders* (Boston: Chapple, 1916), p.1.

40 NPC, *Annual Report*, 1905, p.4.

41 Leo Weinthal to John Jackson, Nov. 4, 1920, NPC correspondence.

42 "The Future of the Falls," *Toronto Star*, reprinted, *NFR*, Dec. 24, 1915.

43 Olmsted report to Jackson, July 10, 1914, NPC correspondence.

44 Writing to Olmsted to inform him of the changes, Jackson said some passages in the report were "hastily dictated" and "scarcely bore out the air of dignity which such a report should have for presentation to the Board." He also reminded Olmsted that the chairman, Mr. Langmuir, was "nearly 80 years of age, [and] has spent more than half a century since the inception of the park in doing everything for its future."

Jackson to Olmsted, July 13, 1914, Frederick Olmsted to Jackson, May 5, 1916, NPC correspondence.

45 *The Niagara Parks Commission Welcomes You*, n.d., c.1920.

46 Jackson to Langmuir, June 20, 1913, NPC correspondence; NPC, *Annual Report*, 1914, pp.36-40.

47 Memo, Jackson to Langmuir, July 6, 1914, Langmuir to Jackson, July 7, 1914, letter, Langmuir to Simpson, July 8, 1914, NPC correspondence; *NFR*, clipping, n.d., c.May 1909; *Mail and Empire* (Toronto), May 25, 1909: *Niagara Falls Record*, July 27, 1909.

48 William Nolan to Jackson, Aug. 5, 1914, Jackson to Nolan, Aug. 8, 1914, NPC correspondence.

49 Ellis to Jackson, June 14, 1920, NPC correspondence.

50 Wilson, *Culture of Nature*, p.25.

51 See, for example, Kasson, *Amusing the Million*; Kathy Peiss, *Cheap Amusements: Working Women and Leisure in Turn-of-the-Century New York* (Philadelphia: Temple, 1990); Valverde, *Age of Light, Soap and Water*; and Carolyn Strange, *Toronto's Girl Problem* (Toronto: University of Toronto Press, 1995).

52 *NFR*, Feb. 23, 1921.

53 Jane Urquhart, *The Whirlpool* (Toronto: McClelland and Stewart), p.46.

54 *Niagara Falls Evening Review* (*NFER*), May 26, 1925.

55 *NFR*, Dec. 20, 1918; emphasis added.

56 Irwin, *New Niagara*, pp.99, 147; Kiwanis Club of Stamford, *Niagara Falls*, pp.36-46, 194; *NFER*, Sept. 9, 1916.

57 *NFG*, Sept. 12, 1912.

58 *NFR*, March 14, 1919, Aug. 11, 1920; "Is Niagara Doomed?" *The Literary Digest*, vol.15, no.21 (September 18, 1897), p.614.

59 *NFR*, July 25, 1919.

60 *NFR*, Feb. 11, 1915.

61 *NFR*, June 1, 1910, May 27, 1910.

62 *NFR*, July 25, 1919.

63 *NFR*, May 11, 1920.

64 Irwin, *New Niagara*, p.228.

65 "Report of the Committee of Landscape Architects," April 13, 1908, quoted in William Irwin, "The New Niagara: The Meaning of Niagara Falls in American Culture, From Discovery to 1920," Ph.D. dissertation, University of Virginia, Charlottesville, 1991, p.291.

66 David Nye, *American Technological Sublime* (Cambridge, Mass.: MIT Press, 1994), pp.136-37.

67 Ferguson to Jackson, Sept. 26, 1917, Jackson to Ferguson, Sept. 29, 1917, American Cyanamid to Jackson, Aug. 27, 1918, NPC correspondence.

68 *NFR*, Aug. 19, 1922.

69 The Hooker Company lives in infamy as the corporation that gave the world Love Canal in the 1970s. Starting in the early twentieth century the company manufactured bleach and caustic soda at Niagara Falls, New York, showing as little regard for the health of its employees as for its neighbours. Working conditions in the Niagara plant were truly horrific. The company piped chlorine, used in the production of bleach, directly into the bleach chambers, with only a layer of lime on the floor to absorb the gas. For their protection workers wore only framed goggles whittled out of wood, and they wrapped yards of wet flannel around their faces during their twelve-hour shifts. Robert Thomas, *Salt and Water, Power and People: A Short History of the Hooker Electrochemical Company* (Niagara Falls, N.Y.: n.p., 1955), p.23.

70 *NFR*, April 27, 1921. Irwin notes that in the early twentieth century the Niagara Falls, New York, press regularly commented on the stench caused by chemical and electro-metallurgical plants. Irwin, *New Niagara*, p.186.

71 Williams, *Niagara, Queen of Wonders*, p.3; *Illustrated Guide to Toronto by Way of Niagara Falls* (Toronto: Canadian Railway News, 1913), p.10; David E. Nye, *Electrifying America: Social Meanings of a New Technology* (Cambridge, Mass.: MIT Press, 1990), p.42; Wells, quoted in Conrad, *Imagining America*, p.25.

72 Nye, *American Technological Sublime*, pp.109-42.

73 *NFG*, May 10, 1906; Shredded Wheat Company, *The Wonders of Niagara, Scenic and Industrial* (Buffalo, N.Y.: Niagara Lithographic Company, 1914); *Burke's Guide and Souvenir Book of Niagara Falls* (Buffalo, N.Y.: C.E. Burke, 1915). See also Irwin, *New Niagara*, pp.179-203.

74 Yvonne Fitzroy, *A Canadian Panorama* (London: Methuen, 1929), pp.101-2.

5 Boom and Bust in the 1920s and 1930s

1 *NFG*, March 7, 1896. On the tourist boom of the 1920s, see also Alphonse Gavin, "Niagara Falls, 1918-1929," thesis, Niagara University, n.d., c.1955.

2 Lynne Marks, *Revivals and Roller Rinks: Religion, Leisure and Identity in Late-Nineteenth-Century Small-Town Ontario* (Toronto: University of Toronto Press, 1996), pp.133-39.

3   Gary Cross, *Time and Money: The Making of Consumer Culture* (London: Routledge, 1993), pp.78-79; Charles M. Mills, *Vacations for Industrial Workers* (New York: Ronald Press, 1927), pp.31, 37, 39, 41, 115, 209.

4   *Star Weekly* (Toronto), July 16, 1921. The four steamships that travelled daily between Toronto and Queenston remained extremely popular until their run was discontinued in 1952. The boats featured drawing rooms, ladies' cabins, dining rooms, private parlours, and an orchestra and took about two hours to reach their destination. See Niagara Navigation Company, *The Niagara River Line*, 1903; and Percy Rowe, *Niagara Falls and Falls* (Toronto: Simon and Schuster, 1976).

5   Jack London, *The Road* (London: Arno Publications, 1967), pp.107-11.

6   William D. Baker, Travelogue, 1906-1908, D67-2, Buffalo and Erie County Historical Society, Buffalo, N.Y.

7   *NFG*, Aug. 19, 1897.

8   *NFG*, March 7, 1896.

9   Thomas Tugby, *Tugby's Illustrated Guide to Niagara Falls* (Niagara Falls, N.Y., 1899); *Niagara Falls: Nature's Grandest Wonder* (Buffalo, N.Y.: Mathews Northrup, n.d., c.1890), p.26.

10 Niagara Navigation Company, *Niagara River Line*.

11 Edward Roper, *By Track and Train through Canada* (London: Allen, 1891); John Edbauer, *New Guide and Key to Niagara Falls and Toronto* (Buffalo, N.Y.: Volksfreund, 1925); Phillip Mason, *Colourful Niagara: Land of the Rainbow* (Niagara Falls, Ont., 1972).

12 *NFR*, July 13, 1925, June 22, 1926, July 8, 1926, July 15, 1926.

13 *New York Herald Tribune*, reprinted, *NFR*, Feb. 1, 1926.

14 Walden, *Becoming Modern in Toronto*, p.291.

15 *NFR*, April 1, 1915, April 15, 1916, July 23, 1918.

16 See, for example, *NFR*, July 26, 1918. The Canadian Pacific Railway made a similar pitch to Americans to promote holidays in the Canadian Rockies during the war. The war had taught the Allies, so the story went, that "they have a common purpose, common ideals and a common humanity." Thus if Americans decide to visit Canada, "they will be more welcome even than in the past." *Travel*, May 1919, p.43.

17 *NFR*, Sept. 10, 1929, June 11, 1926, Sept. 18, 1928; Kiwanis Club of Stamford, *Niagara Falls*, p.197; *NFG*, March 12, 1925; Chamber of Commerce, *Annual Report*, Niagara Falls, N.Y., 1928, pp.23-25.

18 Nye, *American Technological Sublime*, pp.171-72. Niagara had been illuminated several times previously. In 1860 several hundred lights were placed alongside the river bank,

and the Prince of Wales, visiting from England, was given the honour of flipping the switch to light up the waterfall. Greenhill and Mahoney, *Niagara*, p.113. In summer 1907 the General Electric Company used searchlights to light the falls in the evening, which also proved a tremendous tourist attraction. *NFR*, Nov. 29, 1924. On electrical illumination as a tourist attraction in Toronto, see Walden, *Becoming Modern in Toronto*, pp.304-11.

19 *NFR*, May 26, 1925.

20 *NFR*, July 25, 1924.

21 *Manchester Guardian*, cited in *NFR*, Oct. 28, 1925; *New York Herald*, Nov. 29, 1925.

22 *Niagara Falls City Directory*, Niagara Falls, Ont., 1920, 1925, 1930.

23 *NFR*, May 29, 1926.

24 *Belfast Evening Telegram*, cited in *NFR*, Jan. 22, 1912; *NFR*, May 5, 1921; interview with Katie Agar, Niagara Falls, Ont., Dec. 2, 1997.

25 Velma Vetter, "The General Brock," *Canadian Hotel Review*, August 1929, p.10.

26 *NFR*, June 29, 1929, May 31, 1930, Sept. 30, 1930, Nov. 24, 1932.

27 Jackle, *Tourist*, p.121; M.C. Urquhart and K.A.H. Buckley, eds., *Historical Statistics of Canada*, 2nd ed. (Ottawa: Statistics Canada, 1983), p.T147.

28 Jackle, *Tourist*, pp.127-28; John Herd Thompson with Allen Seager, *Canada, 1922-1939: Decades of Discord* (Toronto: McClelland and Stewart, 1985), pp.87-88; Donald F. Davis, "Dependent Motorization: Canada and the Automobile to the 1930s," *Journal of Canadian Studies*, vol.21, no.3 (Autumn 1986), pp.125-27.

29 Warren Belasco, *Americans on the Road: From Autocamp to Motel, 1910-1945* (Cambridge, Mass.: MIT Press, 1979); and Jackle, *Tourist*, pp.120-45.

30 *NFG*, July 1, 1925, July 10, 1925, July 11, 1925, Sept. 1, 1925, July 29, 1929.

31 *NFR*, Aug. 19, 1922.

32 John Davidson, "The Spirit of Service," *Canadian Hotel Review*, May 1928, p.39; Vernon G. Cardy, "Invested Capital versus Unfair Competition," *Canadian Hotel Review*, January 1936, p.10.

33 *Canadian Hotel Review*, November 1935, p.20.

34 *NFR*, March 17, 1925, May 5, 1925, March 18, 1925. The Buffalo reference would have a definite ethnic and class-laden resonance to people in the Niagara Peninsula, because Buffalo's many ethnic, working-class neighbourhoods in the 1920s were the scene of pitched battles—including house bombings—as the Ku Klux Klan established itself in the city. Shawn Lay, *Hooded Knights on the Niagara: The KKK in Buffalo, New York* (Albany, N.Y.: State University of New York Press, 1995).

35 *NFR*, Nov. 21, 1925. The NPC did not open an autocamp in the 1920s, and even by the late 1930s this possibility was still at the discussion stage. NPC, General Manager's Office Correspondence, Jan. 1, 1937 to July 31, 1938, RG 38-3-2, PAO. Thanks to Cecilia Morgan for passing this reference on to me.

36 *NFR*, Aug. 18, 1925.

37 *NFR*, July 5, 1926.

38 *NFR*, July 21, 1926, June 15, 1928.

39 *NFR*, Jan. 28, 1929, July 10, 1928.

40 *NFR*, June 4, 1928.

41 Jackle, *Tourist*, p.257.

42 See, for example, *Canadian Hotel Review*, August 1930, p.13.

43 *Outing and the Wheelman*, January 1891, August 1891, June 1894, September 1897; Archie Wynne-Field, "What Do You Know about Travel?" *Chatelaine*, August 1929; Anita Ritchie, "Helpful Hints for the Autumn Traveller, *Canadian Magazine*, September 1929; Judith Clinton, "All Aboard!" *Canadian Magazine*, May 1930; and Judith Clinton, "Travel Hints That Make for Comfort," *Canadian Magazine*, July 1930.

44 Memo from John Jackson to all staff, Aug. 20, 1920, NPC correspondence; *NFR*, June 13, 1923.

45 *NFR*, Sept. 19, 1929.

46 See, for example, *Canadian Hotel Review and Restaurant*, December 1933, p.3; Senate of Canada, *Report of the Special Committee on Tourist Traffic*, Ottawa, 1934, p.222.

47 Frank Yeigh, "Niagara and Thereabouts," *Canadian Geographical Journal*, vol.4, no.6 (June 1932), p.358; *Manchester Guardian*, cited in *NFR*, Oct. 28, 1925.

48 See, for example, *NFR*, July 17, 1923, Aug. 29, 1923, April 16, 1925, Sept. 22, 1925, Aug. 7, 1928; Davis, "Dependent Motorization," p.124.

49 *NFR*, July 11, 1929, July 12, 1929, Aug. 16, 1929, October 1930.

50 *NFR*, April 14, 1928.

51 Thompson, with Seager, *Canada, 1922-1939*, p.88.

52 In 1928 the Ontario Restaurant Association and the Dominion of Canada Hotel Association were formed. The country's first national tourist promotion institution was created in 1929, when the Canadian Association of Tourist and Publicity Bureaus—an umbrella group of provincial tourist bureaus—was organized. Its main priority was money; it quickly began a campaign to lobby the federal government for more tourist promotion spending. Senate of Canada, *Report of the Special Committee on Tourist Traffic*, pp.47-51.

53 Theodore Morgan, "Five Million Tourists," *Canadian Geographic Journal*, vol.1, no.6 (October 1930), p.482.

54 Marie-Francoise Lanfant, "International Tourism, Internationalization and the Challenge to Identity," in *International Tourism*, ed. Lanfant, Allcock, and Bruner, p.26.

55 Senate of Canada, *Report of the Special Committee on Tourist Traffic*, pp.206, 2.

56 *NFR*, Nov. 18, 1930.

57 *NFR*, Dec. 6, 1924, Dec. 17, 1937.

58 Kiwanis Club of Stamford, *Niagara Falls*, p.195.

59 *NFR*, May 16, 1934; *Canada Senate Journals*, vol.72, First Session of the 17th Parliament, Ottawa, 1934, pp.24-25.

60 On the cultural images of the Dionne family, see Mariana Valverde, "Representing Childhood: The Multiple Fathers of the Dionne Quintuplets," in *Regulating Womanhood: Historical Essays on Marriage, Motherhood and Sexuality*, ed. Carol Smart (London: Routledge, 1992), pp.119-46; and *Journal of Canadian Studies*, Special Issue on the Dionne Quintuplets, Winter 1994. The Dionne parents themselves visited Niagara in 1939, causing a minor flurry of excitement in the town. In keeping with the generally hostile assessment of the couple by the Canadian press and policy-makers, Oliva Dionne, according to the *Review*, "appeared very unenthusiastic" about the waterfall— perhaps the only famous visitor to be described this way for two centuries. *NFR*, Nov. 18, 1939. By contrast Dr. Alan Dafoe, who was created as the hero of the piece, was appropriately excited by his visit in 1943. *NFG*, April 26, 1943.

61 *NFR*, June 6, 1938.

62 *NFR*, Dec. 31, 1932.

63 Standard Hotel Files: New Windsor Hotel, Queen's Hotel, Orchard Inn, Arlington Hotel, Fort Erie Hotel, RG 36, PAO.

64 K. Wisby, Inspector, Unemployment Relief Branch, to NPC Manager, Jan. 12, 1938, NPC correspondence.

65 Chamber of Commerce minutes, Niagara Falls, Ont., Jan. 12, 1938. On the RCMP and tourism, see Michael Dawson, *The Mountie from Dime Novel to Disney* (Toronto: Between the Lines, 1998).

66 *NFR*, Oct. 22, 1931.

67 R. Daville, General Brock Hotel, to W. L. Houck, M.L.A., Sept. 21, 1936, and Howard Fox, Foxhead Inn, to W.L. Houck, Sept. 18, 1936, NPC correspondence; *NFR*, Feb. 16, 1937, March 8, 1938, Aug. 23, 1938.

68 Thompson, with Seager, *Canada, 1922-1939*, pp.88, 348.

69 Low Wages and the Industrial Standard Act Files, File 15-0-29, Hotel Employees, RG 7, PAO; "Je Sais" to Roebuck, Sept. 22, 1934.

70 Low Wages and the Industrial Standard Act Files, Hotel and Restaurant Workers, sample contract from Hotel and Restaurant Employees International Union, Local 168, file 71-0-76, RG 7, PAO.

71 H.A. MacLennan (manager, Royal Connaught Hotel, Hamilton, Ont.), "Problems of Personnel," *Canadian Hotel Review and Restaurant*, June 1936, p.14.

72 Report of Armand Racine and Henry J. Welsh, July 17, 1934, "Niagara Parks Commission Enquiry," NPC Archives; *NFR*, Aug. 1, 1934.

73 Interview with Katie Agar, Dec. 2, 1997.

74 Phil Tongler to Mitchell Hepburn, July 1935, file 71-0-77, RG 7, PAO.

75 Memo from Mr. Marsh to Mr. Prain, Sept. 20, 1935, file 71-0-77, RG 7, PAO.

76 The minimum-wage act applied only in communities with populations of more than 4,000. David Croll to S. Scott, July 15, 1935, file 71-0-77, RG 7, PAO.

77 *NFR*, Sept. 15, 1941; interview with Katie Agar, Dec. 2, 1997.

78 Standard Hotel Inspectors files, 1928-1935, RG 36-1, PAO.

79 *NFR*, May 3, 1938; see also *NFR*, Oct. 20, 1936.

80 *NFG*, July 16, 1930.

81 See, for example, *NFR*, June 27, 1934, Nov. 22, 1935, June 23, 1936, Aug. 22, 1938; Kiwanis Club of Stamford, *Niagara*, p.55; A. Morrison to B. McQueston, Minister, Department of Highways, Sept. 2, 1936, anonymous to NPC, July 17, 1937, NPC correspondence.

82 *NFR*, Sept. 20, 1930.

83 *Canadian Hotel Review*, July 1938, p.27.

84 *Canadian Hotel Review and Restaurant*, December 1933, p.27.

85 T.B. McQueston, Minister of Highways, to J. Bickness, Registrar of Motor Vehicles, Aug. 18, 1938, Sept. 2, 1938, NPC correspondence.

86 Mr. Fisher to W. Houck, MLA, Aug. 15, 1938, NPC correspondence; St. Catharines *Standard*, n.d., c.summer 1938; Chamber of Commerce minutes, Niagara Falls, Ont., July 19, 1938.

87 Harold Lemmer, Detroit, July 1, 1937, NPC correspondence; *NFR*, July 17, 1930, July 8, 1930.

88 Senate of Canada, *Report of the Special Committee on Tourist Traffic*, pp.14, 273.

89 Reuben Lavine, Oswego, N.Y., to NPC, July 7, 1931, NPC correspondence.

90 *NFR*, May 8, 1926, Aug. 20, 1930.

6 "A Laboratory for the Study of Young Love": Honeymoons and Travel to World War II

1 Allan Harding, "The Honeymoon Trail Still Leads to Niagara Falls," *American Magazine*, vol.102 (July 1926), pp.32-96.

2 Ibid., p.92.

3 Wendy Mitchinson, "Medical Perceptions of Marital Sexuality in Canada, 1900-1950," in *The History of Marriage and the Family in Western Society*, ed. R. Phillips (Toronto, CSPI, 1995), p.5.

4 Katz, *Invention of Heterosexuality*, p.85. See also John D'Emilio and Estelle B. Freedman, *Intimate Matters: A History of Sexuality in America* (New York: Harper and Row, 1988); Steven Seidman, *Romantic Longings: Love in America, 1830-1980* (New York: Routledge, 1991); and Veronica Strong-Boag, *The New Day Recalled: Lives of Girls and Women in English Canada, 1919-1939* (Toronto: Copp Clark Pitman, 1988).

5 Charles Everett Hall, *Some Honeymoon!* (New York: George Scully, 1918), p.28.

6 K. Patricia A. Turner, *Ceramic Uncles and Celluloid Mammies: Black Images and Their Influence on Culture* (New York: Anchor, 1994), pp.41-68; Sue Jewell, *From Mammy to Miss America and Beyond* (New York: Routledge, 1993), pp.37-44.

7 Clement Wood, "Honeymoon," in *Americana Esoterica*, ed. Carl Van Doren (privately published, Macy-Masius, 1927), p.258; Graeme Lorimer, "Just Married!" *Ladies Home Journal*, September 1929, p.32.

8 *The Crowd*, King Vidor, director, MGM, 1928.

9 Ella O. Burroughs, "The Bride," *Metropolitan*, December 1913; Stuart M. Emery, *Honeymoon Millions* (New York: Dutton, 1928).

10 Harding, "Honeymoon Trail," p.96.

11 Ernest Groves, *Preparation for Marriage* (New York: Greenberg, 1936), p.106.

12 Editorial, "Blunders on the Wedding Night," *Journal of Sexology and Psychoanalysis*, vol.2 (July-August 1924), pp.232-33.

13 Gladys H. Groves and Robert A. Ross, *The Married Woman* (New York: Greenberg, 1936), p.66.

14 Katz, *Invention of Heterosexuality*, p.88.

15 Dr. G. Courtenay Beale, *Marriage: Before and After* (London: Health Promotion, n.d., c.1920s), p.33; S. Daniel House, "Wisdom for Lovers," *Journal of Sexology and Psychology*, vol.2 (July-August 1924), p.375; Groves and Ross, *Married Woman*, p.52.

16 House, "Wisdom for Lovers," p.384.

17 Bernarr Macfadden, *Talks to a Prospective Husband about Sex* (New York: Macfadden Publications, 1922), p.36; House, "Wisdom for Lovers," p.371; William Robinson, *Married Life and Happiness* (New York: Critic and Guide Company, 1922), p.62.

18 Robert Dickinson, "Marital Maladjustment, the Business of Preventative Gynaecology," *Long Island Medical Journal*, January 1908, pp.1-6. On Dickinson, see also Jennifer Terry, "Anxious Slippages between 'Us' and 'Them': A Brief History of the Scientific Search for Homosexual Bodies," in *Deviant Bodies: Critical Perspectives on Difference in Science and Popular Culture*, ed. Jennifer Terry and Jacqueline Urla (Bloomington: Indiana University Press, 1995), pp.129-69. Dickinson was probably ahead of his peers in his open attitude towards birth control. Only one advice book of this era, *Preparation for Marriage* by Ernest Groves, provided any information about birth control, and Groves simply explained the rhythm method and hinted that doctors could explain other, unspecified contractive possibilities. Groves, *Preparation for Marriage*, pp.99-101. Others either ignored the topic or issued dire warnings of the dangers of unspecified "injurious" or "ineffective" methods of contraception. See, for example, Oliver Butterfield, *Marriage and Sexual Harmony* (New York: Emerson Books, 1938), pp.44-45. Other advice book writers advocated undressing alone; some continued to suggest sleeping separately as well. See, for example, Herman Rubin, *Eugenics and Sex Harmony* (New York: Publishers Guild, 1933).

19 Allan M. Brandt, *No Magic Bullet: A Social History of Venereal Disease in the United States since 1880* (New York: Oxford, 1985), pp.19-20, 147-49.

20 Groves, *Preparation for Marriage*, pp.64-65. Groves was a pioneer of the marriage education movement, teaching the first such course in the United States at the University of North Carolina in 1927. Beth Bailey, "Scientific Truth . . . and Love: The Marriage Education Movement in the United States," *Journal of Social History*, Summer 1987, pp.711-32.

21 Groves and Ross, *Married Woman*, p.65.

22 Christina Simmons, "Modern Sexuality and the Myth of Victorian Repression," in *Passion and Power: Sexuality in History*, ed. Kathy Peiss and Christina Simmons (Philadelphia: Temple University Press, 1989), pp.163-64.

23 Joan Herbert, *Mrs Brown's First Honeymoon* (London: Samuel French, 1934), p.7.

24 See, for example, Katherine Arnup, *Education for Motherhood: Advice for Mothers in Twentieth Century Canada* (Toronto: University of Toronto Press, 1994); and Cynthia Comacchio, *Nations Are Built of Babies: Saving Ontario's Mothers and Children, 1900-1940* (Montreal and Kingston: McGill-Queen's University Press, 1993).

25 Mitchinson, "Medical Perspectives," pp.5-10.

26 Terry, "Anxious Slippages," pp.139-54.

27 James Reach, *The Road to Niagara: A Melodramatic Farce in Three Acts* (New York: Samuel French, 1937).

28 *Honeymoon Hotel*, Merry Melodies, Warner Brothers, Leon Schlesinger, producer, 1934.

29 *Footlight Parade*, Warner Brothers, Lloyd Bacon, director, 1933.

30 Suzanne Morton, "The June Bride as the Working-Class Bride: Getting Married in a Halifax Working-Class Neighbourhood in the 1920s," in *Canadian Family History*, ed. Bettina Bradbury (Toronto: Copp Clark, 1992), p.374; John Gillis, *For Better For Worse: British Marriages, 1600 to the Present* (New York: Oxford University Press, 1985), p.298.

31 "Honeymoon Letters": Gerald and Janet Zoerhof, 1927; May and Bill Lindlaw, 1938; Omar and Frances Stangland, 1935; Charles Bredd and bride, 1938, all in Niagara Falls Public Library, Niagara Falls, Ont. (See chapter 8 for a history of these letters.)

32 Frank Parker Day, *The Autobiography of a Fisherman* (Garden City, N.Y.: Doubleday Page, 1927), pp.112-13. My thanks to Gerry Hallowell for passing this reference on to me.

33 Carolyn Steedman, *Landscape for a Good Woman: A Story of Two Lives* (London: Virago, 1986), pp.12, 23.

34 Michael Lynch, "Walt Whitman in Ontario," in *The Continuing Presence of Walt Whitman*, ed. Robert K. Martin (Iowa City: University of Iowa Press, 1992), p.143.

35 Ina Russell, ed., *Jeb and Dash: A Diary of Gay Life, 1918-1945* (Boston: Faber and Faber, 1993), p.105.

36 *NFR*, March 10, 1930.

37 *NFR*, April 29, 1933; *NFG*, June 13, 1939; *Canadian Hotel Review*, May 1929, p.32.

38 *NFR*, Jan. 16, 1935.

39 *NFR*, May 8, 1931, Oct. 31, 1935, June 2, 1938.

40 *The New York Times*, Aug. 18, 1935; *Toronto Telegram*, May 21, 1937.

41 A.W. O'Brien, "Holiday Daze," *Maclean's*, July 15, 1943.

42 *Ottawa Citizen*, Aug. 10, 1944.

43 O'Brien, "Holiday Daze."

44 *Maclean's*, cited in *Canadian Hotel Review*, Feb. 15, 1940, p.22.

45 Leslie Frost, address to Ontario Post-War Tourist Planning Conference, Toronto, April 14 and 15, 1944.

46 Doug Owram, *Born at the Right Time* (Toronto: University of Toronto Press, 1996), p.9.

47 *Canadian Hotel Review*, March 1942, p.9.

48 *NFR*, Jan. 29, 1940.

49 *NFG*, Sept. 29, Oct. 6, 16, 17, 18, 20, 21, 23, 25, 1941; *NFR*, Oct. 20, 25, 27, 1941.

50 Chamber of Commerce, *Annual Report*, Niagara Falls, N.Y., 1941.

51 See, for example, *The Globe and Mail*, May 1, 1943; *NFR*, May 3, 1943; *NFG*, April 3, 1943.

52 United Church of Canada, Division of Evangelism and Social Services, *Eighteenth Annual Report*, Toronto, 1943, p.68, cited in Gary Kinsman, *The Regulation of Desire: Homo and Hetero Sexualities*, 2nd ed. (Montreal: Black Rose Books, 1996), p.149. More than fifteen million U.S. civilians moved across county lines during World War II for jobs and defence postings, while another twelve million Americans served in the military. Beth Bailey and David Farber, *The First Strange Place: Race and Sex in World War Two Hawaii* (Baltimore: Johns Hopkins University Press, 1992), pp.16-17.

53 *NFG*, April 3, 1943.

54 *NFR*, Oct. 23, 1944; *NFG*, Dec. 3, 1945.

55 "Honeymoon Letters": Ronald Ede, 1944; Fred and Ella Probst, 1942.

56 *NFR*, Oct. 20, 1941.

7 Honky-Tonk City: Niagara and the Postwar Travel Boom

1 Kiwanis Club of Stamford, *Niagara Falls*, p.195; *NFR*, Nov. 15, 1960; *NFR*, Aug. 24, 1967.

2 Dominion-Provincial Tourist Conference, *Report of Proceedings*, Ottawa, 1946, PAO. I explore the postwar tourist industry in Canada in more detail in "Everybody Likes Canadians: Americans, Canadians and the Postwar Travel Boom," in *The Development of Mass Tourism: Commercial Leisure and National Identities in 19th and 20th Century Europe and North America*, ed. Shelley Baranowski and Ellen Furlough (forthcoming).

3 F.H. Leacy, ed., *Historical Statistics of Canada*, 2nd ed. (Ottawa: Statistics Canada, 1983), pp.D318-28.

4 Hal Tracey, "Motel Business Is Booming," *Saturday Night*, Sept. 11, 1951; "Why Tourists Like Ontario," *Financial Post*, Oct. 9, 1954; James Montagnes, "Motel Owners Step up Investment," *Canadian Business*, July 1959; Ontario Economic Council, *Ontario's Tourist Industry*, Toronto, December 1965, p.17; *Canadian Hotel Review*, May 1949, p.66. The number of hotels in Canada dropped during the travel boom, from 5,656 in 1941 to 5,157 in 1952. Elizabeth Hay Trott, "For Hotels, the Boom's Still On," *Monetary Times*, July 1954, p.22.

5 Robert Thomas Allen, "Why U.S. Tourists Are Passing up Canada," *Maclean's*, May 1955; Karal Ann Marling, *As Seen on TV: The Visual Culture of Everyday Life in the 1950s* (Cambridge, Mass.: Harvard University Press, 1994), p.132; Kenneth White, "Is Our

Visitor Industry in for Record Year?" *Financial Post*, June 16, 1951; John Maclean, "Gloom in Playland," *Financial Post*, Oct. 20, 1956. The figures cited for U.S. travel outside the United States pertain to the year 1950. Historian John Jackle cites a similar study done in 1954, which indicates a similar pattern: 5 per cent of Americans travelled outside their country in that year, and 73 per cent of them came to Canada. Jackle, *Tourist*, p.185. When the amount of money spent by U.S. travellers was calculated (as opposed to simply the number of travellers), Canada fell to second place, behind Europe; in 1955 38.5 per cent of U.S. foreign travel expenditures went to Europe, and 27.8 per cent to Canada. *Canadian Hotel Review*, September 1956, p.7.

6   Logan Maclean, "Needed: Travel Promotion," *Saturday Night*, April 25, 1956.

7   Bruce Hutchinson, "The Unknown Country," *Maclean's*, March 1956; Larry Smith, "The Falls, Roaring Trade," *Saturday Night*, Nov. 14, 1950; Forbes Gilbertson, "Niagara Looks Ahead," *Financial Post*, Sept. 1, 1962; "Tourism Just One of 71 Industries," *Financial Post*, Sept. 1, 1962; Ontario Department of Economics and Development, *Economic Survey of the Niagara Region*, 1963, p.58.

8   Chamber of Commerce minutes, Niagara Falls, Ont., Oct. 14, 1954.

9   Memo from T.C. McCall, 1948, Department of Travel and Publicity, Series B-1, Deputy Ministers Office (DMO) correspondence, RG 5, PAO.

10   Summary of Proceedings, Second Annual Ontario Tourist Conference, Niagara Falls, Ont., April 25-27, 1950.

11   Niagara Falls City Directory 1945, 1955, 1965; Ontario Department of Economics, *Economic Survey*, pp.57, 87; Chamber of Commerce minutes, Niagara Falls, Ont., Nov. 19, 1958; *NFR*, Aug. 22, 1961.

12   *NFG*, series on Niagara Attractions, July 2-Aug. 13, 1963, later published by the NFNY Chamber of Commerce, *Official Guidebook*, 1964.

13   Judith A. Adams, *The American Amusement Park* (Boston: G.K. Hall, 1991), p.105.

14   Ibid., pp.94, 97. See also Project on Disney, *Inside the Mouse*.

15   Chamber of Commerce minutes, Niagara Falls, Ont., May 26, 1948, Aug. 31, 1949, Oct. 12, 1949; General Manager to Lynne Spencer, Aug. 16, 1948, NPC correspondence; *NFR*, June 12, 1950.

16   *NFR*, June 14, June 28, 1960.

17   On globalization and cultural uniformity see, for example, Benjamin Barber, *Jihad vs. McWorld: How Globalism and Tribalism Are Reshaping the World* (New York: Ballantine, 1996); and George Ritzer and Allan Liska, " 'McDisneyization' and 'Post-Tourism': Complementary Perspectives on Contemporary Tourism," in *Touring Cultures*, ed. Rojek and Urry, pp.96-112.

18   Interview with Howard Bedford, July 12, 1993.

19   *NFR*, Oct. 10, 1934, June 9, 1936, May 4, 1939, April 14, 1941, June 21, 1948; interviews with Ruth Stoner, Dec. 3, 1997, and Katie Agar Dec. 2, 1997.

20   *NFR*, March 10, 1950, March 31, 1950: *Canadian Hotel Review*, February 1950, April 1950.

21   Chamber of Commerce minutes, Niagara Falls, Ont., April 1954; Standard Hotel Files, Niagara Riding and Driving Club, Series 36-1, RG 36, PAO.

22   See, for example, *Toronto Star Guide*, 1957; and *Travellers Guide*, 1959. Accommodation listings and guidebooks, as well as formal announcements of the opening of hotels and restaurants, indicate that large numbers of Eastern European and Italians owned such establishments; in some listings half the names are non-Anglo.

23   Standard Hotel Files, Caverly; *NFR*, June 11, 1950.

24   Standard Hotel Files, Prospect House; "Where History Helps Sell Beer," *Canadian Hotel Review*, August 1955.

25   Standard Hotel Files, Falls View Hotel; *NFR*, June 3, 1959.

26   See, for example, Standard Hotel Files, Belleview Hotel, Merview Hotel.

27   Standard Hotel Files, Inspectors' Recommendations against Hotels, Victoria Inn.

28   Interview with Olga Ricci, Dec. 1, 1997.

29   *NFR*, Jan. 11, 1949; Standard Hotel Files, Bon Villa.

30   *NFR*, Sept. 21, 1950.

31   *NFR*, Sept. 2, 1949.

32   *NFR*, Jan. 11, 1949; Kiwanis Club of Stamford, *Niagara Falls*, p.58.

33   *NFR*, June 10, 1950, Feb. 21, 1951.

34   *NFR*, March 18, 1952.

35   *NFR*, April 14, 1952.

36   "Niagara screenplay," and "Twentieth Century-Fox," Deputy Minister's Office correspondence, RG 41, Series B-1, PAO.

37   *NFR*, Jan. 2, 19, 21, 27, 28, 1953; Kiwanis Club of Stamford, *Niagara Falls*, p.58.

38   *Variety*, Jan. 21, 1953; *The New York Times*, Jan. 22, 1953; *NFR*, June 20, 1953, July 11, 1953, Dec. 14, 1953; *Financial Post*, July 10, 1954; *Buffalo Courier Express*, Aug. 15, 1953.

39   *NFR*, May 4, 1959, July 10, 1959; Chamber of Commerce minutes, Niagara Falls, Ont., June 1955, June 1960.

40   Krotz uses Belize in the 1990s as an example of this phenomenon. See Krotz, *Tourists*, pp.65-87.

41   "Tips to Travellers," *Holiday*, September 1946.

42   *NFG*, July 26, 1955, Aug. 3, 1962; *NFR*, July 26, 1955.

43 See, for example, *NFR*, July 6, 1948, April 15, 1950, Aug. 7, 1959, Dec. 6, 1960, Nov. 26, 1963, Aug. 21, 1970; James Auld, Speech to Niagara Falls Visitor and Convention Bureau, Oct. 28, 1964, Minister's Office, Series A-8, RG 5, PAO.

44 *NFR*, Aug. 30, 1967.

45 R.I. Wolfe, "The Changing Patterns of Tourism in Ontario," in *Profiles of a Province*, ed. Ontario Historical Society (Toronto: Ontario Historical Society, 1967), p.176.

46 *The Globe and Mail*, Jan. 14, 1995.

47 Thomas, *Niagara's Freedom Trail*, p.6.

48 McCall memo, n.d., 1947, W. Rourke to T.C. McCall, July 7, 1949, and response, July 12, 1949, Deputy Minister's Office correspondence, PAO.

49 Mrs. Whitecotton received a quick apology from the restaurant's manager, who insisted that the problem was not racism but that her party had been queue-jumping. Mrs. E. Whitecotton to Manager, Queenston Restaurant, Aug. 29, 1948, and C. Sheldon Brooker, response, Sept. 4, 1948, NPC correspondence.

50 Chamber of Commerce minutes, Niagara Falls, Ont., May 25, 1949; *NFR*, July 10, 1950. Instead, the couple got a dinner at the NPC-run Refectory.

51 "Niagara" screenplay, Deputy Minister's Office correspondence, RG 5 Series, B-1, PAO. This tribute to the people's Niagara only happened in the movie *script*; it did not make it into the film.

52 NPC, Manager's files, correspondence, 1948; *NFR*, Oct. 24, 1960, Aug. 20, 1959; Anne Chamberlain, "See America First," *Saturday Evening Post*, Aug. 28, 1965.

53 "Authentic Decor from English Pubs Big Attraction at Niagara Falls," *Canadian Hotel Review*, February 1967.

54 Interdepartmental correspondence, C.D. Crowe to Thomas McCall, Deputy Minister's Office, March 25, 1950, Series B-4, RG 5, PAO.

55 Hon. James Auld, Speech to Niagara Falls Visitors and Convention Bureau, Oct. 28, 1964, Series A-1, PAO; *NFR*, March 27, 1969.

56 See, for example, *NFR*, May 26, May 27, May 29, 1952, April 26, 1957, May 11, 1961, July 9, 1961; Niagara Development Committee School of Hospitality Questionnaire, Niagara Falls Public Library, Niagara Falls, Ont.

57 *The Globe and Mail*, May 16, 1985.

58 Minister's correspondence, June 9, 1963, Series A-1, RG 5, PAO; *NFR*, June 27, 1963.

59 *NFR*, June 27, 1960; Anne Chamberlain, "See America First," *Saturday Evening Post*, Aug. 28, 1965.

60 Niagara Falls Public Library Vertical Files, Tourist Industry; *The Globe and Mail*, clipping, n.d., c.1964.

8 Heterosexuality Goes Public: The Postwar Honeymoon

1 Elaine May, *Homeward Bound: American Families in the Cold War Era* (New York: Basic Books, 1988); Winnie Brienes, *Young, White and Miserable: Growing up Female in the Fifties* (Boston: Beacon Press, 1992); Joanne Meyerowitz, *Not June Cleaver: Women and Gender in Postwar America 1945-1960* (Philadelphia: Temple University Press, 1994); Elizabeth Kennedy and Madeline Davis, *Boots of Leather, Slippers of Gold: The History of a Lesbian Community* (New York: Routledge, 1993); Adams, *Trouble with Normal*; Joy Parr, *A Diversity of Women: Ontario, 1945-1980* (Toronto: University of Toronto Press, 1995).

2 Sonya Michel has identified Marie Derry as the "antithesis of the ideal postwar woman." It is certainly possible to read what Michel terms Marie Derry's "excesses" as parts of a whole: she likes nice clothing, travel, dining out in restaurants, and extramarital sex. In proposing that Fred's discharge money be spent on "a real honeymoon" she is again acting as the sexual aggressor and thus stands apart in this tale of redemption through domesticity. It is also noteworthy that not a word about a honeymoon is mentioned during the wedding of the film's sentimental, pathetic couple, the disabled Homer and his loyal girl, Wilma. See Sonya Michel, "Danger on the Home Front: Motherhood, Sexuality and Disabled Veterans in American Postwar Films," *Journal of the History of Sexuality*, vol.3, no.1 (1992), pp.109-28.

3 Romar and Lee, eds., *The Canadian Male: A Manual of Personal Hygiene* (Vancouver, B.C.: Modern Film Distributors of Canada, 1961), p.4; Abraham Beacher, M.D., "Sex Problems of Newlyweds," *Sexology*, April 1957, p.558.

4 Henry Lee, "Should Honeymoons Be Banned?" *Pageant*, December 1955, p.7; Olivier Loras, "Honeymoon Shock," *Sexology*, August 1957, p.4; "Don't Let Your Honeymoon Be Hell!" *Fotorama*, December 1956, p.110; Alfred Tyrer, *Sex, Marriage and Birth Control* (Toronto: T.H. Best, 1943), p.157.

5 Salem Harrison, *Marriage Guide*, vol.1, no.1 (December 1956), p.17; Maxine Davis, *Sexual Responsibility in Marriage* (New York: Dial Press, 1963), p.161.

6 Adams, *Trouble with Normal*, p.10.

7 Theodore H. Van de Velde, *Ideal Marriage* (London: William Heinemann, 1942), pp.256-57; Romar and Lee, *Canadian Male*, p.4; Eustace Chesser, *Sexual Behavior* (London: Corgi Books, 1964), p.103; Davis, *Sexual Responsibility*, p.165.

8 Harry F. Tashman, *The Marriage Bed: An Analyst's Casebook* (New York: University Publishers Incorporated, 1959), pp.176-87; Paul Scholten, "The Premarital Examination," *Journal of the American Medical Association*, Nov. 1, 1958, p.1176.

9 Francis Bruce Strain, *Marriage Is for Two: A Forward Look at Marriage in Transition* (New York: Longmans, Green, 1955), p.86; Margaret Sanger, *Happiness in Marriage* (New York: Blue Ribbon Books, 1940), pp.85, 89.

10 Lois Pemberton, "Before the Wedding Night," *True Confessions*, June 1949, p.12.

11 "Marital Stage-Fright," in *Illustrated Sex Quiz*, ed. Myron Jacoby (New York: Herald Publishing, 1943), p.3.

12 Clifford R. Adams, *Preparing for Marriage: A Guide to Marital and Sexual adjustment* (New York: Dutton, 1951), p.141; Edward O'Rourke, *Marriage and Family Life* (Champaign, Ill.: The Newman Foundation, 1956), p.141; David Keller, *101 Personal Hygiene Questions and Answers* (New York: Popular Medicine, 1942), p.17; Sidney Goldstein, *Marriage and Family Counseling* (New York: McGraw-Hill, 1945), p.115.

13 Loras, "Honeymoon Shock," pp.4-5; Eugene Linton, "Honeymoon Cystitis," *Medical Aspects of Human Sexuality*, August 1971, p.114.

14 Boris Golden, "Honeymoon Sexual Problems," *Medical Aspects of Human Sexuality*, May 1971, pp.139-52.

15 Stanley R. Brav, "Note on Honeymoons," *Marriage and Family Living: Journal of the National Conference on Family Relations*, February 1947, p.60; Jean Libman Block, "Are Those Marriage Manuals Any Good?" *Cosmopolitan*, October 1948; Jerome and Julia Rainer, *Sexual Pleasure in Marriage*, 2nd ed. (New York: Permabook, 1963), p.1.

16 "Honeymooners, Beware," *Time*, Aug. 15, 1955, p.7; Lee, "Should Honeymoons Be Banned?" p.7; Helen Colton, "When Honeymoons Are Dangerous," *Coronet*, June 1954, p.21; Jerome and Julia Rainer, *Sexual Pleasure in Marriage*, pp.168-69.

17 Caroline Bird, "Advice to Honeymooners," *Cosmopolitan*, July 1951.

18 See, for example, Jhan and June Robbins, "Honeymoon Business," *New York Herald Tribune This Week Magazine*, June 6, 1948; June Callwood and Trent Frayne, "A Honeymoon at the Falls," *Maclean's*, Aug. 1, 1950; Bird, "Advice to Honeymooners."

19 *Lucky Partners*, 1940, Lewis Milestone, director.

20 *I Married Joan*, Aug. 12, 1953.

21 *Rear Window*, 1954, Alfred Hitchcock, director.

22 *What's My Line?* CBS, Feb. 27, 1955; *Bewitched*, ABC, Sept. 17, 1964.

23 *Monkey Business*, 1952, Howard Hawks, director; *Lover Come Back*, 1961, Delbert Mann, director.

24 *The Long, Long Trailer*, 1954, Vincente Minnelli, director.

25 *Father of the Bride*, 1950, Vincente Minnelli, director.

26 *A Time to Smile*, 1941; *The Brady Bunch*, September 1969; *My Favorite Wife*, 1940, Garson Kanin, director.

27 Jennifer Ames, *Honeymoon Alone* (London: Hodder and Stoughton, 1940); Jerome Weidman, "Three Men on a Honeymoon," *Cosmopolitan*, March 1949; "Honeymoon for Three," *Cosmopolitan*, September 1946; Jack Woodford, *Savage Honeymoon* (New

York: Woodford Press, 1949); Barbara Dickinson, "Separate Honeymoons," *Women's Home Companion*, October 1953; Robert H. Rimmer, *The X-Rated Videotape Guide*, vol. 2 (Buffalo: Prometheus, 1991), p.251.

28 *To Catch a Thief*, 1955, Alfred Hitchcock, director; *Remember the Night*, 1940, Mitchell Leisen, director.

29 Ontario Department of Tourism and Information, Series B-1, Deputy Minister's office correspondence, Twentieth Century-Fox, "Niagara" screenplay, RG 5, PAO.

30 *Niagara*, 1953, Henry Hathaway, director.

31 "Honeymoon Letters," Bernie and Virginia Hogan.

32 *Ottawa Citizen*, Aug. 10, 1944.

33 *NFR*, June 11, 1949; Chamber of Commerce minutes, Niagara Falls, Ont., Feb. 16, June 29, 1949. "Niagara Honeymoon," written in 1955 by Niagara resident Lucille Hilston, struck just the right note of sentiment and promotion:

> We recall our Niagara Honeymoon!
> Love filled days dear, that ended all too soon;˙
> Where the falls spread a mist
> 'Round us dear as we kissed,
> 'Neath the stars in a dream-land for two;
> We'll return dear, to pledge our love anew.
> By the falls once again we'll say "I Do";
> How it makes our hearts sing,
> We'll return in the spring,
> for our second Niagara Honeymoon!

34 See, for example, *NFR*, July 31, 1951, Jan. 24, 1952, June 15, 1955, Jan. 17, 1950; *The Star Weekly* (Toronto), June 18, 1949.

35 Chamber of Commerce Tourism Committee, *Report*, Niagara Falls, Ont., September 1957, September 1959.

36 *NFR*, Feb. 5, 1949. The two previous prime ministers, William Lyon Mackenzie King and R.B. Bennett, were both unmarried.

37 Interview with Art Blakely, July 1993; *NFR*, Sept. 13, 1948.

38 Lotta Dempsey, "Honeymoon Town," *Chatelaine*, May 1947; Callwood and Frayne, "Honeymoon at the Falls."

39 *NFR*, July 9, 1947; Jhan and June Robbins, "Honeymoon Business"; Monroe Fry, "Cross Section U.S.A.: Honeymoon Town," *Esquire*, June 1957; Henry and Kathleen Pringle, "The Cities of America: Niagara Falls," *Saturday Evening Post*, Oct. 30, 1948; *NFG*, Nov. 12, 1952.

40 Newton, *Cherry Grove, Fire Island*, p.89; Elise Chenier, "Tough Ladies and Trouble Makers: Toronto's Public Lesbian Community, 1995-1965," M.A. thesis, Queen's University, Kingston, Ont., 1995, p.157; Donaldson, *Niagara!*, p.229.

41 "Homosexual Scandal Rocks Niagara Falls," *Hush*, Oct. 27, 1962.

42 "Honeymoon Letters," McAulay, 1945, Calvello, 1946, Coppinger, 1943, Hutton, 1946, Holloway, 1952.

43 Chamber of Commerce minutes, Niagara Falls, Ont., Aug. 31, 1949.

9 Conclusion: The Sublime Becomes Ridiculous

1 *Toronto Star*, Nov. 8, 1991.

2 See, for example, Jeremy Ferguson, "The Wonders of Niagara," *Leisureways*, April 1992.

3 *The New York Times*, Sept. 29, 1996.

4 See, for example, Barry Callaghan, "Honeymoon Suite," *Saturday Night*, January 1987, p.156. See also the documentary film *The Falls*, 1991, Kevin McMahon, director.

5 Trinh T. Minh-ha, "Other Than Myself/My Other Self," in *Travellers' Tales*, ed. Robertson et al., p.22.

6 See, for example, *USA Today*, June 22, 1989; *The Globe and Mail*, Sept. 16, 1991; Calvin Trilling, "Anne of Red Hair," *The New Yorker*, Aug. 5, 1996; and *Fast Forward: Japanese Tourists Abroad*, a film by Barbara Doran and Peter Wintonick, Morag Productions/CBC Newsworld, 1996. See also Douglas Baldwin, "L.M. Montgomery's Anne of Green Gables: The Japanese Connection," *Journal of Canadian Studies*, vol.28, no.3 (Autumn 1993), pp.123-33.

7 *NFR*, Feb. 26, 1970.

8 *NFR*, Aug. 3, 1967.

9 Kiwanis Club of Stamford, *Niagara Falls*, pp.427-29.

10 *Toronto Star*, Dec. 31, 1985; "An Enduring Attraction," *Maclean's*, Oct. 26, 1987; *The Globe and Mail*, Aug. 16, 1986; *Toronto Star*, Sept. 15, 1985; *NFG*, March 31, 1989.

11 Paul Waldie, "Gloom Falls over Niagara," *Financial Post*, Jan. 23, 1993; *Toronto Star*, March 24, 1994; *The New York Times*, Feb. 9, 1997.

12 Cecilia Morgan, "Managing Landscape, Managing History: The Creation of Historical Memory in Niagara-on-the-Lake and Queenston," paper presented to the Canadian Historical Association Annual Conference, St. John's, Nfld., June 1997.

13 *The New York Times*, July 14, 1961; *The Globe and Mail*, Aug. 6, 1970; *St. Catharine's Standard*, Aug. 13, 1990.

14 *The New York Times*, July 14, 1961; *The Globe and Mail*, Aug. 6, 1970; *USA Today*, June 22, 1989.

15 "The Newlywed Game," *Forbes Magazine*, Sept. 2, 1991.

16 "The Honeymoon Isn't Over," *American Demographics*, August 1992.

17 In Canada, 55 per cent of fifteen- to-nineteen-year-olds are "sexually involved," and 87 per cent of single adults have had sexual relations. Some 80 per cent of Canadians approve of premarital sex. Reginald W. Bibby, *The Bibby Report: Social Trends Canadian Style* (Toronto: Stoddart, 1995), pp.70, 66, 69.

18 *Halifax Chronicle-Herald*, Aug. 17, 1998.

19 Moriyama and Teshima Planners, *Ontario's Niagara Parks: Planning the Second Century*, Niagara Falls, Ont., 1988, p.51.

Illustration Credits

Katie Agar, 146, 147, 187

Boeing Company, 243

Buffalo and Erie County Historical Society, Buffalo, N.Y., 72

Brandon Beierle, map, xiii

British Library, London, England, 223

Canada Steamship Lines, 101

Canadian Hotel Review, 133

Canadian Tourism Commission, 209

Mrs. Esther Clarke, 166

Elliott Erwitt/Magnum Photos & Fotofolio, Canal Sta, N.Y., 212

Graham Harrop, 222

Henry Stewart Publishing Co., Buffalo, N.Y., 54, 70

Indiana University Library, 152, 217

Kinsey Institute, Bloomington, Ind., 218

Maclean's, 233

National Archives of Canada, Ottawa, 20, 69

Niagara Parks Commission, Niagara Falls, Ont., xiv, 51, 73, 84, 96, 97, 99, 104, 114, 116, 118, 121, 142, 144, 172, 176, 180, 182, 183, 207, 230

New York Power Authority Niagara Power Project, Lewiston, N.Y., 40

Niagara Falls, N.Y., Public Library, 31, 34, 35, 37, 38

Niagara Falls, Ont., Public Library, 32, 33, 67, 122, 125, 126, 129, 136, 137, 171, 181, 184, 185, 186, 195, 196

Niagara Falls Gazette, Niagara Falls, N.Y., 229

Niagara Falls Review, Niagara Falls, Ont., 42, 208

Personal collection, 18, 47, 68, 163, 238

Proctor & Gamble, 165

Toronto Reference Library, 36, 156

20th Century-Fox, 199

Index

Note: numbers in bold type refer to illustrations.

Adams, Mary Louise, 14, 217-18
Aerocar, 103, **171**, 121, 183
Agar, Katie, 145, **146**, 188
automobile, 172, 128-30

Baker, William and Effie, 119-20, 132
Barnett, Sidney, 64
Barnett, Thomas, 34, 64, 86-88, 183, 210
Best Years of Our Lives, 215
Bewitched, 225
Bird, Isabella, 37, 41-42, 50, 71, 79
blacks, as tourist-industry personnel, 51,
    78-80, 87, 156; as tourists, 150, 204-6;
    community at Niagara Falls, 78-79
Boorstin, Daniel, 16
Brady Bunch, 226
Brassey, Jean, 23, 81
Brock's monument, 34, 103-4
Butler, Captain William, 29

Cardy, Vernon G., 130, 141, **186**, 187-89
Canadian Government Travel Bureau, 170
Carpenter, Edward, 168

Cataract House, 27, 32, 81
Cave of the Winds, **18, 36, 51**, 119; as early
    and key attraction, 34, 91, 120, 183;
    description of tour, 49-52; annoyances
    at, 77; staff at, 79
Church, Frederick, 88
class, tensions at Niagara Falls, 9-10, 56-57,
    89, 108, 128-30, 206, 241; changing mix of
    visitors, 117, 166-67; and honeymoons, 8,
    165-66, 214
Clifton House, **32, 33, 126**, 141
Clifton Hill, 94, **195, 196**, 197
Cornell, Alonzo, 91
Cotten, Joseph, 198, **199**, 201, 228
The Crowd, 157, 198

Davis, Saul, 85-88, 183, 210
Day, Doris, 225, 226
de Grazia, Victoria, 5
Dett, Robert, 79
Dickens, Charles, 39
Dickinson, Dr. Robert, 160, 162
Dionne Quintuplets, 141

Disneyland, 55, 184-86
Dolan, Leo, 170
Du Bois, W.E., 205

Ellis, Philip, 95-98, 105-6

Father of the Bride, 226
Fleming, Gertrude and Sandford, 25, 26
Foucault, Michel, 28
Fox, Howard, 130, 135, 189. *See also* Foxhead Inn
Foxhead Inn, **136, 137**, 198. *See also* Fox, Howard
Francis, Daniel, 66
Furlough, Ellen 12

General Brock Hotel, 166, 231, 236; constructed, 126-27; in receivership, 141; and honeymoon promotion, 172; purchased by Cardy, 186-87; home to actors Monroe and Cotten, 201; and blacks, 205-6; working conditions in, 145-46, 193
Grant, Cary, 9, 227
Groves, Ernest, 160-61
Gzowski, Casimir, 94

hack drivers, 76-78, 98, 148. *See also* taxi drivers
Harrison, Jonathan Baxter, 88, 89-91
Hennepin, Louis, **40**, 41
Hepburn, Mitchell, 98, 99, 100, 143, 145
heterosexuality, 155; and tourism 12-13; creation of identity, 13-14; practising, 27-28; contrasted to homosexuality, 162-63; as a social norm, 213-14, 217-18; changes in the public culture of, 244
homosexuality, satirizing Niagara Falls, 11, 168, 234-35; and tourism 12, 16, 168, 246; and eugenics, 162

honeymoon, origins of, 19-20, 28-30; and sex experts, 20-22, 25, 158, 163, 216-22; and pornography, 23-25; embarrassment during, 27, 154; and masculine anxiety, 156-57, 219-20; and female anxiety, 21-22, 159, 218, 220; promotion of at Niagara Falls, 169-70, 172-74, 200, 230-32; on film 157, 163-64, 215, 222-28, 244; in novels 26, 27-28, 155
Hooker Electrochemical Company, 113, 239
hotels, and honeymoon suites, 26, 163-64; expansion of, 124, 190-91; rivalry with autocamps, 130-31; rivalry with tourist homes, 131-35, 148-49; and gender, 133; working conditions, 143-46; multinational chains, 188
Houck, William, 182, 189, 192, 200, 201, 232
Howells, William Dean, 14, 26, 39, 45, 92, 198

I Married Joan, 224
Ice Bridge, **47**, tragedy of 1912, 48-49
Irish, 75-77, 125
imaginary geography, definition, 4, 30-31; and danger, 41, 45-52, 82; and gender 42-46; and sex 43-46, 49
Irwin, William, 4, 112
Italians, 126, 145

Jasen, Patricia, 4, 62
Jefferis, B.G., and J.L. Nichols, 20, 21, 22
Jews, as tourist industry personnel, 75, 86-87; anti-Semitism at Niagara Falls, 86, 151

Katz, Jonathan, 14, 115
Killan, Gerald, 88
Kinsey, Alfred, 216

London, Jack, 119
Long, Long Trailer, 226

Lover Come Back, 225
Lucky Partners, 223-24

Machar, Agnes, 40, 41-45
Maid of the Mist, 34, 43, 61, 67-71, **70**, **101**,
102, 119, 121, **176**, 183, 203, 236
Malcolm X, 82
marriage manuals. *See* honeymoon, and
sex experts
Martineau, Harriet, 10
McCannell, Dean, 55
McClintock, Anne, 62, 69
McGreevy, Patrick, 4, 46
McKay, Ian, 12
McKinsey, Elizabeth, 4, 29, 35
Monck, Frances, 10, 29
Monkey Business, 225
Monroe, Marilyn, 9, 198, **199**, 200, 201,
227-8
motels, expansion, 178, 183, 193-94; unethical
practices, 204
Mowat, Oliver, 85, 94
My Favorite Wife, 226

national identity, tensions at Niagara Falls,
39-40, 203-4, 241-42; and tourism, 178-79,
210
Native people, as tourist attractions, 43, **54**,
58, 60-71, 83, 103, 142, 184-86; as tourist
industry personnel, 75
New York State Reservation, 88, 186
Niagara (film), impact on Niagara Falls, 9,
198-210; plot, 227-28
Niagara Falls, and industry, 31, 71-75,
101-2, 107-15, 140, 180-81; illumination of
123-24
Niagara Falls Museum, 64, 86, 87, 120, 184
Niagara Parks Commission, and political
corruption, 7, 94-100; origins of, 94;
Refectory, **96**, **97**, 101; Nursery, **104**;

regulations, 105, 141, 149-50, 186; rivalry
with private sector, 106, 134-35, 143; working conditions, 142, 144; other activities
of, 184
Niagara Falls, N.Y., origins of town, 31,
109
Niagara Falls, Ont., origins of town, 109;
black community in, 78; attitudes towards
tourism, 107-8, 110-11, 123, 137-39
Nye, David, 114

Oakes Garden Theatre, 142
Oakes, Sir Harry, 141
Offenbach, Jacques, 62, 64
Ontario, Travel and Publicity Department,
178, 198, 205, 207-8
Olmsted, Frederick, and Central Park, 56;
and Niagara Falls, 88, 89, 90, 92, 102-3,
106; and tourist industry, 112

Pan-American Exposition, 113-14, 115
Pratt, Mary Louise, 58, 59, 65
Prospect Park, Niagara Falls, N.Y., 66, 88

Queen Victoria Park, 95, **85**, **99**, 149, 210,
231, 234; origins of, 88; opening of, 92-93;
activities in, 103, 108-9, 119, 200

Rear Window, 224
Remember the Night, 227
Rickard, Clinton, 63, 83
Rogers, Ginger, 223, 225, 227
Royal Commission to Enquire into Alleged
Abuses Occurring in the Vicinity of
Niagara Falls (1873), 7, 85-89, 98

Sala, George, 63, 65
Sears, John, 15, 93
Senate Committee on the Tourist Trade
(1934), 139, 140, 150

Shredded Wheat Company, 110, 115, 119
"Shuffle off to Buffalo," 227, 234
souvenirs, 65-66, **68**, **180**, 206, 207
Spanish Aerocar. *See* Aerocar
Spirella Corset Company, **114**, 115, 184
Stall, Sylvanus, 21, 25, 157
Stone, Lawrence, 20

Table Rock, 99, **182**; as early and key
   attraction, 34, 39, 86, 103, 120, 183;
   description of tour 49-52; annoyances at
   77; staff at, 79, 86
taxi drivers, 99, 148, 204. *See also* hack
   drivers
Tocqueville, Alexis de, 71
Terrapin Tower, 34, **38**, 71
To Catch a Thief, 227
tourist homes, 119, 131-33, 134;
   and soliciting, 132, 147-48
Tyrer, Alfred, 216

Tuscarora, 61-63
Tussaud's Wax Museum, **196**

Urquhart, Jane, 108
Urry, John, 4, 5, 11, 15, 56

vacation pay legislation, 118-19
Van de Velde, Theodore, 218

Walden, Keith, 81
wedding night. *See* Honeymoon
What's My Line?, 225
Whitman, Walt, 116, 168
Welch, Thomas, 88
Wells, H.G., 52, 114
Wilde, Oscar, 10, 11, 16
women, as travellers, 21-22, 133-34
World War I, impact on tourism 122-23
World War II, impact on tourism, 170-72;
   impact on honeymoons, 174

- | illustrations - refer in text (figure
text
✓ Travellers/visitors -
✓ individ stories
  - mythology
  - stunts

For Better For
Worse -

index of illustr.